PAEDIATRIC CHAPLAINCY

by the same authors

Spiritual Care with Sick Children and Young People
A handbook for chaplains, paediatric health professionals, arts therapists and youth workers
Paul Nash, Kathryn Darby and Sally Nash
ISBN 978 1 84905 389 1
eISBN 978 1 78450 063 4

Multifaith Care for Sick and Dying Children and their Families
A Multi-disciplinary Guide
Paul Nash, Madeleine Parkes and Zamir Hussain
ISBN 978 1 84905 606 9
eISBN 978 1 78450 072 6

of related interest

Assessing and Communicating the Spiritual Needs of Children in Hospital
A new guide for healthcare professionals and chaplains
Alister Bull
ISBN 978 1 84905 637 3
eISBN 978 1 78450 116 7

Spiritual Care in Common Terms
How Chaplains Can Effectively Describe the Spiritual Needs of Patients in Medical Records
Gordon J. Hilsman, D.Min.
Foreword by James H. Gunn
ISBN 978 1 78592 724 9
eISBN 978 1 78450 369 7

The Spirit of the Child
Revised Edition
David Hay
ISBN 978 1 84310 371 4
eISBN 978 1 84642 473 1

Helping Children and Adolescents Think about Death, Dying and Bereavement
Marian Carter
ISBN 978 1 78592 011 0
eISBN 978 1 78450 255 3

PAEDIATRIC CHAPLAINCY

Principles, Practices and Skills

Edited by Paul Nash,
Mark Bartel and Sally Nash

Jessica Kingsley *Publishers*
London and Philadelphia

First published in 2018
by Jessica Kingsley Publishers
73 Collier Street
London N1 9BE, UK
and
400 Market Street, Suite 400
Philadelphia, PA 19106, USA

www.jkp.com

Copyright © Jessica Kingsley Publishers 2018

Front cover image source: Copyright © Clinical Photography and Design Services and Birmingham Women's and Children's Hospital.

All rights reserved. No part of this publication may be reproduced in any material form (including photocopying, storing in any medium by electronic means or transmitting) without the written permission of the copyright owner except in accordance with the provisions of the law or under terms of a licence issued in the UK by the Copyright Licensing Agency Ltd. www.cla.co.uk or in overseas territories by the relevant reproduction rights organisation, for details see www.ifrro.org. Applications for the copyright owner's written permission to reproduce any part of this publication should be addressed to the publisher.

Warning: The doing of an unauthorised act in relation to a copyright work may result in both a civil claim for damages and criminal prosecution.

Library of Congress Cataloging in Publication Data
A CIP catalog record for this book is available from the Library of Congress

British Library Cataloguing in Publication Data
A CIP catalogue record for this book is available from the British Library

ISBN 978 1 78592 076 9
eISBN 978 1 78450 337 6

Printed and bound in Great Britain

This book is dedicated to paediatric chaplains, especially those in the Pediatric Chaplains Network, and the Paediatric Chaplaincy Network – people of inspiration, encouragement and hope who challenge us to be the best chaplains we can be.

Acknowledgements

We are immensely grateful to all of our chapter authors and practice example contributors, who have made this book such a rich and varied resource. We appreciate the professionalism and support of the team at Jessica Kingsley, particularly the enthusiasm of Natalie Watson, our commissioning editor, who encouraged us to pursue our dream of a book specifically focusing on paediatric chaplaincy.

Contents

Introduction: More Than Just Death and Dying 11
Paul Nash, Senior Chaplain, Birmingham Women's and Children's Hospital, UK, and Mark Bartel, Manager of Spiritual Care, Arnold Palmer Medical Center, USA

Section 1: Principles and Core Practices

1. Child Spirituality and Faith Development 23
   Rebecca Nye, Children's spirituality researcher and consultant, UK

2. Insights from Child Development for Pediatric Chaplains 37
   Dan Roberts, Chaplain Supervisor, McLane Children's Medical Center–Baylor Scott & White Health, Temple, USA

3. Spiritual, Religious and Pastoral Care of Children and Their Families 48
   Claire Carson, Head of the Chaplaincy–Spiritual Care Department, St George's University Hospitals NHS Foundation Trust, UK

4. Models of Chaplaincy in a Multicultural World 60
   Paul Nash, Senior Chaplain, Birmingham Women's and Children's Hospital, UK

5. Screening, Assessment and Charting 73
   Mary Robinson, Director of the Chaplaincy, Boston Children's Hospital, USA

6. Approaches and Skills for Working with Children and Young People 85
   Ryan Campbell, Program Manager, Center for Spirituality of Children, Children's Medical Center, Dallas, Texas, USA, and Sally Nash, Research Lead, Centre for Paediatric Spiritual Care and Chaplaincy, Birmingham Women's and Children's Hospital, UK

7. Working with Families 99
   Krista Gregory, Director, Dell Children's Resiliency Center, Austin, USA

8. Staff Care and Self-Care 110
   Kathryn Darby, Chaplain, Birmingham Women's and Children's Hospital, UK, and Carl Aiken, formerly Manager of Spiritual Care, Women's and Children's Hospital in Adelaide, Australia

9. Chaplain to the Institution 124
   Jim Linthicum, Senior Chaplain, Great Ormond Street Hospital, UK

10. Managing and Developing the Chaplaincy Provision and Team 136
    Paul Nash, Senior Chaplain, Birmingham Women's and Children's Hospital, UK

11. Medical Ethics: Practice and Decision-making 152
    Mark Bartel, Manager of Spiritual Care, Arnold Palmer Medical Center, USA

Section 2: Specialisms and Specific Skills

12. Giving Voice to the Story: Working with Patients Who Cannot Speak 167
    Daniel Nuzum, Healthcare Chaplain and Clinical Pastoral Education Supervisor at Cork University Hospital and Marymount University Hospital and Hospice, Ireland

13. Working in Mental Health 177
    Kathryn Darby, Chaplain, Birmingham Women's and Children's Hospital, UK

14. Working with Trauma and Abuse 190
    Bob Flory, Director of Spiritual Care and Bereavement Services, Children's Hospital Colorado, USA

15. Major Incidents 201
    Naomi Kalish, Coordinator of Pastoral Care and Education, NewYork-Presbyterian Morgan Stanley Children's Hospital, USA

16. Palliative and End-of-Life Care 214
    M. Karen Ballard, Director of Chaplaincy Services, Akron Children's Hospital, USA

17. Bereavement Care 225
    Edina Farkas, Pediatric Chaplain, Velkey László Center for Child Health in Miskolc, Hungary, and Stephen Harrison, former Chaplain at Helen and Douglas House Hospice, Oxford, UK

18. Transition: Journeying with Pediatric Patients into Adult Care: The Chaplain's Role 234
    Kobena Charm, Paediatric Chaplain, LeBonheur Children's Hospital, Memphis, USA

19. Paediatric Spirituality, Space and Environment 246
    Wyatt Butcher, Chaplain to Mental Health Service, Canterbury District Health Board, New Zealand, and Lindsay B. Carey, Palliative Care Unit, School of Psychology and Public Health, La Trobe University, Australia

20. Paediatric Chaplaincy and Research 258
    Daniel H. Grossoehme, Associate Professor of Pediatrics, University of Cincinnati, USA, and Lindsay B. Carey, Palliative Care Unit, School of Psychology and Public Health, La Trobe University, Australia

21. Through These Dark Valleys: A Pediatric Chaplain's Response to the Problem of God and Evil 271
    Kathleen Ennis-Durstine, Manager of InterFaith Pastoral and Spiritual Care, Children's National Health System in Washington, DC, USA

22. Perspectives on Suffering from Major Faith and Worldview Traditions 283
Emma Roberts, Research Assistant, Birmingham Women's and Children's Hospital Chaplaincy, UK

Conclusion 293

APPENDIX 1 BEING A PAEDIATRIC SPECIALIST IN A GENERAL HOSPITAL 297
Deborah Louise Wilde, Chaplain, Oxford University Hospitals, UK

APPENDIX 2 USEFUL WEBSITES FOR PAEDIATRIC CHAPLAINS 300

AUTHOR BIOGRAPHIES 302

SUBJECT INDEX 307

AUTHOR INDEX 317

Introduction
More Than Just Death and Dying
Paul Nash and Mark Bartel

PRACTICE EXAMPLE I.1: IMPROVISING A RESPONSE

This Saturday was a little bit different to usual. Being on call usually means responding to an emergency. However, this had all been planned the day before. I did a baptism for a young child according to Romanian custom, complete with the herb basil, and followed this with a betrothal ceremony for the parents. This all took place in our Victorian chapel, which makes an excellent setting for photographs of such auspicious occasions. The child died a couple of weeks later. While it had not been possible to arrange the wedding that the parents wanted once they realised how sick their child was, they do have photographs and memories of their child present on a very special day.

The Revd Paul Nash, Senior Chaplain, Birmingham Women's and Children's Hospital, UK

Every day in hospitals and hospices around the world chaplains engage in creative responses to the situations which confront them. The hope for this book is to capture and celebrate some of this creativity and best practice and provide a text book to inform and encourage the development of chaplaincy with children and young people in a healthcare setting. Paediatric chaplaincy is a discipline practised by those who are trained and endorsed to offer religious, spiritual and/or pastoral care to anyone from a newborn to whatever the cut-off age is for a children's hospital or hospice – usually between 16 and 25.

We hope this book will not only highlight the breadth and depth of what we do but also give evidence of all that our service could be. When some of us meet others from different countries or contexts, we have realised that we do things differently, don't have some of the resources, methods, approaches, etc. that others have as a normal part of their work. We hope to explain and critique the key ones of these and help make them accessible to the rest of us.

The readership of this book will mostly be either in stand-alone children's hospitals or covering paediatrics in general hospitals, hospices or in a few specialist units (such as rehabilitation). Some of us have suggested that, as difficult as it is to do paediatrics all day, it is a different type of difficultly to get your foot in the door of the children's ward in the protective environment of a general hospital. We hope this book will equip, resource and support regardless of context. We are separated by a common language and want to apologise now if we do not use your preferred spelling or concept. We have written it in such a way that it should be accessible to those of any faith or belief. The authors and practice examples are drawn from a wide range across several continents, and we were only able to work with what we received, despite extensive networking. The skills and knowledge, we hope, are transferable to many contexts and also across other disciplines engaged in spiritual care.

Background to paediatric chaplaincy

The myth of chaplaincy is that we come in useful only when there are dying patients. 'Get the chaplain; this is their area' is what was most commonly heard, and, in some situations, is still the prevailing perceived need and role. Our role has developed into so much more than this and the spectrum of our work is wide and deep and, even when related to death and dying, seeks to be creative and appropriate for the particular patient and family, as the story that starts this chapter shows.

In the UK, the development and origins of our hospitals are with religious communities and go back to the eleventh century (Swift 2009, pp.9–27) and can be traced for the next 1000 years. The clergy played a crucial role in this and the role evolved into that of chaplain we have today. Early prototypes of children's hospitals existed through orphanages in the fifteenth century, which included some health care, and foundling hospitals in the seventeenth century in England. Hospitals as we know them today developed in the nineteenth century. The first children's hospital was founded in Paris in 1802; London followed in 1852, Philadelphia in 1855, Edinburgh in 1860, Birmingham, UK, in 1862 and Toronto in 1875. There are records showing local clergy acting in roles that would become chaplains in the UK from these early days and becoming formalised under the National Health Service (NHS) in the late 1940s. These were mostly Church of England priests, and the service has continued to evolve into the multifaith provision it is today. Paediatric chaplaincy is now an acknowledged role in healthcare and is highlighted in the NHS Chaplaincy Guidelines (NHS England 2015). In the United States, the healthcare accrediting body Joint Commission likewise mandates spiritual care to be provided to patients of all ages.

> ### PRACTICE EXAMPLE I.2: A CHILD IN THE MIDST
>
> We were commissioned to write a series of four booklets for three- to seven-year-olds, covering a visit and stay in hospital, a life-limiting condition and a bereaved sibling. We were asked to find a title for the overall series. Through the influence of the Child Theology Movement, as publishers, editors, writers and designers sat around, I came and figuratively placed a sick child in the middle of our space and said, 'So, what can we say to this child?' We threw around lots of ideas of what we could say with both theological and pastoral integrity and compassion. We came up with 'hope' and then tried to figure out what type of hope this child might ask us for. The unanimous agreement was 'Held in Hope'. This is what we felt we could say to the child and, more importantly, what the child might want from us and God. If I did it again, I might try to bring some real patients into the midst of the discussion.
>
> *The Revd Paul Nash, Senior Chaplain, Birmingham Women's and Children's Hospital, UK*

As we have approached the task of compiling and editing this book, we have been very conscious of having the child in the midst of our thinking as, ultimately, paediatric chaplaincy is about making a difference for our patients, and much of the other work we may do has that end as a goal.

What is distinctive about chaplaincy with children and young people?

At the beginning of a vocation to chaplaincy, it is very helpful to think about and articulate how chaplaincy is different to other types of work or ministry. Around the world, chaplaincy with children and young people can be found in education, justice systems, uniformed organisations, leisure and sports, hostels, as well as health and hospice care. But what makes chaplaincy different from other types of ministry?

- **Authority.** It is key to remember that our client groups are not in our setting because of the chaplain. They are here for another reason – that of medical care. The client/patient 'inherits' the chaplain by coming to the hospital. Whereas the family's chosen religious tradition holds a religious authority in their lives, the hospital chaplain was 'inherited' when they arrived at the hospital. Thus the chaplain does not have the same authority, and the role instead is one of accompanying them through the experience and seeing to any unmet spiritual needs during the stay. In some cases, patients or families feel freer to discuss spiritual distress with the chaplain precisely because we are *not* their religious leader.

- **Navigation.** It is not our ground or patch. It belongs to someone else, but it may not be their familiar ground either. Far from abdicating all spiritual care only to the family's faith tradition, the chaplain can assist both the family and their faith leaders in navigating the complicated world of modern medical care.

- **Transition.** Often paediatric chaplaincy happens around times of transition, whether from illness/injury back to health, or from life into death. The spiritual needs are magnified in such transitions, and chaplains are present to identify and serve those needs.

These characteristics of chaplaincy with children and young people are important for us to reflect on as it will help us discern why we might be struggling (Nash and Roberts 2016).

PRACTICE EXAMPLE I.3: A DIFFERENT CALLING

A severe drug reaction landed a school-age boy in our PICU. As I met the family, it became clear that they were very involved in their church, whose pastor visited them at the hospital. However, the pastor admitted that he felt out of his element. He was grateful that I could be present for him as he served this family. I listened to his concerns and sadness for this child's impending death as we both took a turn in his room so the parents could rest.

Chaplain Mark Bartel, Manager of Spiritual Care, Arnold Palmer Medical Center, Orlando, Florida, USA

Another contribution to articulating the distinctiveness of paediatric chaplaincy involved a systematic literature review (see Nash and McSherry 2017). Four representative databases were searched using key words and Boolean searches: Proquest Nursing and Allied Health Source, Psychinfo, Cumulative Index of Allied Health Literature (CINAHL) and American Theological Library Association (ATLA). Inclusion and exclusion criteria were applied to identify pertinent literature. The search resulted in the identification of 96 items. These were retrieved and reviewed and four broad themes emerged.

- Theme 1: Relating to and supporting families including palliative, end-of-life and bereavement care.
- Theme 2: Relating to and supporting children and young people.
- Theme 3: Chaplaincy as part of a multidisciplinary team.
- Theme 4: Staff support and self-care of paediatric chaplains.

This book will explore these areas but also embrace much more specific elements of the role of a paediatric chaplain which is much less reported in existing literature. We are grateful to be able to build on some significant earlier writing in the field (cf. Bull 2016; Burleigh 2011; Friesen 2000; Fosarelli 2012; Grossoehme 1999; Hesch 1987; Shelly 1982; Sommer 2012; Vandecreek and Lucas 2001).

Spectrum of the work of a paediatric chaplain

What we hope to show, celebrate and inspire is the full spectrum of paediatric chaplaincy. Many of the following chapters will go further into this. However, there are three practices that are core to what paediatric chaplains offer:

- Religious care is care offered in relation to the tenets, practices, rituals and conventions of a particular religious faith, taking into account age and capacity.
- Spiritual care concerns itself with the big questions of life involving connectedness, who someone is, their purpose, their destiny, their identity and any relationship with the transcendent.
- Pastoral care is a term used beyond a Christian context – for example, in schools – and refers to care given to address the

cares, concerns, problems, needs and issues of an individual or family that impacts their wellbeing.

(Adapted from Nash 2011)

It is interesting to note that different countries use these words differently and some interchangeably. One of the objectives of this book is to be clear in what we mean by each term, so that we can present our work consistently across contexts and countries. Many of us are also involved in training our staff in multifaith care, diversity and self-care. Some of our institutions have this training as their core activity. One of the pieces of work we are involved in at Birmingham Women's and Children's Hospital is to create a taxonomy of paediatric chaplaincy drawing on the work of the Advocate team in Chicago (Massey *et al.* 2015) to help find a shared vocabulary for both chaplains and multidisciplinary staff which will help with charting and explaining what we do.

Spiritual care specialists

With spiritual care being explicit or implicit in multidisciplinary healthcare staff's job descriptions, it has become even more important that chaplaincy clarifies what our and other healthcare professionals' roles and responsibilities are. We can be confident, or at least grow into it, that we are a peer professional with unique skills and knowledge to bring to the hospital and bedside. The idea of generalist and specialist spiritual carers supports our distinctiveness. Chaplains are the specialists, and other relevant professionals are the generalists.

Scope of care: patients, families, staff, institution, community

Expanding the scope of those for whom we care, support, train and equip brings clarity and depth to our work:

- **Patients.** In both the UK and the US, the early default focus of care was with parents. This was not only because many patients were too young or too sick to engage with reciprocally, but because engaging with adults was the normative skill most new chaplains brought with them.

- **Families.** However, many of us have built up skills and resources in relating with patients from neonates to adolescents. The stresses and strains families feel when a child is ill are often apparent, and it is clear that the wellbeing of the parent impacts their child. Thus work with families is an integral part of the role.

- **Staff.** While sometimes considered 'indirect care' of the patient, staff care is critical for the ongoing provision of healing in our facilities. A strong, spiritually healthy staff is the best hope for the children who come to us for treatment. A growing number of facilities now have chaplains assigned directly to the spiritual care of staff, such as St Jude's in Memphis.

- **Institutions.** We are not only the chaplain for and to the individual patient and their families, but also to the whole institution. This might be a part of the historical establishment of the hospital or hospice or unit, or it might be something that has had to be worked at or does not really exist. Care happens day to day but also in palliative, end-of-life and bereavement contexts. Some hospitals will have chaplains allocated to individual units or wards who are specialists in, for example, trauma, mental health or neonates.

- **Community.** As the wider community realises and understands what we do, and we reflect on what the realities are of supporting sick patients and their families in their communities and homes, we are able to see how we can support each other.

Standards and competencies from around the world

There are several countries that have very helpfully developed specific standards and/or competences for chaplaincy, and learning from each other may mean an even sharper set. See, for example:

- **USA:** Pediatric Chaplain Demonstrated Competencies and Pediatric Chaplains Network Code of Ethics (http://pediatricchaplains.org/about/professional-standards). These are the most useful as they are specifically for the paediatric context.

However, there are some core and generic skills across chaplaincy contexts, and these examples offer approaches to consider:

- **UK:** UK Board of Healthcare Chaplaincy, Chaplaincy Standards (www.ukbhc.org.uk/publications/standards)

Standards of Practice for Professional Chaplains in Hospice and Palliative Care (www.professionalchaplains.org/files/professional_standards/standards_of_practice/standards_of_practice_hospice_palliative_care.pdf)

Association of Hospice & Palliative Care Chaplains, Chaplaincy Standards (www.ahpcc.org.uk/employment/chaplaincy-standards)

Catholic Healthcare Chaplains, Standards for Certification (www.catholicbishops.ie/wp-content/uploads/2014/01/Standards-for-Certification-in-Healthcare-Chaplaincy-1-January-2014.pdf).

- **Australia:** Spiritual Health Victoria, Standards and Framework (www.spiritualhealthvictoria.org.au/standards-and-frameworks).

Overview of the book and how to use it

This book can act as a resource both for existing chaplains and in the induction of new chaplains, and may function as a text book for the growing number of courses in paediatric chaplaincy as well as resourcing volunteer training. It is one that can be read from cover to cover or dipped into for insights on particular topics. We hope it will be useful for teams to discuss and develop their own practice and also give insight into the role of a paediatric chaplain to other multidisciplinary staff. Each chapter will contain several practice examples, engage with relevant theory and include future research needs and reflection questions. We are using 'children' as an inclusive term to cover all paediatric patients, and when we say 'hospital' or 'institution', this includes all healthcare contexts including hospices and community provision. What the book does not cover is some of the basic chaplaincy skills such as reflective practice or generic pastoral care which are covered in other texts.

The book is in two sections: principles and core practices, and specialisms and specific skills. The first two chapters respectively focus on spirituality and faith development (Rebecca Nye) and child development (Dan Roberts). Chapter 3 explains and discusses the key terms of spiritual, religious and pastoral care through case studies (Claire Carson), and Chapter 4 explores models of paediatric chaplaincy (Paul Nash). Chapter 5 provides a helpful overview of screening and assessment (Mary Robinson). Chapter 6 draws on theory and practice from work with children and young people (Ryan Campbell and Sally Nash). The next four chapters pick up some of the non-patient-focused work: work with families (Chapter 7, Krista Gregory), staff care and self-care (Chapter 8, Kathryn Darby and Carl Aiken), the role of chaplain to the institution (Chapter 9, Jim Linthicum) and managing and developing chaplaincy provision (Chapter 10, Paul Nash). In the final chapter of this first section, we delve into the work of ethics committees and ethical decision-making (Chapter 11, Mark Bartel).

In the second section, we learn about working with patients who cannot speak (Chapter 12, Daniel Nuzum), in mental health contexts (Chapter 13, Kathryn Darby), in trauma and abuse cases (Chapter 14, Bob Flory), and chaplaincy during major incidents (Chapter 15, Naomi Kalish). The next two chapters look at palliative and end-of-life care (Chapter 16, M. Karen Ballard) and bereavement care (Chapter 17, Edina Farkas and Stephen Harrison). Chapter 18 focuses on the chaplain's role in patient transition to adult care (Kobena Charm). Space and environment are discussed in Chapter 19 (Wyatt Butcher and Lindsay B. Carey). Chapter 20 focuses on research (Daniel H. Grossoehme and Lindsay B. Carey), Chapter 21 explores theodicy (Kathleen Ennis-Durstine) and the final chapter explores perspectives on suffering from major faith and worldview traditions (Emma Roberts). Appendix 1 gives a perspective on paediatric chaplaincy in a general hospital (Deborah Louise Wilde) and Appendix 2 is a list of helpful websites.

Pseudonyms have been used in all the practice examples unless specific permission has been given to do otherwise.

Future development and research needs

- A taxonomy of what paediatric chaplains actually do.
- Universal standards, guidelines for good practice for paediatric chaplaincy.
- Training and development of resources based upon core and prioritised distinctives.

Summary

Paediatric chaplaincy is a richly diverse discipline that is expressed by a deep commitment to person-centred care and professional conduct. To date, our work has developed in silos, and apart from the occasional cross-visit by some of our members on study grants or attending conferences, it has not developed in its research and agreed values, standards and practices; perhaps this is acceptable given its diverse contexts around the world. At the time of writing, there are signs that this is changing and we can look forward to a more synergised vocation.

Questions for reflection

- Do you recognise the distinctive themes and spectrum of work in your context?
- How would you assess your service against these themes?
- What would be the priority in your context to address and develop?

References

Bull, A. (2016) *Assessing and Communicating the Spiritual Needs of Children in Hospital.* London: Jessica Kingsley Publishers.

Burleigh, B. (2011) 'Sheffield Children's Hospital NHS Foundation Trust.' In M. Threlfall-Holmes and M. Newittt (eds) *Being a Chaplain.* London: SPCK.

Friesen, M.F. (2000) *Spiritual Care for Children Living in Specialized Settings: Breathing Underwater.* New York, NY: Haworth Pastoral Press.

Fosarelli, P. (2012) 'The Care of Children.' In M. Cobb, C.M. Puchalski and B. Rumbold (eds) *Oxford Textbook of Spirituality in Healthcare.* Oxford: Oxford University Press.

Grossoehme, D.H. (1999) *The Pastoral Care of Children.* Binghamton, NY: Haworth Pastoral Press.

Hesch, J. (1987) *Clinical Pastoral Care for Hospitalized Children and their Families.* New York, NY: Paulist Press.

Massey, K., Barnes, M.J., Villines, D., Goldstein, J.D. *et al.* (2015) 'What do I do? Developing a taxonomy of chaplaincy activities and interventions for spiritual care in intensive care unit palliative care.' *BMC Palliative Care 14,* 10, https://doi.org/10.1186/s12904-015-0008-0.

Nash, P. (2011) *Supporting Sick and Dying Children and Their Families.* London: SPCK.

Nash, P. and McSherry, W. (2017) 'What is the distinctiveness of paediatric chaplaincy? Findings from a systematic review of the literature.' *Health and Social Care Chaplaincy 5,* 1, 16–32.

Nash, P. and Roberts, N. (2016) *Chaplaincy with Children and Young People.* Cambridge: Grove Books.

NHS England (2015) NHS Chaplaincy Guidelines. Accessed on 21/11/2017 at www.england.nhs.uk/wp-content/uploads/2015/03/nhs-chaplaincy-guidelines-2015.pdf.

Shelly, J.A. (1982) *The Spiritual Needs of Children.* Downers Grove, IL: InterVarsity Press.

Sommer, D.R. (2012) 'Pediatric Chaplaincy.' In S.B. Roberts (ed.) *Professional, Spiritual and Pastoral Care: A Practical Clergy and Chaplain's Handbook.* Woodstock: Skylight Paths.

Swift, C. (2009) *Hospital Chaplaincy in the Twenty-first Century.* London: Routledge.

Vandecreek, L. and Lucas, A.M. (2001) *The Discipline for Pastoral Care Giving.* New York, NY: Routledge.

Section 1

Principles and Core Practices

Chapter 1
Child Spirituality and Faith Development
Rebecca Nye

Introduction

An understanding of child spirituality and child faith development is vital for chaplaincy. In some senses, childhood spirituality and faith development run alongside each other, but they can also pull in opposite directions, even concealing different views of childhood itself. In the popular mind, spirituality and faith tend to be seen quite differently: whereas spirituality is associated with openness and flexibility, faith is considered a more fixed or set pathway. And in research, faith development and spirituality tend to address different things and in different ways.

For a child, however, spirituality and faith are likely to be a complex mixture, where it is difficult to be clear about where one thing ends and the other begins. So, although in practice it can be tempting to seek a distinction between spiritual care and faith-based care, these may be adult categories of convenience. A child with ostensibly no faith in particular or who is at a very early stage of 'faith development' may have a surprisingly deep faith of their own making fuelled by natural spiritual sensitivity. Equally, a child whose family has a clear faith context will not necessarily find their faith is a source of spiritual solace, but may be engaged in their own exploration of spiritual life.

Faith development

Perspectives

'Faith development' represents the idea that there may be predictable time-related patterns in how a person's faith is expressed – for example, their ideas about God, prayer or sacred stories. As psychology has charted distinct stages in children's cognitive, emotional, social and moral development, it seems plausible to consider whether faith might be stage-like too, or at least affected by development in other domains.

It can certainly be helpful to be aware of the general patterns in child development and how these may affect the child's understanding of faith issues. For example, until the age of about 10–11 children's thinking tends to be quite literal, so more abstract concepts of God might be difficult. Similarly, when younger children's language development is relatively basic, they might struggle to talk explicitly about religious material (such as a Bible story or prayer) but they may readily latch on to a key emotion or salient image.

> PRACTICE EXAMPLE 1.1: THE PARABLE OF THE LOST SHEEP – RECONCILIATION THROUGH GODLY PLAY
>
> Several times I made use of a Godly Play parable box within my pediatric ministry. On one occasion, I visited an eight-year-old girl who had been brought to the hospital on pretense by her mother and left to have surgery; she had not spoken to her mother for two days despite her mother's pleas for forgiveness – she was angry and hurt. I brought in the gold box and after gently introducing myself, and getting to know her a bit, I asked if I could tell her a story. Intrigued by the box, she nodded and watched the story unfold out of the corner of her eyes. Later she sat up and said she wanted to do the story. She retold the story, naming the sheep that the Shepherd found; the biggest sheep was her baby brother and she was the baby sheep. Her mother got the message – she had treated her daughter without regard for what she could handle at her age, and the mother named it, saying, 'I treated you like a baby, didn't I?' They played with the story that evening, finding comfort in the retelling, and finding reconciliation and reframing for their relationship.
>
> *Mary D. Davis, Regional Director, Spiritual Care and Education, CHRISTUS Santa Rosa Health System, San Antonio, Texas, USA*

However, a faith development perspective requires caution. First, developmental models can encourage a hierarchical mindset where 'lower' stages are seen as less valid, and later stages as more mature and 'real'. This risks seeing a child's understanding of faith (of prayer, a story, God) as half-baked or error-prone, rather than deeply authentic on its own terms. Second, following the models of development in other psychological domains also means a tendency to characterise children negatively, in terms of their limitations compared with an adult norm, rather than perceiving the strengths that only childhood confers. Studies of children's spirituality have helped to challenge this bias, showing that children often have spiritual capacities that are much harder to engage in adulthood. Third, although there are interesting models of faith development (e.g. Fowler below) that chart potential changes across the whole life-span, these have been informed by adult-based research, and may also lack sufficient sensitivity to gender and religious tradition. And finally, reaching a psychological stage in cognitive, social or emotional development does not guarantee that faith development will match that. In fact, many adults exhibit a faith stage typically associated with childhood, and conversely some features of the earliest childhood stages also reappear in the 'highest' stages. As a result, faith development models need to be applied carefully in chaplaincy with children to avoid untoward side-effects.

Principles, values, research

Developmental psychology helps us to see that children differ not only in terms of how much they know but also in terms of how they think. Inspired by Piaget's account of different stages in the structure of children's thinking, Goldman (1964) and others explored how this affects thoughts about faith. This suggested there are three phases – loosely related to preschool, primary and early teens onwards (see Nye 2001, and Table 1.1).

TABLE 1.1: DEVELOPMENT THEORY AND FAITH

Stage 1 Intuitive religious thinking Age 2–5	Scripture: given to magical explanations of religious events; takes in images rather than a narrative sequence.
	God image: a magical power.
	Prayer: a wishful, magical activity.
	Religious identity: automatic, unquestioned, like my name (e.g. Jew).
Stage 2 Literal religious thinking Age 5–11	Scripture: engrossed by narrative but can't extract meaning; metaphors are opaque.
	God image: anthropomorphic (e.g. man with beard, sits on cloud).
	Prayer: instrumental; bargaining to get things I'd like.
	Religious identity: literal logic (I'm Christian because my family is, so our cat must be too!).

Stage 3 Abstract religious thinking Age 11+	Scripture: can use symbolic, metaphorical levels of meaning to make sense; deeper concepts are possible (e.g. salvation, sacrifice).
	God image: can be abstract, multifaceted (e.g. love, creative force, Trinity, judge).
	Prayer: exploration of oneself before God; communicative.
	Religious identity: outcome of making a personal choice.

James Fowler's life-span 'stages of faith' model (Fowler 1981, 1987) is widely used in pastoral care, and is intended to apply to any faith. With adults, a person's stage is ascertained through a lengthy interview process that considers their current and past faith. It is not intended to be a simple capture of key features – observing details and conversation still matter. However, having a general idea of the early stages (0–3) in Fowler's model may provide a useful heuristic. Fowler draws on Piaget's understanding of the typical stages in a child's intellectual development, Erikson's understanding of psychosocial development and Kohlberg's work on moral development – recognising that the context for a child's faith includes their cognitive, emotional and social worlds.

FOWLER'S STAGES OF FAITH

Stage 0: Primal or Undifferentiated Faith tends to characterise infants up to three years. Faith emerges as a sense of trust, pre-verbally, and positive early relations help to create a sense of being 'in relation' and safety.

Stage 1: Intuitive–Projective Faith is typical in children aged three to six years. Their faith is led by imagination and feelings, mystery and curiosity. There is an intuitive attraction to strong images on to which children can project overwhelming feelings of power or powerlessness, good or evil, and these help to contain those issues.

Stage 2: Mythic–Literal Faith emerges from about age six to twelve. Faith starts to be a kind of simple thinking, rather than 'just' feelings. Crucially, stories (rather than images) can now help to hold together sequences of ideas, feelings or values. However, there may be little interest in meanings or reflection outside the story: the literal narrative demands all of a child's attention.

> **Stage 3:** Synthetic–Conventional Faith may develop from adolescence, aided by new capacities for abstract thought and teens' experience of wider social networks. Faith becomes a form of loyalty, influenced by self-awareness and awareness of others. There is a growing sense of meaning to be found beyond the literal – for example, in parable, in drawing ideas together. Faith is expressed in personal relationships with like-minded people, and affirmed in feeling part of the consensus. It is common for God and the church/synagogue (etc.) to be viewed in interpersonal terms, as a new form of family, and faith role-models can be influential. According to Fowler's research, many adults remain at this stage their whole lives. However, a further four adult stages are possible (see Nye 2001 or Fowler 1981).

Implications

Goldman's (1964) portrayal of steps in religious thinking can provide some useful clues for practice. For example, it might suggest only cautious use of 'miracle' and similar stories which inadvertently foster a magical view of God. The way a child's religious identity develops also reminds us that phrases like 'as a Muslim/Sikh/Christian' may hold very different meanings in conversations with children. Realising that younger children may see prayer merely as a list or bargaining exercise, rather than an extension of normal 'communication', suggests caution when moving from conversation into prayer. The model also suggests that petitionary prayer is something younger children may find confusing, whereas prayers of thanksgiving sit very naturally in a child's mind (Cavalletti 1992). Notice in the example below how the girl transforms the prayer into a thanksgiving even though her faith issues seem pointed to things with which she wanted help.

PRACTICE EXAMPLE 1.2: WHY DOES GOD HATE ME?

I was called to support a young girl. 'Why does God hate me?' she asked. This was an understandable question given that she suffered from a chronic illness, limiting her from many activities she would enjoy and longed to participate in. She wondered why God would give her this disease. Why did God withhold from her the many pleasures other kids enjoy? It didn't make any sense. We talked about the things she missed, her frustrations and sadness. We talked about expressing some of these feelings to God. I mentioned a written prayer we sometimes give to people at the

> hospital when they are going through a difficult time; it expresses some of the pains and challenges she was naming. She wanted to see it. The expressions in the prayer were geared towards an adult's understanding. We decided it could be worthwhile rewriting the prayer in her own words. Surprisingly, what emerged was quite a different prayer: one of gratitude for the many things she enjoyed and cherished in her life! We printed out a copy of the prayer and posted it on the wall of her room so others could read it. She was glowing with pride and a sense of accomplishment.
>
> *Linda Wollschlaeger-Fischer, MTS Spiritual Health Leader, Spiritual Care Counsellor, British Columbia, Canada*

Fowler's model has many implications for pastoral care too. For those working with children, the model indicates the 'dominant mode' (or super-power!) of faith at each stage – trust and a pre-verbal world of relationships (0–3 years), image and feelings (3–6 years), the power to be 'in' a story (6–12 years) and faith as expression of 'meaning' and interpersonal identity (12+). Given the potential for up to four seismic changes in faith in just 12 years, care might also involve supporting children's transitions between stages and the potential sense of loss, doubt and search that each change entails. Many psychologists identify stage-changes as a process of deconstruction and reconstruction often precipitated by a crisis, and it is possible that a health crisis could be the catalyst for faith changes.

However, evidence also suggests that faith development tends to lag behind other areas of the child's development, perhaps unsurprisingly since faith comprises such complex issues. This can mean that although a child might 'just about' manage story-based support because they are school age and generally enjoy stories, when their energies are low it might be more comfortable and satisfying for them to slip back into an earlier mode of faith – pre-verbal or image- and feelings-based. Similarly, the teenage capacity for reflective awareness and dealing in abstract concepts such as hope, peace or forgiveness might not yet be very robust or might require too much effort to be really supportive, so they may appreciate interventions that take a step back to faith preferences at an earlier stage.

On the other hand, it's important that faith development models don't lead to underestimating children's faith. Hull (1991, p.11) makes the case for the 'power of a child's concrete theology', describing how despite using a very literal kind of thinking, if we pay attention to the details, subtext and tone of voice, children often express ideas with direct equivalents in theological discourse. This 'theology of children' capacity is being increasingly recognised (Lindner 2004; Zimmerman 2015) and alerts chaplaincy to the significant role of autonomy and agency as children constantly attend to the construction of their faith. Indeed, at times the chaplain might need to provide a buffer between the family's faith (including an atheistic stance) and the child's own, hard-to-articulate, perspective.

> ### PRACTICE EXAMPLE 1.3: A CHILD'S INSIGHTS
>
> Trevor is an eight-year-old who was in the PICU with a recent leukemia diagnosis. He was having a hard day, and his nurse asked me to see him. I walked into the room, looked at him and said, 'Hi, are you Trevor?' He nodded, and I explained I was the chaplain, greeting his dad at the same time. 'Have you ever met a chaplain before, or do you know what that is?' He shook his head no. I asked if he'd ever met a pastor or minister before, and he said yes, his eyes brightening a little. 'Well, I'm like a pastor, but instead of working at a church, I work here at the hospital. I listen to people, talk to people, sometimes I even pray with people. Do you ever pray at home?'
>
> 'Oh yes,' Trevor said. 'I just talked to God the other day. I told him it wasn't fair that I'm sick.'
>
> 'It's not fair,' I agreed.
>
> 'But God told me that he picked me because I'm strong and I can get better,' Trevor said. 'He said it really wouldn't be fair to make another kid get sick who couldn't get better.'
>
> 'That makes sense!' I said, and our conversation continued on, talking a little about God, a little about Iron Man, and a lot about Lego®.
>
> Toward the end of the visit, having confirmed that Trevor came from a Christian family and was well connected to his faith, I asked if he had any favorite Bible stories. He told me the whole story of David and Goliath. Suddenly, he became thoughtful, 'You know, being here is kinda like David and Goliath, except instead it's Trevor and cancer.' His dad had tears in his eyes.
>
> Two years later, Trevor is in remission.
>
> *Joshua Andrzejewski, Chaplain, Virginia Commonwealth University Health, Richmond, Virginia, USA*

In summary, the use of faith development models requires rather a critical and flexible approach, but they can provide some helpful categories to sort out what can seem quite chaotic expressions and evidence of children's faith issues.

Children's spirituality

Perspectives

Spirituality is no longer synonymous with aspects of a person's religious life, but includes many different ways that people may encounter fundamental issues of existence. Often this requires the individual to define 'what is spiritual' for themselves. This means it can be especially hard to think about children's spirituality; we may need to see both spirituality and childhood differently. First, it helps to have a generous view about what 'spirituality' entails, to see things from a child's point of view, even though they might not have the words we normally use to self-define spiritual life. And, second, it helps to have a generous view of childhood, not just to see it as a set of limitations or stages, but to recall the feel of childhood and its distinctive qualities and capacities.

The dominant contemporary view is that childhood provides very auspicious conditions for spirituality, seeing it as a natural, rich and early childhood capacity (Hay and Nye 1998; Nye 2009), even in babies (Surr 2012). This firmly rejects the image of the child as a spiritually empty vessel or as spiritually dormant. In fact, evidence points to how naturally spirituality arises in childhood, and to its tendency to diminish or become suppressed over time (Hay and Nye 2006), possibly because sociocultural factors like education or materialism easily choke an instinctive spirituality.

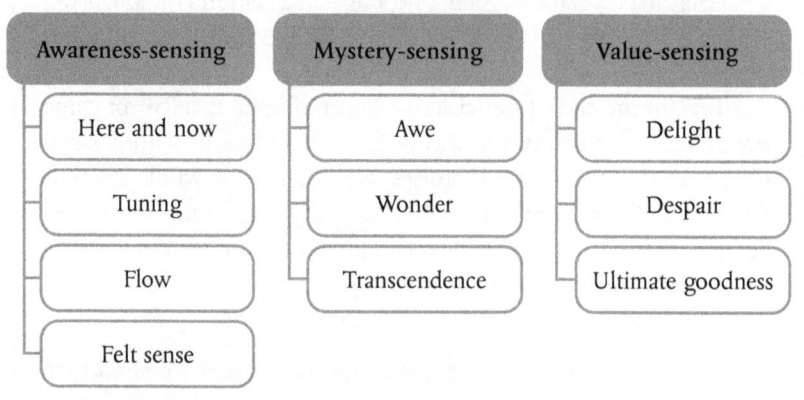

Awareness-sensing	Mystery-sensing	Value-sensing
Here and now	Awe	Delight
Tuning	Wonder	Despair
Flow	Transcendence	Ultimate goodness
Felt sense		

Figure 1.1: Mapping the natural spiritual strengths of children
Source: Hay and Nye 2006

Hay and Nye mapped out areas where spirituality might be found, even in the youngest child, by looking for the overlaps between their characteristic psychological strengths and features commonly associated with adult spiritual life (Figure 1.1). For example, children's awareness-sensing is naturally supported by their acute engagement in the 'here and now', as well as an ability for 'tuning in' things around them. These may give children a heightened sense of being connected to things – for example, with nature or a deep sense of belonging. Children's constant work to master new skills – from breast-feeding to riding a bike – also provides natural opportunity for grace-like experience of 'flow' when previously the activity had required effort and attention. Likewise, children pay more attention to bodily knowing, an intuitive 'felt sense' of things on which spiritual sensitivity often thrives.

Children's capacity for 'mystery-sensing' is an asset for potentially spiritual encounters, too. Because of their limited experience and weaker understanding of how things work, their days are filled with opportunities for awe and wonder.

'Value-sensing' refers to ways in which childhood privileges feeling and emotions, before intellect and reasoning move in to dominate things. This makes children's sensitivity to delight, despair and a (child-like) sense of ultimate goodness (or evil) particularly acute.

Research, principles and implications

This way of seeing childhood as naturally attuned to many aspects of spiritual life is confirmed by research across the world (Watson, de Souza and Trousdale 2014). Chaplaincy will benefit from critically auditing its activities and mindset and considering how best to:

- think imaginatively about the experience of each child
- cultivate a 'high-expectations' view of the spirituality of childhood
- ensure that practices live up to the quality and potency of children's spirituality.

The following research-based principles and implications may help meet these needs.

PRINCIPLE 1
Spirituality permeates children's everyday lives and can be found in a wide range of everyday experiences and exploration such as children's play,

daydreaming, storytelling and curiosity to question and make meaning. In this way, spirituality can be less obvious, but more prevalent. An implication of this is for chaplaincy spiritual care activities to focus primarily on who the child is and how their spirituality is revealed in their everyday being and doing. This includes being mindful that providing 'special activities' could sometimes unintentionally distract us from doing that. Another implication is the need to be on high alert for the ways that the 'big spiritual issues' (e.g. Who am I? What determines things? Do things make sense/have meaning? What's after the ending?) are manifest in children's ordinary play and reactions. And being an advocate for the deep, spiritual undercurrents of simple things such as being called by their preferred name, being given some sense of control or the validity of 'irrational' fears or questions.

PRINCIPLE 2

Spirituality has an important function in children's wellbeing, supporting their need for meaning, purpose and connectedness both now and in the future (Hyde 2008). By implication, if spirituality is neglected or denigrated in childhood, there is a risk of dysfunction and resilience suffers (Lipscomb and Gersch 2012). For chaplaincy, this confirms that the child's own spirituality is an integral part of health care, which may require some advocacy, as others may have the view that chaplaincy mostly provides for the spiritual care of the affected adults around the child. The important function of spirituality in wellbeing also implies that poor or absent spiritual care could add to a sick child's distress. Evaluation of spiritual care encounters should include reflection on ways that input or avoidance may have left a negative trace.

PRINCIPLE 3

Spirituality is strongly non-verbal, even when children have good language skills. Children most easily express and experience spiritual matters through gesture, image, laughter, tears and silence, and in sensory ways (light, sound, touch). Being less tied to a 'head-centred' and verbal mode, children's spirituality can be especially connected to their physical body and their physical world. To allow space for spirituality to emerge in an encounter, it will help consciously to limit how much you speak, regardless of whether the child can understand words well or hardly at all. Listening can include valuing and paying attention to the silences in your encounters – the gift of being quiet together may be especially treasured in a noisy ward. Equally, children's need to use words should be kept to a minimum, with non-verbal alternatives offered and modelled (art, image, play). It may be important to assure children that these alternative expressions are fully valid, and don't necessarily need to be talked about either.

PRINCIPLE 4
Children's spirituality comes out of, and leads deeper into, forms of relational awareness. Mounting evidence shows that, from infancy, children have astute relational sensitivity (Nye 2018). Children's spirituality arises as a sense relation to what is 'other' – other people, a sacred Other, a different sense of themselves – a deep Self, and their environment (Hay and Nye 2006). This implies that good practice might make particular provision for children to focus on 'others', not just themselves. For example, their spiritual work could include acts of care for others (a family member, another patient or the chaplain) or thanksgiving opportunities, since these give the child a much-needed focus beyond their immediate (sick) self. And through such moments of compassionate relatedness to others, children may activate the 'self-soothing' effects of calm and inner peace (Gilbert 2010).

PRINCIPLE 5
Children often feel their spirituality needs to be private, secret or hidden. Perhaps this stems from the paradox that they enjoy heightened spiritual sensitivity, but the 'world' does not seems to notice or affirm their capacity for this. Children report feeling quite alone with their spirituality, and older children assume that no one else considers or experiences these things (Hay and Nye 1998). Adults recalling their childhood spirituality often admit that they spoke to no one about it at the time, intuiting that they would be misunderstood or considered weird. This highlights the fragile nature of spiritual care. Children require assurance of very safe space, confidentiality and a sense of intimacy in order to share the depths of their spiritual life. These things are often lacking in hospital settings, and providing them will require imagination and determination. Although a private physical space may be impossible, the safe boundaries and thresholds into and out of spiritual encounters can be created by simple rituals which will frame each meeting, or special parts within it. Similarly, chaplains can encourage children to value anything produced (pictures, writing, etc.) as out-workings of a personal process, rather than products for display.

PRINCIPLE 6
Childhood spirituality may have an unpredictable relationship with faith. Even within faiths there may be a wide range of views about children's spiritual capacity, and sometimes inconsistency between what is said about and done with children. In many traditions, there are some who adopt a

'generous' view of the child's spirituality, seeking to honour the child's ways of spiritual knowing despite their relative lack of knowledge and understanding about their faith. For others, knowledge 'about' faith is the gateway to spirituality, so child spirituality is regarded as a matter of learning to follow adult practice and language. Evidence suggests that sometimes children find their religious context inhibits their spirituality, although children outside a faith tradition will readily reach for religious ideas or practices to furnish their spirituality (Hay and Nye 2006). A key practice implication is to avoid assumptions, be relaxed about unorthodox ideas and provide as much openness as possible. Furthermore, regardless of their faith context, the upset of being hospitalised may add to the child's natural need to exercise spiritual agency and to find their own voice/outlook. This spiritual autonomy may affect the balance of power between adults and children – for example, where a child may have spiritual concerns or needs that his family doesn't share, or wishes to be avoided with the child, or vice versa.

Future development and research needs

- Are there universal spiritual needs of children?
- How might spiritual needs, understanding and principles change according to different illnesses, ages and conditions?
- Spiritual history, screening and assessment models for different illnesses, ages and conditions.

Summary

Being equipped with an informed (but wary) attitude to faith development models and striving for generous and curious expectations of children's spirituality will provide chaplains with a powerful internal compass for devising and evaluating their own sensitive spiritual care practices. There are some specific resources which are already informed by wisdom and research in these domains.

- The Centre for Paediatric Spiritual Care has a growing list of activities (CPSC 2017), many of which support children's need for non-verbal or creative exploration.
- For accessible practice guidelines about 'Facilitating Spiritual Conversations' with children, see Nye's suggestions in Nash, Darby and Nash (2015, pp.173–177).

- Nye's (2009) illustrated child spirituality checklist, 'S.P.I.R.I.T.', can help in the planning or evaluation of sessions. Its key components act as prompts to ensure that the highest qualities of Space, Process, Imagination, Relationship, Intimacy and Trust govern the use of any chosen method or resource.
- Finally, 'Godly Play' provides both a method and ready-made resources which have stood the test of time over four decades (www.godlyplay.uk; see also Chapter 7). Its roots lie in Berryman's work as a hospital chaplain (described in Berryman 2013, p.111), and it encompasses a particularly thorough approach to all the principles discussed in this chapter.

Questions for reflection

- What insights have you gained about how to engage with a child's spirituality while they are in hospital?
- How might we critique and apply child spirituality theory to our practice?
- How might you use the principles listed above to help other healthcare professionals understand child spirituality?

References

Berryman, J. (2013) *The Spiritual Guidance of Children: Montessori, Godly Play, and the Future.* Denver, CO: Morehouse Publishing.

Cavalletti, S. (1992) *The Religious Potential of the Child: Experiencing Scripture and Liturgy with Young Children.* Chicago, IL: Liturgy Training Publications.

CPSC (2017) Centre for Paediatric Spiritual Care Resources. Accessed on 21/11/2017 at http://bwc.nhs.uk/centre-for-paediatric-spiritual-care.

Fowler, J. (1981) *Stages of Faith.* New York, NY: Harper & Row.

Fowler, J. (1987) *Faith Development and Pastoral Care.* Minneapolis, MN: Augsburg Press.

Gilbert, P. (2010) *The Compassionate Mind.* Edinburgh: Constable.

Goldman, R. (1964) *Religious Thinking from Childhood to Adolescence.* London: Routledge and Kegan Paul.

Hay, D. and Nye, R. (1998) *The Spirit of the Child,* first edition. London: Fount.

Hay, D. and Nye, R. (2006) *The Spirit of the Child,* revised edition. London: Jessica Kingsley Publishers.

Hull, J. (1991) *What Prevents Christian Adults from Learning.* Philadelphia, PA: Trinity International Press and London: SCM Press.

Hyde, B. (2008) *Children and Spirituality: Searching for Meaning and Connectedness.* London: Jessica Kingsley Publishers.

Lindner, E. (2004) 'Children as Theologians.' In R.B. Pufall and R.P. Unsworth (eds) *Rethinking Childhood.* New Brunswick: Rutgers University Press.

Lipscomb, A. and Gersch, I. (2012) 'Using a "spiritual listening tool" to investigate how children describe spiritual and philosophical meaning in their lives.' *International Journal of Children's Spirituality* 17, 1, 5–23.

Nash, P., Darby, K. and Nash, S. (2015) *Spiritual Care with Sick Children and Young People.* London: Jessica Kingsley Publishers.

Nye, R. (2001) 'Religious Development.' In F. Watts, R. Nye and S. Savage (eds) *Psychology for Christian Ministry.* Abingdon: Routledge.

Nye, R. (2009) *Children's Spirituality: What It Is and Why It Matters.* London: Church House Publishing.

Nye, R. (2018) 'The Spiritual Strengths of Young Children.' In C. Trevarthen, W. Dunlop and J. Delafield-Butt (eds) *The Child's Curriculum.* Oxford: Oxford University Press.

Surr, J. (2012) 'Peering into the clouds of glory: Explorations of a newborn child's spirituality.' *International Journal of Children's Spirituality* 17, 1, 77–78.

Watson, J., de Souza, M. and Trousdale, A. (2014) *Global Perspectives on Spirituality and Education.* Abingdon: Routledge.

Zimmermann, M. (2015) 'What is Children's Theology? Children's theology as theological competence: Development, differentiation, methods.' *HTS Teologiese Studies/Theological Studies* 71, 3, http://dx.doi.org/10.4102/hts.v71i3.2848.

Chapter 2

Insights from Child Development for Pediatric Chaplains

Dan Roberts

PRACTICE EXAMPLE 2.1: ARE YOU FIVE YEARS OLD?

Our CPE [Clinical Pastoral Education] students have an optional opportunity to serve as camp counsellors for a summer camp serving children who have or had cancer. An international student participated as a counsellor with the 5–6-year age group. He learned that his comforting skills left a bit to be desired when he sought to reason with a child, inconsolable due to homesickness. The student said. 'Look at me; I am all the way from Africa. I also miss my parents. But do you see me crying?' The child sobbed, 'Yeah, but are you five years old?'

Mary D. Davis, Regional Director, Spiritual Care and Education CHRISTUS Santa Rosa Health System, San Antonio, Texas, USA

Chaplains desire to build relationships with the patients we serve. While the duration of these relationships might be short or long, they can be significant regardless of length. The goal of this chapter is to provide some understanding of development theory to give us insight into the relationships we create and build as chaplains. While I acknowledge that there exist extensive critiques of many of the development theories most frequently taught, there can be some value in having theoretical frameworks that may bring some insight to our work. For example, Vygotsky (1978) talks about the Zone of Proximal Development (ZPD) which is the difference between what someone can do on their own and what they would be able to do with support or collaboration. Spiritual caregivers can offer this support as the following story illustrates.

> ### PRACTICE EXAMPLE 2.2: NOT JUST FOR ADULTS
>
> Ministering in pediatric intensive care, there is no shortage of scared and anxious kids. One early morning, while I was doing rounds in the PICU, I came across a little cherubic nine-year-old who was alone in her room and looking very scared. As I entered, I introduced myself and asked if she would like some company, and she nodded yes. As I sat next to her bed, she willingly explained she was having surgery today and was waiting on her mom to come. I affirmed her anxiousness and asked about her family and how she calms herself when she is afraid. She said she didn't know. I asked if she had a special place or experience that made her smile every time she thought about it. She said she did, with a hint of a smile. I asked if she could tell me about it, and she told me about her love of the beach and the waves of the ocean, and how they make her feel happy and free. I told her I too loved the beach and the power of the waves – I call it my happy place – and how it helped me with calmness. I asked if she would like to try something called meditation, which can help de-stress, relax, and connect with her own inner source of calm. She said she would like to try, so we began by starting with getting in a position of comfort (she put her stuffed bunny on top of her tummy), noticing our breathing, and then visualizing her happy place at the beach. Directing her to use the inside of her forehead as a screen, I asked if she could see with her mind's eye her favorite beach and asked her to listen for the waves, all the while calling attention to her breathing. She was able to hold her focus for nearly five minutes, and she was so much calmer. About the time we finished her mom walked in, and she said, 'Mommy, I went to my "happy place", and I could hear the waves.' She explained her experience and her anxiety had melted away.
>
> *Peggy Huber, Lead Pediatric Chaplain, The Children's Hospital of San Antonio, Texas, USA*

In the remainder of the chapter, I will look at the different stages of development and seek to make some connections to human development theory and how it might illuminate our work.

Infancy

Infancy is a busy time of physical growth and development, but it is also a time of great relationship growth and faith development. Infants are also new to this scary world. This world is made even scarier if he or she is receiving treatment for medical issues. Thus, feeling loved and cared for are critical for their future physical, mental and spiritual development. Even though they can't verbalize their needs, infants need spiritual care as much as older children and adults, although it is delivered in different ways.

Lisa Miller, the director of the Clinical Psychology Program at Teacher's College, Columbia University, believes that people are innately spiritual. She does not downplay the role that socialization plays in spirituality, but she argues that twin studies show that a significant amount of spirituality is innate. In other words, we are biologically wired as spiritual beings from birth. Our environments either foster or suppress our spirituality (Miller 2015).

Issues of attachment are significant at this stage and hospital stays may impact this. As Mooney observes, we need to 'acknowledge his [Bowlby's] work as the foundation for all of us who study children and families and who view emotional connections as critical to healthy human development and success in adult life' (2010, p.24). For example, chaplains should encourage medically appropriate touch between infants and parents. Parents sometimes fear holding or touching their medically fragile babies. While this fear is understandable, the absence of parental touch can be detrimental to the patient's physical, emotional and spiritual development. Attachment research shows that physical touch from a parent is needed for the child to appropriately develop emotionally and mentally. Research also suggests that medically appropriate touch may be instrumental in spiritual development. Attachment psychologist Bonnie Poon Zahl posits that 'relational patterns developed in early childhood continue to influence other close relationships across our lifespan' (Poon Zahl 2016, p.87). Pehr Granqvist and Lee A. Kirkpatrick (2008) explain that people can have attachment relationships with divine being(s) of their faith, including anxious, avoidant or secure attachments with God. Research continues to show that attachment during our early relationships, especially with primary caregivers, can have a great impact on how we view the divine (Poon Zahl 2016).

In addition to encouraging medically appropriate touch between parents and their infants, chaplains should also interact with these patients themselves. Parents often cannot and often should not be with their hospitalized infant 100% of the time. Chaplains should encourage parents to rest from caregiving for the parents' own health and wellbeing. During these times of parental absence, chaplains have the opportunity to minister directly to the infant. Grossoehme (1999) describes a situation in which a minister shared her frustration of attempting to visit the parents of a hospitalized infant from her parish. However, Grossoehme points out that the minister completely missed the opportunity to minister to the infant during those times by talking to and allowing them to grip their finger because we represent the divine.

Toddlerhood

Toddlers are growing in many dimensions and are engaging with their environment in new ways. They have learned how to travel through crawling and walking. I have a nephew who is currently a toddler. I recently watched him play on a playground, and I was reminded about how toddlers often exhibit a high level of determination and a lack of caution.

At the toddler stage, children begin to establish their independence. Saying 'No!' and learning to walk allow them more freedom from their caregivers. Chaplains can foster relationships with toddlers at this stage by supporting their desire for autonomy (Erikson's (1995) second stage). Giving the child choices, such as asking whether the child wants to color or play with trains, allows the child to express his or her autonomy and helps establish a positive relationship.

Play is the best gateway into a child's world. Play is a way for children to form new relationships with others. At this age, play might be as simple as scribbling with crayons or playing with a plush animal. Grossoehme (1999) encourages chaplains to carry a 'magic visiting bag' filled with play items for a variety of ages with them when they visit children. This bag can contain items such as crayons, paper, travel-size board games, dinosaurs, dolls, etc. Chaplains can also use electronics, such as an iPad or Android tablet, loaded with games and other age-appropriate resources. With all items brought into the room, appropriate infection-control protocols should be used between each patient visit.

Talking to patients on their eye level is important at all ages from a toddler to an elderly patient. Be sure to talk to them on their eye level and use simple words. This could range from standing beside their crib or bed to sitting on the floor with them. Another way to engage toddlers is with simple stories, in language the toddler can understand. Letting the toddler tell you about their pets, favorite toys and loved ones can build and deepen a relationship of trust between the chaplain and the toddler. Focusing on the child can also lead to better relationships with caregivers, because the caregiver sees that you care about their child.

Preschool

Preschoolers' language skills are developing rapidly. Preschoolers can use complete sentences to communicate, are learning the alphabet and sight words, and often enjoy being read to by caregivers. A preschooler's imagination is also a great playground for them. During this stage, toys, coloring and simple games on a tablet are still great tools to connect with patients.

Stories that capture the child's imagination can be another valuable tool to connect with children at this age. During his preschool years, my son began to enjoy stories about superheroes and the epic story of *Star Wars* that occurred 'a long time ago in a galaxy far, far away…' Sharing stories from scripture or holy books is also a great resource for chaplains to connect to the spiritual aspect of children at this age.

Chaplains can also build relationships with their preschool patients by empowering them during ministry as well. When ministering to preschoolers, chaplains can ask for their input in prayers, ask the child what activities he or she wants to do, and allow them to lead the dance of spiritual care. This helps them develop their initiative and agency, which Erikson (1995) sees as a foundational element of this stage. Another important element to consider when building relationships with preschoolers is the need to ask patients for their permission and input from this age group and older. Beginning at this stage, chaplains should not only ask for the patient's parents or guardians permission to enter the room or interact with the patient, but they should also ask for the patient's permission. Often, pediatric patients feel powerless in the hospital: they are not given an option of what medicines to take or when to take them; people come in and out of their rooms all the time without permission; they often cannot wear their own clothes or participate in their normal activities. Chaplains can confront this sense of powerlessness and empower the patient by asking for permission. Sometimes the child will exercise their right to refuse, even to the embarrassment of their parents, but the chaplain can establish a relationship of trust with the child by respecting the child's desire and informing the parents that the child's response is fine.

Grossoehme (1999) also suggests that you should ask the child's permission to talk to the parents or caregivers outside of the room. I appreciate this sentiment, but I respectfully disagree with him. I will ask the caregivers if they would like to talk outside of the room in the hallway or in our consult room. I think that it is important to give the pediatric patients autonomy by allowing them the option of receiving spiritual care, but I do not think that it is appropriate to give them the power to permit or deny others the opportunity to receive spiritual care outside of their room.

School age

Many children of this age tend to focus on fairness and are more thoroughly developing their understanding of right and wrong than at earlier ages. I have an older brother and, at this age, I constantly thought that it was unfair that he was allowed to do things or participate in activities, when I was told that I could not. Looking back, I realize that it was appropriate for him to have these opportunities, since he was older. When I got older, I was able to participate in similar opportunities. As a school-age child, I struggled to understand this concept.

Their understanding of fairness often informs the understanding of right and wrong of children at this age. If something is unfair, then it is wrong, and if it is fair, it is right. My son is seven years old, and he thinks that I am unfair and am treating him wrongly when I do not allow him to watch certain shows that a peer might get to watch. On the other hand, I view it as being a good parent by not letting him watch shows whose target demographic is adults.

At this age, children are developing the mental faculties that allow them to grow in their understanding of right and wrong. This is also a time in which caregivers focus on teaching moral behavior such as do not lie, steal, cheat, etc. This exploration of fairness and right and wrong is often a fertile land for spiritual care with patients in the hospital. As Turiel (1983) suggests, a child's moral development focuses around considering how the effects of actions have an impact on wellbeing, and core concepts that help structure thinking are harm, welfare and fairness. They might think they are being punished with illness or injury due to misdeeds, or struggle with feeling loved by their higher power due to the unfairness that they are ill or injured. This can lead to spiritual distress as they struggle to fit their experience within the framework of their worldview.

School age is also a time when children expand their social networks. The friends they make at school can greatly influence them, and they often want to be liked and accepted by their peers. Illness can have a profound impact on how school-age patients are perceived by other children. Patients might not be able to do certain activities, and they may have times of separation from their peer group due to hospitalization. During this time, children might feel isolated, unaccepted or anxious because of differences in how they look, walk, talk, etc. While chaplains are not a substitute for a supportive peer group, spiritual caregivers can provide a relationship where the child feels accepted as he or she is and encourages the child that he or she is worthy of acceptance and love by others and his or her higher power.

At this age, children often look at how their parents and other adults around them react to gauge the severity of their situation and how they should respond. Children often have the same emotions as adults when coping with health-related issues. The statements and questions children have might be different, but they are often dealing with the same feelings that adults encounter, such as fear, guilt, sadness, anger, etc. In nurturing relationships with school-age children, chaplains should recognize that children may have complex emotions surrounding their illness and work toward building a rapport with the child that acknowledges the child's feelings and creates a safe environment for the child to express their emotions.

> ### PRACTICE EXAMPLE 2.3: COREY AND SOCIAL CUES
>
> Corey was a school-age child being treated for a difficult cancer and was hospitalized for chemotherapy. When I knocked on the door and introduced myself, Corey's father enthusiastically welcomed me into the room, but Corey's response was more subdued. I asked Corey if he knew what a chaplain was. He indicated that he did not, and I explained the chaplain's role in a hospital. At this point, he seemed to relax a little bit. It is important to explain who we are and why we visit to pediatric patients. I have often found that patient's parents do not know either. Corey saw my bag that contained activities and games. He asked, 'What do you have in the bag?' I stated that I was glad he asked, and I pulled out a few of the games. I asked him if he wanted to play a game, and he pointed to one of the games. At this point, the patient's father started working on his laptop, but I could tell he was listening to our conversation. At first, I asked Corey questions to help me get to know him, then we began to talk about his illness and hospitalization. When I asked Corey how his illness made him feel, Corey's father set his laptop down and started listening intently. Corey told me that he was afraid.

> He said that he knew he had cancer, and that it was a bad illness, but no one really talked to him about it, which made it scarier. At that point, Corey's father came over to the bed and, with tears in his eyes, told Corey that he could talk to him about it whenever he wanted. Corey asked his father a few questions, and then he told us that he was tired. I told him that I would let him rest.
>
> Corey's father followed me out of the room and began to weep. Corey's parents had not talked to Corey about his illness because they struggled to keep their own emotions under control when discussing it, and they did not want to scare Corey. Corey's father explained that they thought that Corey was handling his illness fine because he had not talked to them about it; however, the opposite was true. In reality, Corey was following the social cues of his parents, which left Corey facing his fear alone.

Adolescence

Adolescents are in a state of personal awakening and questioning. The journey to independence comes to full expression in adolescence and may be accompanied by religious rites of passage where a child transitions into adult responsibilities at an age different to that determined by a country's legal system. For example, in Islam this occurs at puberty or age 15 if there are not other signs (Nash, Parkes and Hussain 2015). This journey towards independence is important for them to travel on their path to adulthood. It can be a source of frustration and conflict for both adolescents and their caregivers as a teenager is becoming their own person. During this time, most adolescents are figuring out what they personally believe about most, if not all, areas of life, instead of believing without question what they have been taught. Miller writes that according to research, 'spirituality is *the* most robust protective factor against the big three dangers of adolescence: depression, substance abuse, and risk taking' (2015, pp.208–209). She also writes that there is 'clinical and genetic evidence…[for a] surge of spiritual awakening' that occurs alongside the physical and emotional developmental surges during adolescence (p.4). It is important for us to take this 'surge' into account when providing spiritual care to teenage patients.

During this period of spiritual awakening, it is important to create a space in which teenage patients can share with spiritual caregivers outside the presence of family or friends. Adolescent patients might want to discuss subjects they are not comfortable sharing with their parents in the room concerning their anxieties, fears, spiritual questions or topics that their parents are not ready to discuss. It is a significant period of identity development (Erikson 1995), and being ill may affect this in a variety of ways which a spiritual caregiver may be able to support working through.

> ### PRACTICE EXAMPLE 2.4: WHOSE FAITH?
>
> Julia was a 16-year-old who was in the hospital after a reoccurrence of cancer. On this day, a nurse had referred Julia for a chaplain visit because she seemed to be having a difficult day. When I arrived for the visit, Julia was alone, as her father was at work and her mother had gone home to get more clothes. The visit started with polite small talk, but it did not take long for Julia to build up the courage to tell me she was wrestling with questions about her faith, treatment options, loneliness and fear. As Julia started to share, it was as if her dam of inner thoughts burst. She was afraid she might die. She was facing more cancer treatments, and she thought that death might be better than living through the hell of chemotherapy and surgeries again. When Julia tried to talk to her mother, Julia's mother shut down any conversations because she believed that God would heal Julia if they had enough faith, and talking about death was a sign of lack of faith. Julia also could not talk to her father because emotionally he was not at a place where he could contemplate Julia's possible death with her.
>
> Julia expressed that her family was very active in a church, but well-meaning church people tried to encourage her by saying things like 'God still works miracles', 'You just have to pray and God will give you strength', or 'We know that God is going to heal you, because we are praying for you daily'. Julia then stated that she had very few friends anymore, because during her first bout with cancer, she was unable to go to school or participate in extra-curricular activities. Slowly, all of her friends stopped visiting, except one. Julia continued talking about her doubts and fears until her mother entered the room, at which point Julia abruptly ended our discussion. Julia was at a point where she was doubting everything she grew up believing about her spirituality, including the existence of a higher power, and she was only able to share this without fear because her parents were not present.

Teenagers can often find it hard to start a conversation with an adult chaplain. Therefore, discussing things that interest them, such as music or movies, can be a great icebreaker that allows patients to feel comfortable enough to open up about deeper issues. If a patient can go to our teen lounge, I routinely ask if they would like to play video games. I often find out more about the patient in ten minutes of playing video games together than I would have discovered if I had talked to the patient for an hour in their room. These mutual interests and activities allow a spiritual caregiver to meet the patient where they are and build a relationship with them.

Recognizing the significance of rites of passage is another important aspect of providing spiritual care to teenagers. Many faith traditions have rites of passage to recognize that teenagers are transitioning from childhood to adulthood. Culturally, teens often view other significant events, such as getting a driver's license, getting a first job and going to prom, as important rites of passage on their way toward adulthood. Teenagers with chronic and terminal illnesses often miss out on some of these rites of passage that allow them to have more freedom, more responsibility, or mark an important milestone. Spiritual caregivers should be aware of the losses teens experience from being unable to participate in these rites. The inability to experience these anticipated rites of passage may leave teenage patients with the sense that they are being robbed of these experiences. It is important for chaplains to be mindful of the patient's need to grieve these losses. In addition, chaplains can assist with facilitating spiritual rites of passage for adolescent patients.

Future development and research needs

- Critique child development theories in the light of illness.
- Understand the synergy of how insights from child development stages intersect with spiritual care in hospital with children and young people of various conditions and illnesses (case studies).
- A clearer understanding and practice of autonomy and child development and personal faith.

Summary

'Pediatric patients are not just small adults' is a common adage used by pediatric care providers. This adage is true for spiritual care with pediatric patients too. They often feel the same emotions as adult patients and interpret these events through the lens of their own worldview. This different worldview will impact what is important to them, why they are angry or sad, how they communicate their concerns and fears, and how they cope. In order to provide effective care, pediatric spiritual caregivers need to engage patients on their level with love, curiosity and authenticity in a way that affirms them and what they are experiencing.

Questions for reflection

- How might we apply and critique child development theory in our practice?

- How has a particular patient's child development needs been affected by their illness?

- How might we be able to support and facilitate normative transitions and rites of passage?

References

Erikson, E.H. (1995) *Childhood and Society*. London: Vintage.
Granqvist, P. and Kirkpatrick, L.A. (2008) 'Attachment and Religious Representations of Behavior.' In J. Cassidy and P.R. Shaver (eds) *The Handbook of Attachment: Theory, Research, and Clinical Applications*, 2nd edition. New York, NY: Guilford Press.
Grossoehme, D.H. (1999) *The Pastoral Care of Children*. Binghamton, NY: Haworth Pastoral Press.
Miller, L. (2015) *The Spiritual Child: The New Science on Parenting for Health and Lifelong Thriving*. New York, NY: Picador.
Mooney, C.G. (2010) *Theories of Attachment*. St. Paul, MN: Redleaf Press.
Nash, P., Parkes, M. and Hussain, Z. (2015) *Multifaith Care for Sick and Dying Children and Their Families*. London: Jessica Kingsley Publishers.
Poon Zahl, B. (2016) 'Attachment Theory and Your Relationship with God.' *The Mockingbird*, Vol. 8 (ed. Ethan Richardson). Accessed on 13/01/18 at www.mbird.com/2016/10/attachment-theory-and-your-relationship-with-god.
Turiel, E. (1983) *The Development of Social Knowledge: Morality and Convention*. Cambridge: Cambridge University Press.
Vygotsky, L.S. (1978) *Mind in Society: The Development of Higher Psychological Processes*. Cambridge, MA: Harvard University Press.

Chapter 3

Spiritual, Religious and Pastoral Care of Children and Their Families

Claire Carson

Listening attentively to a person's story is at the heart of what spiritual and religious care is all about. It is also at the heart of developing relationships with the people we are caring for. How we communicate and allow space for them to tell their stories is crucial for the work we do as healthcare chaplains. It is about valuing and respecting who people are, their beliefs, their culture, their relationships with significant people in their lives and the world around them. It is about making connections.

Spiritual care

Spiritual care is:

> that care which recognises and responds to the needs of the human spirit when faced with trauma, ill health or sadness and can include the need for meaning, for self-worth, to express oneself… Spiritual care begins with encouraging human contact in compassionate relationship, and moves in whatever direction need requires. (NHS Education for Scotland 2009)

Spiritual care may include religious care if that aspect of a person's life is important to them, but spiritual care is not always religious and is for everyone of any faith or belief. As Kelly states, 'The spiritual aspect of our human personhood is that element which seeks meaning and purpose in life. Such a dimension is not confined to persons of religious faith, but is part of what it is to be human' (2012, p.100). Spiritual care includes religious, pastoral and spiritual aspects.

Religious care

Chaplains are involved in offering specifically religious care to children and their families, which may involve ritual, prayer, worship – formal and informal, by the bedside or perhaps in a chapel or prayer room. As Cobb suggests, religious care can be seen as 'a distinct subset of spiritual care and has a clear focus: the practices, doctrines, narratives, experiences, ethics, social organizations and material aspects of a faith tradition' (2005, p.41).

Pastoral care

Pastoral care has expanded over the years to embrace different faith traditions; however, its origins lie within Christianity. Lartey talks about pastoral care as 'deep concern about what it is to be human'. This includes what you can observe about someone, as well as that aspect which is hidden. 'The hiddenness lies in the heartfelt desire for humanity to be truly and fully human. It is all encompassing passion that all people might live to the fullest of their potential' (1997, p.5).

The care we offer as chaplains can be spiritual, religious and pastoral. For some people, their faith tradition is integral to their lives and who they are. Chaplains can enable people to continue following their religious traditions and practices while in hospital. For example, the Muslim chaplain would ensure that the religious requirements of the patients they are looking after are met, such as maintaining a halal diet, helping with prayer and facilitating worship; or perhaps it would involve listening to patients' beliefs and faith connected with their illness and stay in hospital. In many faiths there are specific traditions around birth and death which people may also wish to follow (see Nash, Parkes and Hussain 2015).

It is essential that we do not make assumptions about what spiritual, religious and pastoral care means for a patient and their family. It can be different for everyone. We cannot say what faith means to a specific person without listening to who they are and what is important to them. For those who are not religious, we cannot say what gives their life value and meaning and what is significant to them, if we do not first listen to their story. Attentive listening is crucial, and, as Lartey says:

> the person who listens actively and creatively does not remain silent throughout the process. There comes a time when the listener reflects with the other person, seeking to clarify what has been heard... When listening is deep, real and penetrating the experience can be awe-inspiring for it has to do with core being-in-encounter. (1997, p.63)

Initiating contact, making connections, building relationships

How we initiate relationships and approach patients, their families and significant people in their lives can vary greatly depending on the context and how we come to meet them. As chaplains, we frequently meet children and their carers on the wards as we walk around without specific referrals. A smile and a hello can be so important, or perhaps a comment about something you notice by the bedside: a cuddly toy, or game, a card or painting. Often this will enable people to start a conversation. Sometimes first encounters can be brief, but develop over time as you pass by more. Often then at a time of crisis the conversation may deepen. Other times chaplains may be called by a nurse, doctor or other healthcare professional because the family has requested a visit and support.

It is important for us to reflect upon and understand good practice and institutional policies in engaging with patients. This is part of a wider discussion of how we and our service are perceived by our institutions. Some of us are understood to be there in our own professional right and have automatic permission to engage. Others can only have contact with the child if we are given clear permission. Sometimes we might know or sense that the nurse is the gatekeeper to the child. This is always alongside asking the child if they would like us to visit.

Being able to make connections, build rapport, listen attentively and stay with how someone feels is incredibly important. Acknowledging and being able to stay with someone's pain, fear, anxiety and uncertainty is both challenging and necessary. When people are facing difficult situations, such as trauma, pain or distress, or when they have to make difficult decisions about end-of-life care, a chaplain's ability to hold a space for them, no matter how they are or what they want to say, is a vital part of spiritual care.

In offering spiritual, religious and pastoral care, chaplains need to be inclusive, valuing diversity and being respectful of how people choose to live their lives, being open and hospitable and engaging in multifaith dialogue and complex ethical issues. In order to offer truly holistic, compassionate care which is appropriate and sensitive, chaplains should never be working alone in a healthcare setting, but rather be fully engaged in multidisciplinary teams – for example, with doctors, nurses, play specialists, psychologists, to name a few.

Making connections with families, children and young people in hospital can be challenging on many levels. Family relationships may have broken down, people may not be speaking to each other, or family members may have significantly different beliefs about treatment choices and end-of-life care options, or their religious beliefs may differ. Working in teams can be beneficial in these circumstances, as it may be more appropriate for two different chaplains to offer care to family members. Needs vary greatly. Trauma and distressing situations can profoundly affect relationships. Being aware of family dynamics, holding boundaries and maintaining confidentiality are all part of offering the best possible spiritual and religious care.

Stories

The following are two very different stories of relationships I have developed with families and their children. One shows both spiritual and religious aspects of care, while the other is more reflective of spiritual care without a specifically religious element.

PRACTICE EXAMPLE 3.1: WILLIAM'S STORY

William's mum and dad, Dawn and Mark, write:

> In September 2014 William suddenly stopped breathing whilst at home. There was no obvious reason, no accident, no sign of illness. Thankfully I was able to deliver CPR and managed to keep him alive while waiting for an ambulance. William was admitted to St. George's Hospital, intubated and placed in intensive care. William recovered and after a month was discharged, but without a clear explanation. Two days later it happened again: William stopped breathing and this time my husband Mark delivered CPR. Once again William was taken into intensive care and intubated. Looking back, we were both in a state of shock. We had no idea why this had happened, the doctors could not offer an explanation and we were not sure how to deal with the situation. We had to split our family, so one of us could always be at the hospital with William, staying with him day and night, and the other trying to provide a sense of stability to our four-year-old daughter at home.

The staff called me to see William and his parents on the paediatric intensive care unit (PICU). They briefly explained the situation to me from a medical point of view and said the family would like to speak with a chaplain. I went to introduce myself to William's parents with no agenda other than to listen to them and how they were feeling. Then we would decide together where we went from there.

> Dawn writes:
>
> The chaplain came to speak to us whilst we were staying on the PICU ward. With her very calm and open demeanour I was able to share a lot of these thoughts and feelings with her and ended up talking to her over the next few months when times were tough. We went from unanswered questions to a potential diagnosis that was life-limiting. This was the most horrific and heartbreaking news that we had ever received. The consultants presented us with information that was both technical and confusing. There was no thought to our feelings and how we were going to cope as we were told that we'd be staying for the next few months in hospital whilst more tests were conducted. The chaplain helped us to make sense of the situation and to shape our perspective. Our relationship with the chaplain and psychologist that we spoke to on a weekly basis made a dramatic change to the way we handled the situation. I still look back and remember the advice that we were given and reflect on it when times are tough.

I continued to visit Dawn and Mark during William's stay on the PICU. Being there with them, building trust, giving them space to think, talk and be were the most important aspects of care, rather than the words I said. In the terrifying, heart-stopping moments, words seem so inadequate and in reality are not always helpful.

One day as William's discharge from hospital was drawing close, Dawn and Mark asked me about baptising William. I talked about what that meant for them. They were keen to have the baptism in the hospital, although he was being discharged. Hospital had become a safe place for them, especially as the situation with William had been so unsure. Although William would be going home, he still required 24-hour care and lots of support. Being surrounded by people who understood their situation was incredibly important to them: a source of strength and closure of a very traumatic time.

There is no fixed boundary between spiritual and religious care, and William's story highlights this very well. As chaplains, we enter the space of the family empty-handed and wait for cues from them as to what their needs are. Overall, we can offer spiritual care, and that may become more specifically religious care at times when required. The baptism for them was an important part of their family tradition and their faith. This was not explicitly talked about in earlier conversations, but when the time was right for them, they raised the question of whether a baptism in the hospital was possible. We have to be flexible in the care we offer and the ways we respond. The chaplain must use their skills of observation, listening and intuition. Often there is no straightforward path and we have to be able to hold all of the different emotions people bring. Staying with the difficult feelings, the tensions, the pain, is enormously important for the care we offer.

Dawn concluded:

> We spent 11 of William's first 15 months at St. George's Hospital, and it felt right that we held his Christening at the chapel in the hospital. Whilst we have strong connections to our church at home, William's connections were at St George's: he had made friends with so many of the staff, consultants and nurses; his walks were not around the park but around the hospital grounds; his trips out were to the hospital canteen not to the local coffee shop; on a Saturday morning William and his dad would sit watching the steady stream of people from the benches at the front of the hospital enjoying a moment in the sun together. The chaplain knew our story and over those 11 months had supported our family so much that we were delighted when she agreed to carry out the baptism. It was the most happy and peaceful gathering of our very close friends and family, a moment that helped to close our experience at St George's. I know that we can always visit the chapel and have a special connection there, a memory of happiness after a turbulent journey.

PRACTICE EXAMPLE 3.2: TIA-GRACE'S STORY

I met Tia-Grace and her grandma in the school room on the children's ward. We chatted very informally and frequently said 'Hi' in passing. Then one day I was visiting on the ward and popped into Tia-Grace's room. Tia-Grace and her grandma said, 'Hi', but Tia-Grace's mum was visibly in shock. Without hesitating, she asked me why I was visiting and what did I know. I calmly reassured Sandra that I was just passing by to say hi and see how things were going. I explained that I did not know anything about their particular situation. We continued to talk, and I could see Sandra relax as time went on. It had indeed been a very difficult and traumatic time for them. Tia-Grace had been very unwell on paediatric intensive care.

Tia-Grace's mum, Sandra, writes:

> Tia-Grace suddenly became seriously ill, and we were thrown into devastation, fear, heartbreak and certainly the unknown. We didn't

know if she would even survive. The feeling of hope and safety both Tia-Grace and I got from the hospital chaplain is beyond words. Once Tia-Grace had survived a coma due to the seriousness of her sudden condition, we had to remain in hospital for the following year. Our journey was horrific as my once so very healthy daughter could no longer move and was totally paralysed from head to toe. No words can explain the fear that runs through you when you are told your daughter will be left with a life-limiting condition and she may never walk, talk or eat again.

My heart hit the floor, and I could hardly hold back the tears, as I believed that the chaplain had been sent to talk to us by the doctors. Once I had relaxed and realised there was no motive behind her visit apart from saying hello, both Tia-Grace and I looked forward to seeing the chaplain whilst we lived at the hospital. Tia-Grace would ask daily to go to the chapel just for a few minutes once she had regained her speech and a little movement in her body. For some reason she felt so very safe there and after a visit to the chapel Tia-Grace always appeared happier and stronger.

The comfort and calmness I got from visiting the chapel during our year-long stay was unbelievable. It truly became my safe haven. Had the chaplain not visited Tia-Grace's bedside that day, I can honestly say I would never have even thought about visiting the hospital chapel. The visits from the chaplain got us through some of our darkest days. We had many laughs along the way and normal conversations, too.

My visits with Tia-Grace and her mum reminded me how important building relationships is, through patience and listening, without an agenda, but with an open and non-judgemental presence, often not saying much at all, but accompanying them through extremely tough times. Making connections with people requires openness and vulnerability. A lightness of spirit can create a space where people feel free to be themselves: a safe space where they can be honest and real. Humour can be important too as it allows us to deal with incredibly difficult situations and get to the heart of human experience. 'Giving people permission to laugh in the midst of adversity can lead to storytelling, reframing and re-interpretation. Used with wisdom and discernment, our sense of humour can help deepen people's exploration of their story, not just to avoid its reality' (Kelly 2012, p.48).

Stories from other contexts

The care we offer, whether it is called spiritual, religious or pastoral care, depends on the context and type of healthcare setting we work in, whether it is a paediatric department within an acute hospital, a children's hospital or a hospice. However, there are many commonalities which the following stories show.

> ### PRACTICE EXAMPLE 3.3: A CHILD IN A RURAL SOUTH AFRICAN CONTEXT
>
> For many months a child with an extreme case of hydrocephalus was in a ward. His mother had been frustrated with the lack of treatment offered nearby and the more distant hospital she had gone to had not referred her on, so she took it upon herself to bring this child to the Children's Hospital in Cape Town. She had come from a very distant rural place on a bus. His head was so large that he was unable to roll over or sit up and she had learned to carry him alone.
>
> The surgeons put in a shunt and kept a watch to see if it would reduce the size of his head, which over time it did, minimally. They assessed that he would not survive an operation, that he would die if the pressure was surgically released. After some months, when no active treatment was being given, they moved the mother out of the ward as there is always a risk of the child picking up some virus or infection. Due to the difficulty of transporting him, even in an ambulance, the mother chose to stay locally rather than go home till the next check-up. She lived with him in a room in a block for parents' accommodation where the facilities were fairly basic. The pastoral care team kept in touch. We saw their needs and how she was bound to his side as she was now the sole caretaker. To enhance the experience in their room, we made arrangements to lend them a TV and some other things to make their stay more comfortable. The pastoral care worker often took a portable CD player and played songs that the child could sing along to. This led to a really close bond with the pastoral carer. Eventually, however, the child did need to return home. The head size had reduced somewhat. With a buggy that supported his head, he could now be wheeled rather than carried and could sit up for limited periods of time.
>
> Mostly, the expectation was that in due course he would die. However, the care and capability of this determined mother led to them returning for the next check-up six months later. He is a bright

little boy. He learned quite a lot of English in the hospital stay the first time, but he had limited movements. The chaplain found him playing with his mother's old push-button phone. It struck the chaplain that he would probably be able to look at a tablet screen quite well, so she sought a donor and was able to buy him a tablet. Sadly, their transport left the hospital just an hour before this arrived. But music and games are being loaded on to it in the meantime, and we look forward to seeing him back again in six months' time.

The Revd Lynn Pedersen, Chaplain, Red Cross War Memorial Hospital, Cape Town, South Africa

---

PRACTICE EXAMPLE 3.4: A CHILD'S NEED TO STAY CONNECTED TO HIS 'NORMAL LIFE'

A little guy about nine years old came to our PICU after suffering traumatic injuries from a car accident. Several days into his stay he was regaining consciousness and asking for his parents and his friends at school. The next few days were filled with anxiousness and confusion for him, and agony for his parents who were at a loss as to how to soothe him. Each visit we would pray, and he would add the names of different friends to our prayer. One day after a visit I asked to talk with his parents privately and suggested we connect him to his classmates, if possible, and I asked if they would allow me to contact his teacher and see if we could connect on Skype. After getting care team approval and conferring with his teacher, it was arranged, and he was connected to his classmates by Skype. That same day, just before we connected, the Vice Principal of his school delivered a huge sack of cards, letters and drawings from the schoolmates. The patient was overjoyed and had a renewed spirit, and his mother wallpapered his room with all the letters, cards and drawings. Skype connections were done on a regular basis throughout his three-month hospitalization. He was motivated and encouraged by connecting to what he called his 'normal life'.

Peggy Huber, Lead Paediatric Chaplain, The Children's Hospital of San Antonio, Texas, USA

PRACTICE EXAMPLE 3.5: A DISCHARGE BLESSING

Significant moments of healing, struggling, hoping and releasing happen every hour in a neonatal intensive care unit. Those hours add up, and when the day has come for a baby and family to be discharged home, it is important to claim time and space to reflect on what that neonatal stay has meant for all involved. Last spring, each time a baby was discharged home, I gathered as many people from the care team as possible at the bedside and offered a blessing. The blessing has multiple aims and intends to address the individually unique yet often universal emotional and spiritual needs of each patient, family, and staff.

The blessing itself is straightforward and doesn't last a very long time but it holds a great deal of intensity and in many ways, summarizes the beautiful and difficult dynamics of what being in a hospital means for all of us. The blessing focuses on themes of fragility, vulnerability and resilience – all important parts of our shared humanity. The blessing begins with a time of remembering (the chaotic birth, anxious mother, distracting hum of jet ventilator). Then there is a time for celebrating (the night that death was near but morning came, the surgery that repaired the heart valve, the first time baby opened her eyes). There is also a time for thanking (the nurse who stayed late not to administer a medication but to swaddle the baby just so, the father who brought doughnuts in). There is a time for hoping (for continued healing and growing, for deepened family life, for days of rest). Finally, there is a time for saying goodbye.

At its best, the discharge blessing is a moment in time and space where the precious life of a child is acknowledged, the deep connections a family has to that child are encouraged, and the contributions of the medical team are lifted up as healing. Each and all part ways feeling known, appreciated, and ready for the journey ahead to continue.

Hadley Kifner, Paediatric Chaplain, UNC Health Care/
North Carolina Children's Hospital, USA

Future development and research needs

- Paediatric models for religious, spiritual and pastoral care.
- Contextual resources for patients and their families for religious, spiritual and pastoral care.
- Refined definitions of religious, spiritual and pastoral needs and care for hospitalised children and their families.

Summary

While offering spiritual, religious and pastoral care may differ depending on the faith tradition or beliefs of the family, or indeed the circumstances and context, there are common underlying principles which apply. All spiritual, religious and pastoral care we offer should be about:

- making connections which are meaningful for those we are caring for
- creating a safe space which is reflective, open, nurturing and sustaining
- offering appropriate and sensitive care according to the tradition, beliefs and values of the child and family
- attentive listening without an agenda
- being respectful and non-judgemental
- celebrating and valuing difference
- seeking human flourishing
- honouring experience.

Questions for reflection

- What is the core best practice in offering religious and spiritual care?
- Can you give examples of how you have offered and engaged in assessment and interventions in the differences between religious, spiritual and pastoral needs and then care?

- With regard to permission to approach, how might we safely and professionally offer religious, spiritual and pastoral care to children and their families in our setting?

References

Cobb, M. (2005) *The Hospital Chaplain's Handbook.* Norwich: Canterbury Press.

Kelly, E. (2012) *Personhood and Presence: Self as Resource for Spiritual and Pastoral Care.* London: T & T Clark International.

Lartey, E.Y. (1997) *In Living Color: An Intercultural Approach to Pastoral Care and Counselling.* London: Cassell.

Nash, P., Parkes, M. and Hussain, Z. (2015) *Multifaith Care for Sick and Dying Children and Their Families.* London: Jessica Kingsley Publishers.

NHS Education for Scotland (2009) *Spiritual Care Matters: An Introductory Resource for all NHS Scotland Staff.* Edinburgh: NES.

Chapter 4
Models of Chaplaincy in a Multicultural World
Paul Nash

> **PRACTICE EXAMPLE 4.1: GOD AND BUDDHA**
>
> I was once called to the room of a seven-year-old girl who was Asian-American and Buddhist. A long-term cancer patient, she and her mother had just been given the news that the cancer was now incurable. When I entered the room, I saw the beautiful, bald-headed little girl in her pink princess dress, magic wand in hand. She looked up at me, and we spoke for a few minutes. Soon she said, 'Please pray to your God because Buddha cannot help me.' My heart sank as I thought of the pain and fear she was feeling. After spending more time listening to them, I invited us to sit together and all pray aloud (a practice common to both our religions) to all that would hear…God, Buddha, ancestors, nurses, doctors, and so on. We poured out hopes, fears, feelings, tears, and much more. There would be no miracle healing of her body, but there was a presence of creativity, nurture, faith, compassion, and love that healed all our spirits. I do not have fancy words for it, and it does not fit into tidy doctrinal statements, but I can only describe that as God's work and presence. She may use different language, but the net effect was the same. We joined in loving each other and healing happened. No other story captures my faith and understanding of God so clearly.
>
> The Revd Lavender Kelly, Staff Chaplain, Ann & Robert H. Lurie Children's Hospital of Chicago, now at Children's National Health System, Washington, DC, USA

Introduction

There is no agreed or universally used model of paediatric chaplaincy, and, as this story shows, encounters will not always fit neatly into a model anyway. However, in seeking to articulate what it is we do and in developing service provision, the language of models does have its uses. We are using the term 'model' to mean something that is followed or can be imitated and summarises how we work.

An initial helpful summary of generic chaplaincy models is offered by Miranda Threlfall-Holmes (2011, p.118) who suggests that secular models include:

- provider of pastoral care
- spiritual carer
- diversity model
- traditional/heritage model
- a meta-model of specialist service provider which offers several of these elements.

From a Christian theological perspective, she offers the metaphors of missionary, pastor, incarnational or sacramental, historical–parish, and those which draw on the idea of being an agent of change which includes prophet, jester and social activist.

When thinking about models, there are a range of other concepts which merit consideration. Embedded chaplaincy seeks to be part of an organisation, a critical friend from within rather than a prophetic voice from without. Chaplains are professional peers in a multidisciplinary team which is a collaborative model. Some chaplains work within a screening, assessment, intervention approach which reflects a medical model and may help us to be integrated and embedded into our contexts. However, there are few screening or assessment tools fit for purpose in a paediatric context. There is increasingly a debate about evidence-based models and a growing focus on research to help develop this (see Chapter 20). The concept of presence in chaplaincy remains important and would be integral to any model. Related to this is the notion of wandering with intent. This is a proactive and intentional way of walking around the hospital, and while it looks casual, it is far from it – it is facilitating my availability. Adopting an asset-based rather than a deficit model is an area which is increasingly being considered (Hopkins and Rippon 2015).

Different models and approaches to chaplaincy

It can be important to distinguish between models for the sake of clarity in our explanations to our teams, other staff and the development of service provision. It would usually be the case, however, that whatever model is preferred, chaplaincy care is available to those of any faith or none on request or referral. Ford highlights the need for a fourfold deepening for chaplains who work in multifaith contexts: the need to go deeper into one's own tradition/faith; deeper into those of others; deeper into engagement with the institution; and deeper into mutual understanding among the team (2011, p.14).

Three main approaches are multifaith, interfaith and generic:

1. Multifaith

A multifaith model would seek to offer religious care to members of individual faith groups mainly through adherents of the same faith (see Nash 2015, pp.16–30, for a full explanation of how we use it at Birmingham Women's and Children's Hospital).

PROS

- Chaplains are able to offer appropriately focused provision to a religious family/community.
- They take seriously the distinctiveness of beliefs between different faith and belief groups.
- They avoid offending people by marginalising, minimising or misinterpreting their faith.
- They celebrate diversity.

CONS

- People can feel excluded, as it can look exclusive.
- One cannot cover every variety of faith in a team or tradition within a faith.

> ### PRACTICE EXAMPLE 4.2: I HAD MY PRAYER SCARF UNDER MY PILLOW
>
> Many of us have seen the emotional support prayer scarves, shawls and hats can bring to those patients that are seriously ill. While chaplain at CHRISTUS Santa Rosa Children's Hospital of San Antonio, we had a prayer scarf ministry. The prayer scarves were made by school children who were taught the art of knitting and crocheting by their parents. As the children made the scarves, they prayed for the person that would receive their 'work of love and prayer'. I gave one of the beautifully made scarves to a 12-year-old patient who had cystic fibrosis. I explained that the scarf was made by someone his age and that the person had prayed for him while making the scarf. The patient held the scarf tenderly and thanked me for giving it to him. I went to see my patient the next morning and asked how he had slept in the night. He eagerly replied, 'I slept good last night, Chaplain Maggie. I had my prayer scarf under my pillow.'
>
> *Maggie Jones, Chaplain, CHRISTUS Santa Rosa Hospital, New Braunfels, Texas, USA*

2. Interfaith

Interfaith is where a religious provision of service or an event is provided for everyone of any faith. This is often used in bereavement events in particular and increasingly in designing multi-use religious space in hospitals.

PROS

- It is inclusive.
- It can make staffing easier to manage.

CONS

- It may not be relevant or appropriate enough to meet specific religious needs.
- It can seek to achieve and be motivated by political correctness and not person-centred care.
- Some feel you end up with the lowest common denominator, with most participants dissatisfied.

> ### PRACTICE EXAMPLE 4.3: AN INTERFAITH PRAYER FOR PEACE
>
> Rather than having prayers from a range of religious traditions in a service, another option would be to use an interfaith prayer. This is one for peace:
>
> *Lead me from death to life,*
> *from falsehood to truth.*
> *Lead me from despair to hope,*
> *from fear to trust.*
> *Lead me from hate to love,*
> *from war to peace.*
> *Let peace fill our heart, our world, our universe.*
>
> *(www.weekofprayerforworldpeace.com/prayers_all_faiths.html)*

3. Generic spiritual care

Spiritual care is predicated on the assumption that everyone has a spiritual dimension to their life regardless of any religious belief.

PROS

- It is inclusive.
- It does not assume religious belief and is clearly a universal service.

CONS

- It may not esteem religious care.
- The person offering it may not have specialist religious care background, so needs to make more referrals.

All these approaches have something to offer in the spectrum of our work in multifaith and multicultural contexts. A key value of paediatric chaplaincy is that we do not have to believe the same or agree with the religious beliefs of our patients and families to offer them supportive care, as this story illustrates:

> ### PRACTICE EXAMPLE 4.4: WHY DID THIS HAPPEN?
>
> Following a brief conversation with a mother in Special Care, I learned that her baby had Down syndrome and that she was Hindu. The conversation had felt inadequate. I tried to see her again, but we missed each other. Many weeks later, one evening I had a call from the children's ward asking if I had seen the mother of P in SCBU. She was asking to see me. She had begun conversations with Social Services about having the baby adopted.
>
> I came in – she wanted someone to listen, and it was important to her that it was a person of faith. I assured her that I could listen, but that I could only talk from my perspective of faith. That was fine with her. Her starting point was 'the gods are punishing me'. We explored the concept of a loving God; suffering; her family; her upbringing (and why she felt she might be being punished). I listened, reflected back, and she talked and talked. Finally I pointed her toward the peer support offered by the Down's Syndrome Association. After nearly two hours she went off to look after her baby again, expressing gratitude. I thanked her for trusting me. She had evidently known she could trust me when we first met, but wasn't able to speak then.
>
> It was a powerful encounter for us both, as we explored the depth of her pain from our different perspectives. Sadly, her baby died a few months later, but our common humanity had transcended faith differences. What I had experienced as an inadequate conversation, she had experienced as meeting someone 'safe'.
>
> *Jane Hatton, Chaplain, East and North Hertfordshire NHS Trust, UK*

We are proposing that there is not just one model of and for paediatric chaplaincy, but that we discern the contexts in which we find ourselves and develop a model that is appropriate for the context. Pastoral care is integral to all of the models and the following story is one example of an intervention with a sibling.

> ### PRACTICE EXAMPLE 4.5: BEING WITH JIMMY
>
> When I met Jimmy, I could see from his expression that he was completely stunned. Shock had come over him. How could it be that

his brother was dying? Only hours earlier they were out together, having a good time, likely bugging and annoying one another, but full of brotherly love nonetheless. How surreal it must have been to be standing in a hospital room, talking about what would unfold in the next few hours. Like a tight lid on a pot, things were being covered, held in until it could be covered no more. Jimmy's mom and dad were talking, crying, caressing his brother – they had found a way to let their emotions out. Suddenly, Jimmy bolted from the room, out of the unit and down the hall. Not sure of where he was going or what he was doing, I followed him. Outside he stopped beside a wall. At last the cries, the swearing, the screaming, the tears flowed from his being. He kicked the wall, more swearing, disbelief, exhaustion. I stood and held the space, nodded occasionally, so that he knew he was heard. We walked slowly and silently back to the unit and back to his brother's room. The family requested a bedside prayer. We incorporated a ritual with water – for each family member to bless him with their love and have an opportunity to say some words to him before his last breath. After giving the family some time alone, I went to say my goodbye. Jimmy threw himself into my arms. 'Thank you,' he said softly. For what exactly he was thanking me, I am not completely sure, but I think it had to do with giving him space, widening the perimeters and yet containing and holding all he needed to express.

Linda Wollschlaeger-Fischer, MTS, Spiritual Health Leader, Spiritual Care Counsellor, British Columbia Children's Hospital, Canada

Values

Child-centred care

My early experience of observing chaplains in a paediatric hospital was seeing them engage far more with families than the patient. I began to wonder how we could place the child in the centre of our care. Spiritual play is the shorthand we have given at Birmingham Women's and Children's Hospital to our assessment and intervention model, Interpretive Spiritual Encounters (ISE). This is a model that seeks to use activities to engage patients in exploring their spiritual needs. This model takes seriously the interests and developmental capacity of the children. It uses activities that have been specifically developed to assess the children's spiritual needs (see Chapter 5). The values and practices of this model are participation and empowerment, two things patients do not always feel in hospital.

Godly Play is another approach used (see Chapter 6). While the practice of a chaplain going to see patients empty-handed with no agenda is a valuable and widely used approach, when we place a child in the centre of our care, it may be more helpful to have at least some available resources with which to engage.

> ### PRACTICE EXAMPLE 4.6: PATIENT-FOCUSED CARE
>
> We are at the service of the patients, and although we are trained in our specific fields, my experiences have taught me that listening to the needs of patients can benefit both the patients and the medical staff. For instance, I had an encounter with a 13-year-old girl with a tumor on her leg who would not speak or visit with the medical team. When the team came by in the morning during rounds, the patient would stay under the covers and not respond, while also keeping the lights turned off and the shade down. The team thought she might benefit from a visit from a psychiatrist; however, the nurse manager referred her to me, the chaplain, for an assessment.
>
> I asked the reason she was under the covers and not responding to the doctors. She told me, 'They give me a lot of information which I don't understand and my mother gets upset with me when she comes in the evening because I can't remember what they said.' The girl's mother was a single mom with two other small children, and due to her work schedule could not visit until the evening. I suggested to the team that it might be helpful during rounds if they added the mother to the conversation via telephone. They took this suggestion, and this relieved some of the stress on the patient, her mother and the medical team. As I continued to visit with the patient, I then inquired why she had the lights off and the shades down, and she said, 'When I get up to use the potty, I think someone is looking at me across the street from the apartment building.' After hearing this, I decided to make another suggestion to the team regarding moving her to a different room, and after doing so, the patient felt comfortable to keep the lights on and shades up.
>
> Finally, I asked if there was anything else I could do to make her feel more comfortable while hospitalized, and she said, 'All my friends are at McDonald's, and I would like to have a McFlurry, cheeseburger and fries.' So I checked with the dietitian to make sure she was not on a restricted diet, checked in with the nurse manager to make sure it was okay, and then I went out and got what she

> requested. The girl's demeanor shifted, and she became more upbeat, talkative and attentive, so much so that a staff member approached me and asked what I did, and I replied, 'I gave her spiritual care, I listened, and she told me what she needed.' When the medical team and even family members discuss what the person's needs are, they all mean well, but they may not realize that in most cases, the patient can tell us best what they need. We must learn to listen and ask the right questions, and if we listen long enough, they will tell us exactly what they need.
>
> *Yusuf Hasan, Board-Certified Chaplain, and Synchana Elkerson, Mental Health Counsellor Muslim Institute for Chaplaincy, New York, USA*

Missional not evangelistic

This is not particularly a paediatric issue, but it does need mentioning as it is at the core of professional ethical healthcare chaplaincy. It can be argued that for healthcare chaplains who are also faith representatives, chaplaincy is missional; we are sent, sometimes by our denomination, to offer pastoral, spiritual and religious care. We are seeking to support people on a spiritual or faith journey with the resources of our faith. As a Christian, I would say this involves the love of God, although other faith groups may express this differently. However, as practitioners, we need to ensure that we are working with the faith tradition of the child and family, and that our ways of engagement do not overstep the line of responding to questions and challenges with an overt expectation of personal response. This is particularly a danger with engaging with children, who are exploring and developing their normative identity and beliefs. What we often do encounter is a misunderstanding of what chaplains do.

> ### PRACTICE EXAMPLE 4.7: GOOD OR BAD DAY?
>
> Within our Trust there is very little religious need. The main people we support are those who would say they have no religion. I remember very vividly one mum whose trust I had gained. She was very suspicious of religious people and shared with me, 'Kathy, I bet you have a really bad day if you don't manage to convert someone.' I replied, 'I would have a bad day, I'd be sacked since that's totally against the Chaplains' Code of Conduct.' We then went on to have

> a wonderful conversation about how you don't need to be religious to have support from chaplains.
>
> Sister Kathy Green, Church Army, Chaplaincy Team
Leader, Sheffield Children's Hospital, UK

Hospitable

To offer hospitality is a common value in healthcare chaplaincy. The words 'hospitable' and 'hospitality' have the same roots as 'hospital', which means shelter for the needy. To be welcoming of everyone, to provide appropriate prayer and worship activities that express our care for their needs is at the heart of hospitality (see Boyce 2010 for a model of chaplaincy for children and young people in a multicultural school setting).

The make-up of our teams, faith symbols on our walls and notices of cultural and religious celebrations all contribute. Many of us will make a point of engaging with visitors who look lost. A few years back we started a hospitality team in our chapel. We have volunteers available for those passing by or dropping in, to make them feel welcomed, cared for, listened to. We offer refreshments, a chat, a prayer.

Non-judgemental

When a dead child is brought into our emergency department accompanied by parents and several police officers, it is easy to jump to conclusions. A useful mentality I have found is to assume nothing and approach the family with compassion in mind. If they are guilty, they will need support; if they are not guilty, they will need support. The outcome is the same: offer support. This is an extreme example, but there are many situations which may be difficult emotionally, theologically or personally and offering a non-judgemental presence is part of what the role of a chaplain may entail.

Crossing boundaries

Sometimes our faith and context and that of a patient or a family may present a challenge because of historical or cultural issues, as this next story illustrates.

> ### PRACTICE EXAMPLE 4.8: ATTENDING TO A FAMILY – A DOUBLE MITZVAH
>
> My pager beeped loudly in the large Texas children's hospital: a five-year-old boy had fallen three storeys and was on his way to the hospital. I waited with the team. No one knew how serious the injuries would be.
>
> A few minutes later, the stretcher barrelled through the doors. Mom followed, tears streaming down her face, blood staining her clothes. I showed her to a chair. She mumbled, 'No English.' When I asked what language she spoke, she replied, 'Arabic.' I used a phone translator, asking basic questions. The translator's stammered answer to my first question stopped me cold: the family was from Palestine…the West Bank…Israel, she said. 'Yes,' I replied. 'I'm Jewish. I understand.'
>
> For generations, refugees from the war that created the state of Israel have been fighting for their independence. Israel is the enemy. Here I was, a Jewish chaplain in Dallas during Chanukah, menorah and dreidel earrings dangling from my earlobes, and Mom a Palestinian on the eve of Ramadan. Dad arrived with a Palestinian friend. Mom went home and the men politely excused me and waited for tests to be completed. Later in the evening, I returned to the boy's bedside. He had been lucky: just a broken clavicle and bruising. A nurse asked Dad questions as the friend translated. The friend and I eyed each other. He gave me an imperceptible smile. Tonight, we were allies.
>
> Throughout the night, I updated the men. They were gracious and grateful. Chaplaincy work is always a mitzvah (good deed). On this night, I was able also to do the mitzvah of bridging a difficult cultural and emotional gulf. The work affirmed, yet again, that our humanity can connect us even when religion and politics do not. It was a double mitzvah.
>
> *Robin Kosberg, Chaplain, Children's Medical Center, Dallas, Texas, USA*

Partnership

While chaplaincy always works in partnership as part of a multidisciplinary team in a hospital, it can apply outside too. Patients and their families have communities that they come from and go back to, and one of the challenges can be to help faith communities support them at each stage of their journey (see Hill-Brown 2016 for ways of encouraging this).

> ### PRACTICE EXAMPLE 4.9: CHURCH/ HOSPITAL PARTNERSHIP IN AFRICA
>
> One of the CURE (www.cure.org) essential standards for ministry is that we are part of the Christian Church. We therefore take partnership with local churches very seriously. One of the key responsibilities of the Spiritual Ministry Director, a board-level post, is forging such partnerships. The rationale is that our patients come from and return to communities where local churches are part of the same communities. Church leaders are community leaders and they have served as our ambassador, educating their communities on disability, mobilising children with disability and bringing them to the hospital and then following them up to encourage adherence to treatment.
>
> In turn, spiritual directors help these church leaders use the medical services of the hospital to serve their communities by bringing children with orthopaedic and neurosurgical problems. This has worked perfectly to bring religious tolerance to communities that are hostile to Christians like in Niger and some parts of Kenya. Local church pastors are also taught a theology of disability and this has helped them teach their congregations to be Christian in the way they view disability.
>
> *Victor Nakah, Senior Vice President for Spiritual*
> *Ministry with CURE International, Zimbabwe*

Future development and research needs

- Comparing and contrasting patient satisfaction and wellbeing within different models.
- Research into the efficacy of chaplaincy may help the strategic development of provision.
- Audit or patient satisfaction of our values.

Summary

There is not one way to do chaplaincy, and while models can offer a language to explore and develop provision in a one-to-one encounter, we often make a choice as to what is the appropriate response to this person at this time. However, multifaith, interfaith and generic spiritual care are three paths that different chaplaincy provisions sometimes use.

Values of chaplaincy that can be seen in whatever model we adopt include being child-centred, missional, hospitable, working in partnership and crossing boundaries.

Questions for reflection

- What, if any, is your preferred model of chaplaincy? In what ways do you see the different models manifested in different elements of your work?

- What other values would you add to the list? Which is most significant in your context? How do these values shape your practice?

- What are the pros and cons of these approaches in your context?

References

Boyce, G. (2010) *An Improbable Feast: The Surprising Dynamic of Hospitality at the Heart of Multifaith Chaplaincy*. Lulu.com.

Ford, D.F. (2011) *Theology and Chaplaincy in a Multi-Faith Context: A Manifesto*. Cardiff: Cardiff Centre for Chaplaincy Studies. Accessed on 22/11/2017 at www.stpadarns.ac.uk/wp-content/uploads/2016/06/Cardiff-Chaplaincy-f-2011-Prof-David-Ford.pdf.

Hill-Brown, R. (2016) *Supporting Families with Sick Children*. Birmingham: Red Balloon Resources.

Hopkins, T. and Rippon, S. (2015) *Head, Hands and Heart: Asset-based Approaches in Health Care*. London: The Health Foundation. Accessed on 22/11/2017 at www.health.org.uk/sites/health/files/HeadHandsAndHeartAssetBasedApproachesInHealthCare.pdf.

Nash, P. (2015) 'Five Key Values and Objectives for Multifaith Care.' In P. Nash, M. Parkes and Z. Hussain (eds) *Multifaith Care for Sick and Dying Children and Their Families*. London: Jessica Kingsley Publishers.

Threlfall-Holmes, M. (2011) 'Exploring Models of Chaplaincy.' In M. Threlfall-Holmes and M. Newitt (eds) *Being a Chaplain*. London: SPCK.

Chapter 5
Screening, Assessment and Charting
Mary Robinson

Spiritual screen: there is a role for all caregivers

In pediatric settings, chaplains must tend to the spiritual needs of the child, siblings, parents, and often distressed grandparents, all gathered at the bedside or in the waiting room. How can a pediatric chaplain respond to so many different needs?

One growing approach has been to utilize the generalist/specialist model in providing spiritual care in the hospital setting. While most healthcare givers appreciate the importance of spirituality in patient-centered care, few have received adequate training to undertake it skillfully (Balboni *et al.* 2013). Increasingly, chaplains, the spiritual specialists, are providing training for non-chaplains, the spiritual generalists, to embed a basic spiritual screen into their nursing, psychosocial and medical intakes (Thiel and Robinson 2016). Healthcare professionals of many disciplines can learn to complete a spiritual screen, provide basic level spiritual care and refer to the specialist for more in-depth assessment and complex spiritual care (Baldacchino 2015; Handzo and Koenig 2004; Massey, Fitchett and Roberts 2004).

The goals of a basic spiritual screen are to (Thiel and Robinson 2016):

- identify spiritual sources of wellbeing (beliefs, behaviours and supportive relationships that contribute to resilience) that the patient and family bring to a medical crisis

- inquire if/how the patient would like to incorporate them into the plan of care

- notice signs of spiritual distress or struggle

- refer to a chaplain those requiring follow-up or more specialized care.

In the basic screen, spiritual distress or struggle would automatically generate a referral to the chaplain, as research has indicated its negative impact on quality of life, adjustment to hospitalization and illness, and recovery (Fitchett 1999; Fitchett and Risk 2009). Other indicators for a referral to the chaplain or spiritual specialist include: transition to palliative care; request for prayer, sacrament or ritual in the hospital; assistance with Sabbath observance or funeral planning; need for devotional materials; or request for ethical consultation from a religious perspective.

If we think of spirituality as a life-giving relationship to something greater than one's self that is trustworthy and inspiring, highly valued or sacred, then it becomes clear that religion is only one spiritual expression among many. In fact, there is a growing demographic of younger generations in the US and in Europe who identify as 'spiritual-but-not-religious' (Pew Research Center 2015; Smith 2012). Many in this demographic are unfamiliar with or averse to religious language, while having rich spiritual lives and legitimate spiritual needs. For this reason, the spiritual screen should utilize inclusive – that is, secular – language. Should a patient or parent respond in religious language, then the spiritual generalist can adopt the other's terminology (Thiel and Robinson 2016).

PRACTICE EXAMPLE 5.1: TEACHING SPIRITUAL SCREENING

One hospital offered full-day, simulation-based workshops to prepare interprofessional clinicians to function as capable, confident and ethical spiritual care generalists (Robinson *et al.* 2016). Over the course of five years, more than 350 spiritual generalists from many areas of the hospital have completed a program that included didactics, visual slideshows, simulation of common clinical scenarios, and debriefings. The curriculum included such topics as: an inclusive definition of spirituality (both religious and secular forms), current research on the positive impact of spirituality on healing, patient satisfaction, costs of care, and resilience; hospitality for all spiritual practices and religious traditions, the FICA screening tool (Borneman, Ferrell and Puchalski 2010) in both religious and secular versions, training to hear spiritual distress expressed in secular and religious language, ethical guidelines for providing basic spiritual care, and indicators for a chaplaincy referral. Thus,

> basic spiritual screening in this hospital is increasingly included in nursing, social work and medical intakes and care plans, evidence-based referrals to chaplaincy have increased, and the resources of trained chaplains are used more effectively in spiritual assessments and complex care.

Spiritual assessment: first, cultural and spiritual humility

Spiritual assessment is a more in-depth and nuanced encounter than a spiritual screen, and is a chaplain's task. The term 'assessment' can be misleading if it implies that there is a universal ladder of spiritual advancement. Fowler's research (1981), once an accepted universal hierarchy of spiritual development, has increasing been challenged as being culturally, developmentally, and religiously limited. Current research is exploring the inner world of children in many global cultures and traditions, their unique voices and perspectives, and the diversity of spiritual practices and aspirations (Adams, Hyde and Woolley 2008; Yust *et al.* 2005). Above all, chaplains must cultivate cultural and spiritual humility, not only because that is the professional standard of ethical practice, but also because the true intent of spiritual assessment is to visit another's spiritual world with reverence, respect and compassionate curiosity. Another's inner world – its unique landscape, beauty, safety, history and stories, joys and rituals – is sacred ground. The chaplain enters only if invited as a guest and, above all, must do no harm.

Listen, observe, but don't frisk!

A chaplain may choose from an abundance of published assessment models for use with parents and young adults in the hospital setting (Cadge and Bandini 2015; LaRocca-Pitts 2012). All assessment models are best used as a silent guide for listening attentively to another's narrative. This approach is time-intensive and other-centered, so the spiritual caregiver must be a patient and engaged listener.

Spiritual issues only emerge when a context of trust and safety has been established. This may require preliminary conversation before any assessment can take place. As one listens to the parent or patient's narrative, what themes emerge? What has been said with emotion, perhaps deserving more attention? What themes have not been mentioned? The latter may inspire the chaplain to inquire gently, if time permits, or follow-up with another visit.

Assessment tools can be misused if applied as a tool for 'frisking' for information, as with a clinician-centered checklist. Another's spiritual/inner life is perhaps the most private of zones, more intimate even than those examined in a medical exam. All in a chaplain's care should be permitted to decline or limit a spiritual assessment, particularly as some may have experienced spiritual or religious trauma in their past.

Interpretive Spiritual Encounters: assessment through facilitated expressive play

Spiritual assessment of a child more resembles an art than a task. Children may not express their spirituality verbally or use religious language. Most children have rapidly changing foci of attention and curiosity. Because their primary mode of exploration and expression is play, that is the medium best suited to spiritual assessment.

The chaplain engages a child in expressive play or creative activities that are fun, affirming, developmentally appropriate and sensitive to the patient's abilities and condition. The chaplain offers the occasion and materials, but the child remains free to select play options from the chaplain's bag or decline altogether. In the context of safe and patient-centered play, spiritual themes or concerns may be expressed by the child and observed by the pediatric chaplain. A chaplain can inquire gently during the play or offer wondering questions to invite further narrative, but the child is the leader of the play, maintaining control over the process and the content.

Important spiritual themes among children include: love, forgiveness, trust, hope, anger, guilt/punishment, security/safety, loneliness/connection, why/meaning, wholeness/identity and legacy (Thayer and Nee 2009). Nash, who coined the term Interpretive Spiritual Encounters or ISE (Nash, Darby amd Nash 2015), reports that this approach not only gives the chaplain a window into the child's inner world, but also often functions as a therapeutic intervention in and of itself. A child can explore feelings or concerns, and experience relief by simply expressing them to an attentive and compassionate listener. Often the chaplain can identify a misunderstanding that could benefit from further explanation, or concerns that warrant reassurance. Nash, Thayer and Berryman all offer a wide variety of activities and materials well-suited to ISE.

BEADS
The child selects and strings beads to create a customized bracelet. Colors of the beads can represent spiritual themes such as love, hope, worry or peacefulness. Alternatively, beads can used by a child to make a story of

'what has happened during my hospital stay' or to represent 'the people who love me'.

DOLLS

Children create stick dolls by drawing pictures of themselves and others on tongue depressors. The child is invited to talk about whom they have drawn, what makes each of the persons happy or sad, or to put on a little play using the stick dolls.

BOXES

A child can be offered a small wooden box to paint or decorate with markers and glitter glue which becomes a 'hope and happy box'. The chaplain can invite the young child to draw, cut out magazine photos or select dollhouse-sized items that recall happy aspects of their life outside the hospital. The patient can even select photos from a parent's mobile phone that can be printed by the chaplain for inclusion in the box. Some children will want to make more than one box, such as a box for prayers or a box to put away one's worries. If the child cannot yet write words to describe a worry, the chaplain can volunteer to be a scribe.

BUBBLES

Another tool that easily fits inside a pediatric chaplain's pocket is a small bottle of bubbles. A chaplain can stand outside the doorway or bed curtain and blow bubbles into the patient's line of sight. Since this is both novel and non-medical, it often facilitates curiosity and trust. 'I am a chaplain. I wonder if you know what that is? ... No? I have the best job in the hospital. I just get to make friends and play with kids... I wonder if you like bubbles? Just watching or catching them can be fun... I wonder if you would like to wish upon these bubbles? What hopes or wishes should we put inside our bubbles?' A child can also be invited to put worries inside the bubbles and blow them away. If items in the room or conversation suggest religious affiliation, the chaplain can inquire, 'I wonder if there is anything you want to talk to God about today? We can put our prayers inside the bubbles and blow them up to God!' Family members may wish to participate as well. Leaving the small bottle of bubbles behind with the child affirms that God is always available to receive our prayers another time.

GODLY PLAY

Jerome Berryman's Montessori-based religious curriculum of Godly Play (Berryman 2013) can also be adapted for use in an ISE. For example, the Good Shepherd lesson (Berryman and Stewart 1989) can be adapted for use with Christian or Jewish patients. Alternately, a customized lesson can be created using Berryman's pedagogy (see more in Chapter 6).

> ### PRACTICE EXAMPLE 5.2: PREPARING A ROOM
>
> This chaplain, for example, developed a lesson based on John 14.2 for a Christian child nearing end of life. The patient used a variety of blocks to make a house, then selected or drew the items she wanted to have available in her room inside the big house. The chaplain offered some wondering questions: 'I wonder if the people are happy in this house? I wonder how many people could live in this place? I wonder who takes care of everyone in this house? I wonder where this house could really be?'

CHATS WITH A STUFFED ANIMAL OR ACTION FIGURE

While a chaplain can carry interpretive materials to the bedside, the creative chaplain can also notice and make use of items already in the child's room. 'Can you introduce me to everyone here in your room?' 'Who isn't here?' (A child can tell you about their siblings, pets, step-parents or supportive circle.) The chaplain can then ask for an introduction to the patient's stuffed animal (or action figure), and speak to it directly. Keeping eye contact with the stuffed animal conveys that you are taking this conversation seriously. Often a stuffed animal or action figure can be quite talkative, when the child is otherwise silent or shy. While shaking its paw (or hand), the chaplain can inquire, 'Tell me, Boo Bear (or Spiderman), how are you feeling today? Are we taking good care of you here? I wonder what you and your buddy do for fun when you're not in the hospital? I wonder what could make the two of you happy today? Do you ever worry about stuff? Even a bear (or Spiderman) worries about stuff sometimes. I wonder what worries you?'

A VIRTUAL TRIP HOME

An older child or teen patient's computer can often facilitate an interpretive encounter.

> ### PRACTICE EXAMPLE 5.3: TACO BILL
>
> A 12-year-old boy introduced the pediatric chaplain to the large stuffed dog sitting on his pillow, named Taco Bill. 'He goes with me

whenever I go to the hospital. He's grouchy because he hasn't had any tacos in five days. They are not on the menu here. Do you know where I can find him some tacos?' 'Hmmm. Where would you go if you were home? Can you take me for a visit?' asked the chaplain. The patient proceeded to pull up Google Earth on his computer screen, showing the chaplain his hometown in western Texas, nearly half a continent away from his hospital room in Boston. He pointed out his house while tracing the route to school with his finger, identified the field where he plays soccer with his friends, as well as the place where he is taking guitar lessons. He invited the chaplain to see his church and his grandmother's house, where his favorite dog lives. Photos of the dog, grandmother and friends were pulled up on Facebook accompanied by lively commentary. Eventually, the patient also identified the two best places for tacos in town and planned whom he would invite to his homecoming taco dinner.

BIBLIOTHERAPY

Chaplains can assemble a carefully selected library of picture books for interpretive spiritual bibliotherapy. Books for this bookshelf are selected with care, reflecting a range of developmental levels and cultural inclusivity. The quality of illustrations is just as important as the words and themes of the story.

The chaplain typically selects three books for a bring-to-the-bedside bag, keeping a particular patient in mind. Included is a book that facilitates getting acquainted, one that is simply fun and fanciful, and a third book with a story that is engaging on its own merit, but also contains characters, situations or spiritual themes with which the patient can identify, if he or she chooses. Arriving at the bedside, the chaplain can invite the patient to choose a book to read together. The chaplain sits near the patient and holds the book, and reads with the patient, offering occasional wondering questions to open the conversation wider. Often children may connect their own story to that of the picture book. Listening with care, the chaplain can often discern the spiritual challenges or strengths within the child's inner world, and offer compassionate listening and affirmation.

DRAWING

Drawing can also be a window to a child's inner world and a fun activity in the hospital playroom or at the child's bedside. The chaplain can draw or color in parallel.

> ### PRACTICE EXAMPLE 5.4: GOD'S FRIEND
>
> Seven-year-old Sarah asked the chaplain, 'My mom says you are God's friend. Have you ever seen God?' The chaplain replied, 'No, but I sometimes wonder what God looks like.' Sarah began to draw with focused energy, commenting, 'Soon you'll know, because I am drawing his picture!' The drawing looked quite a bit like a daisy with eyes and a smile in its center. The chaplain watched with anticipation. 'See, God has lots and lots of ears. More than 20, so he can hear everyone's prayers!' Sarah exclaimed. The chaplain inquired, 'I wonder if you want to draw some of those prayers?' Sarah shook her head vigorously. 'No, they are private between God and the kids here! Kids don't have to say their prayers out loud, but God's ears can hear them anyway. God has awesome ears that never stop listening. God always listens to all children. God likes children best!'

VIDEO GAMES

An ISE can be utilized effectively with adolescents and young adults as well using 'a third focus' to facilitate building a relationship. Instead of a face-to-face conversation with eye contact, the chaplain can ask to sit down near the patient's side, and focus together on a common activity. If the adolescent is in the midst of a video game, the patient can be invited to instruct the chaplain. Giving a patient a moment of mastery and authority in a hospital setting is therapeutic in and of itself. If the chaplain is willing to be an active and curious listener, a climate of trust and safe communication may be established, in which the chaplain can inquire, 'How's it going for you here in the hospital? I wonder what bothers you most about being here in the hospital? I wonder what you are hoping for? I wonder what you would want your doctors and nurses to understand in order to take better care of you?' Keeping the visual attention on the 'third focus' often facilitates the adolescent's ease in sustaining an ongoing conversation.

SMART PHONES

Hospitalized adolescents usually have their phone handy. Phones are an essential social lifeline to peers, but also contain favorite apps, songs and photos. The chaplain can ask about favorite apps, or express a desire to learn more about what music the patient likes best. As they establish rapport, the chaplain might ask, 'Can you play me the song that makes you most happy?' Other possibilities might be 'the song that helps you calm down when you are stressed out' or 'the song that matches how you are feeling today'. As in other interpretive spiritual encounters, the chaplain must be a patient and engaged listener, and would do well to express gratitude for the chance to learn something new from such a good teacher. In this paradoxical encounter, the patient is not only in charge, but the more knowledgeable provider of information.

JOURNALS OR VIDEOS

Adolescent patients with chronic or life-limiting illnesses are often pondering the meaning of their illness and suffering, as well as wondering about their legacy (Thayer and Nee 2009). Many adolescent patients with cystic fibrosis have given thought to their own funeral, having attended the funerals of fellow patients. Some have given up on a God who they believe has caused or permitted their illness, or perhaps is really powerless. Teens may be seeking and finding spiritual strength from non-theistic sources. Adolescents who may choose to protect their parents from such musings may well welcome a chance to journal privately or write poetry about their journey. A chaplain can offer a choice of handsomely bound journals, thus conveying respect for the patient's wisdom and narrative. With the help of technology-savvy volunteers and the support of the chaplain, the patient may be invited to make a video about themselves or their medical journey. Some patients have chosen to post theirs on their own Facebook page, or to invite their care team to a bedside viewing party.

Charting: communicating spiritual care and concerns with the team

How and what should the chaplain chart? In one sense, the writing of a note is the next step in the ISE process. Charting provides the chaplain the opportunity to reflect further upon the visit, and distil what is most important for the other team members to know. What spiritual resources or strengths were identified? What spiritual concerns or needs were expressed or observed? What was the chaplain's response or intervention?

What is the follow-up plan? Who will be the primary chaplain providing follow-up spiritual care?

Charting should be efficient as well as effective in communicating with the team. Our staff reviewed a variety of chaplaincy charting models and, in coordination with our information department, designed three templates that would embody best practices, be efficient to write and read, and communicate relevant information to other clinicians while respecting the 'need to know' criteria of privacy. The three templates offer the choices of brevity or depth, check-off or free text within an outline format. In the template utilizing check-off options, those items not selected are automatically deleted from the final note. The templates are easily accessed from within the medical record program by chaplains on any hospital computer or tablet. Once signed, chart notes are readily accessible to other caregivers.

Selected fields from these templates also feed into a computer-generated daily chaplaincy census which is updated in real time, listing a patient's name, location, medical record number, spiritual identity(s), level of priority, length of stay, days since last chaplain visit, primary chaplain, and language. When appropriate, the census also includes an asterisk indicating risk factors necessitating a careful review of the chart prior to visiting, or a family's preference for no further chaplaincy visits. Much of the demographic data is retained for future visits, but can be edited at any point, should, for example, the primary chaplain or priority change.

The use of this daily chaplaincy census has contributed to increased efficiency, reliability, communication and accountability within multi-person chaplaincy departments. For example, when a patient transfers to a new floor, the receiving chaplain can identify the prior chaplain of record, and coordinate an effective hand-off. In the case of patients receiving palliative care, the primary chaplain will follow the same patient and family over the course of many admissions or transfers within the hospital. Finally, the primary chaplain can readily triage patients' needs utilizing priority and days since last visit data.

Future development and research needs

- What are the most effective screening and assessment tools for children in hospital and hospices? Also in the light of different abilities, conditions, etc.?

- What are the best-fit research models for researching our screening and assessment tools? Efficacy, reliability, narrative/case study?

- A universally agreed, accessible charting content, including taxonomy, types of needs, interventions, plan.

Summary

- Spiritual screening can be performed by many members of the healthcare team and serves as the initial record of spiritual and religious needs and struggles.
- Spiritual assessments go deeper and are performed by chaplains. They find the deeper spiritual issues and serve as guides to appropriate spiritual care interventions and follow-up.
- Many methods of play can be used to assess a child's spiritual life and needs, from young children to adolescents.
- Charting what has been assessed then communicates to the rest of the medical team what the chaplain's plans and interventions and outcomes have been. Charting also ensures communication and continuity within the team of chaplains.

Questions for reflection

- Critique the screening, assessment tools and charting format for children and their families with different abilities and conditions in your context.
- What is the role of the spiritual care generalist and specialist in screening and assessing needs? And how might the communication between them be improved?
- How might you be able to develop your screening and assessments using play and questions?

References

Adams, K., Hyde, B. and Woolley, R. (2008) *The Spiritual Dimension of Childhood*. London: Jessica Kingsley Publishers.

Balboni, M.J., Sullivan, A., Amobi, A., Phelps, A.C. *et al.* (2013) 'Why is spiritual care infrequent at the end of life? Spiritual care perceptions among patients, nurses and physicians and the role of training.' *Journal of Clinical Oncology 31*, 4, 461–467.

Baldacchino, D. (2015) 'Spiritual care education of health care professionals.' *Religions 6*, 594–613.

Berryman, J. (2013) *The Complete Guide to Godly Play*, vols 1–8. New York, NY: Church Publishing Incorporated.

Berryman, J. and Stewart, S. (1989) *Young Children and Worship*. Louisville, KY: John Knox Press.

Borneman, T., Ferrell, B. and Puchalski, C.M. (2010) 'Evaluation of the FICA Tool for Spiritual Assessment.' *Journal of Pain and Symptom Management 40*, 2, 163–173.

Cadge, W. and Bandini, J. (2015) 'The evolution of spiritual assessment tools in healthcare.' *Society 52*, 5, 430–437.

Fitchett, G. (1999) 'Screening for spiritual risk.' *Chaplaincy Today 15*, 2–12.

Fitchett, G. and Risk, J. (2009) 'Screening for spiritual struggle.' *Journal of Pastoral Care and Counseling 63*, 1–12.

Fowler, J. (1981) *Stages of Faith: The Psychology of Human Development and the Quest for Meaning*. New York, NY: Harper and Row.

Handzo, G. and Koenig, H. (2004) 'Spiritual care: Whose job is it anyway?' *Southern Medical Journal 9*, 7, 1242–1245.

LaRocca-Pitts, M., (2012) 'FACT, a chaplain's tool for assessing spiritual needs in an acute care setting.' *Chaplaincy Today 28*, 1, 25–32.

Massey, K., Fitchett, G. and Roberts, P. (2004) 'Assessment and Diagnosis in Spiritual Care.' In K. Mauk and N. Schmidt (eds) *Spiritual Care in Nursing Practice*. Philadelphia, PA: Lippincott, Williams and Wilkin.

Nash, P., Darby, K. and Nash, S. (2015) *Spiritual Care with Sick Children and Young People*. London: Jessica Kingsley Publishers.

Pew Research Center (2015) 'U.S. Public Becoming Less Religious.' Accessed on 22/11/2017 at www.pewforum.org/2015/11/03/u-s-public-becoming-less-religious.

Robinson, M., Thiel, M., Shirkey, K., Zurakowski, D. and Meyer, E.C. (2016) 'Efficacy of training interprofessional spiritual care generalists.' *Journal of Palliative Medicine 19*, 8, 814–821.

Smith, T. (2012) 'Beliefs about God across Time and Countries.' National Opinion Research. Accessed on 22/11/2017 at www.norc.org/PDFs/Beliefs_about_God_Report.pdf.

Thayer, P. and Nee, R. (2009) 'Spiritual Care of Children and Parents.' In A. Armstrong-Dailey and S. Zarbock (eds) *Hospice Care for Children*. Oxford: Oxford University Press.

Thiel, M.M. and Robinson, M. (2016) 'Spiritual care of the nonreligious.' *PlainViews*, 1.2. Accessed on 13/01/18 at https://plainviews.healthcarechaplaincy.org/articles/Spiritual_Care_of_the_Nonreligious.

Yust, K., Johnson, A., Sasso, S. and Roehlkepartain, E. (2005) *Nurturing Child and Adolescent Spirituality: Perspectives from the World's Religious Traditions*. New York, NY: Rowan and Littlefield.

Chapter 6

Approaches and Skills for Working with Children and Young People

Ryan Campbell and Sally Nash

Introduction

> **PRACTICE EXAMPLE 6.1: PLAYING WITH SITA**
>
> Sita spent several weeks in hospital with a mental health issue, and I visited her regularly. She was initially reluctant to engage with me and told me that she didn't like the fact that everyone kept asking her questions, so I promised to ask no questions but suggested that she might like to play a fun card game to help while away some time. Sita enjoyed the game, and as we played, she became more open with me and began to talk about the things in her life which were important to her. All through our game we talked about faith and our understanding of it and many other things too.
>
> *Susy Insley, Chaplaincy Youth Worker, Queen's Medical Centre, Nottingham, UK*

This is an everyday occurrence for children and youth workers who create spaces where children and young people feel comfortable to explore the issues that are important to them. In this chapter, building on the discussion of children's spirituality in Chapter 1, we explore some of the relevant core concepts, approaches and skills.

Safe and healthy environments

Hospitals usually have a policy to safeguard the welfare of patients (sometimes known as child protection policies), and it is important that chaplains work within this. A significant concept for chaplains is that of spiritual abuse which can be understood to mean:

> the mistreatment of a person by actions or threats when justified by appeal to God, faith or religion. It includes:
>
> - using a position of spiritual authority to dominate or manipulate another person or group
> - using a position of spiritual authority to seek inappropriate deference from others
> - isolating a person from friends and family members
> - using biblical or religious terminology to justify abuse.
>
> (General Synod of the Anglican Church of Australia 2016)

From a Christian perspective, the Churches' Child Protection Advisory Service (CCPAS) conclude their theological reflection on safeguarding with the following statement: 'However, it is clear that protecting children and all who are vulnerable, weak and oppressed is central to God's character. Jesus demonstrated that children are to be cherished, valued and protected' (www.ccpas.co.uk/theology). Chaplains and spiritual caregivers need to be alert to the potential of religion to be used inappropriately and be willing to advise institutions on this issue if it arises in the care of a patient as well as ensuring that the concept is clearly taught as part of induction for both staff and volunteers.

Beyond this, there is much that can be done to help children and young people *feel* as well as *be* safe. Harris uses the term 'holding environment' to describe a safe and secure context and identifies five key elements (2011, p.69):

- safe attachment and protection
- reliability and consistency
- attempts to understand
- empathic attunement
- safe limits and boundaries.

Within such a context a person can explore strong feelings in a safe setting. Chaplains may be one of a small number of healthcare staff who can offer such a holding environment, as they have time to listen and the opportunity to build relationships and are not usually focused on compliance.

Relationships with youth workers have been described as 'like a friend' (Young 1999, p.72), but clearly there are different parameters to other friendships and it is important to understand the professional boundaries and codes of practice that one works within. Richards (2014, p.124), discussing the role of the youth worker, distinguishes between being 'friends of' rather than 'friends with'. Chaplains have similar issues in articulating the nature of relationships with patients or their families and need to reflect carefully on appropriate boundaries.

Understanding loss

Underpinning much of the work with sick children and young people is an understanding of loss. There are at least six areas where loss may be significant (Doehring 2006):

- material
- relational
- intrapsychic (loss of symbol or ideal in relation to inner world)
- functional (disability)
- role
- systemic (change in how system functions).

One can argue what is the most used and useful theory in paediatric chaplaincy. Some would propose loss theory. It connects and brings insights to so many aspects in the life of children and their families in hospital: loss of hope, future, aspirations, abilities, achievement, identity, health, relationships, purpose, carers, financial security, etc. When we understand that all these potentially might be going on in one pastoral encounter, we are better equipped to understand the strains and sadness and respond more compassionately and appropriately. Some of us have set up funds for families to apply for, to facilitate significant achievements and wishes, to advocate for ongoing support, to sit and listen for longer to the lament of the significance of the loss of the final hope of a child, the physical inability of no longer being able to play sports to a professional level due to the loss of limbs, of potential further damage to delicate bones. The list goes on, as does our empathy to see loss beyond our own perception. Both the child and the caregiver can be liable to such loss and the grief which accompanies it.

Experience matters

When it comes to children, we are not in relationship with theories; we are in relationship with other people. Our own personal experiences matter – *as* children as well as *with* children. We, from our many roles, have a fountain of wisdom to draw from simply by reflecting on our experiences, and being open to what that wisdom communicates to us (often beyond words).

As a Clinical Pastoral Education (CPE) student, my supervisor told me the following bit of wisdom:

> In the midst of crisis, no matter how old you are, two things are going to happen to the people you are caring for as a chaplain. The first is that people will revert to the theology of their childhood in the midst of crisis. The second is that it won't matter what words you use with them, because in the end they don't remember who said what, they only remember who was there to care for them.

The first maxim in this bit of wisdom is not a new idea, but it is important, and we may recall relating to God through prayer or meaning-making, bargaining or hoping for the best possible outcome as we may have done when younger. Also important is that our presence precedes our words when we are with other people experiencing crisis. We may have life-changing conversations with people *when they are ready*, but crisis is not generally one of those times. The same goes for children in the hospital – we may have important conversations with them, as with Sita above, but only when they are ready. Our first act of caring for children in the hospital is showing up and letting them decide when they are ready and what they are ready to engage in. Knowing a bit about what happens in ourselves will help us to leave enough space for the children we serve to connect to their own experiences and needs.

If you want to work with children, you need to spend time around them. Neuroscience uses the term 'limbic resonance' (Lewis, Amini and Lannon 2000). Research suggests that our brains are affected by, and affect, the brains of those around us. This is all going on in the background, and we are interacting, often without any awareness of it, with one another's 'vibes'. Much of the popular conversations surrounding limbic resonance focuses on romantic love and institutional leadership, but it all starts in childhood. The effect of a parent's silent gaze into the eyes of an infant, the simple joy of being with a child engaged in a common activity, sitting with another person in the midst of crisis without trying to fix things – all of this can have scientifically measurable effects on the brains of those who are sharing physical space together. We engage in 'a symphony of mutual exchange and internal adaptation whereby two mammals become attuned to each other's inner states', meaning our brains can literally 'learn' to be in a kind of 'harmony' with children when we are around them in an open and authentic manner (Lewis *et al.* 2000, p.16). As spiritual carers of children in a clinical setting, embracing both the observable and explainable as well as the mysterious and ineffable, and the tension that sometimes appears to exist between the two, is tantamount to our being fully present with children. After all, sometimes we can see the sacred, and sometimes we can only feel it, but, either way, we know it's there in the midst of a shared experience.

Another key aspect of *experience* is that theologically there is an exchange that takes place between the adult spiritual caregiver and the child – what Berryman calls a 'mutual blessing' (2013, p.1). Such relationships requires presence – presence not only to children in physical space, but also to children in their ways of being and knowing and loving, as well as to the children within ourselves who are still growing spiritually. The experience, then, of being with ourselves, of being with children and of being present to all the mysterious ways in which our presence affects the presence of others (and vice versa) cannot be found in theory alone. It can only be found by showing up!

Play

Think about the last time you had a conversation with a young child or, better yet, the last time you played with a child. Play can be just as serious and meaning-making as can conversation. Note that in the story above it was through play that Sita was able to find herself comfortable enough to begin conversing with her visitor. Play is an incredibly valuable and simple tool in the kit for paediatric spiritual caregivers.

Play is pre-verbal, pre-conscious, occurs across species, is necessary for life in sentient beings and seems to defy being confined to a specific context or description. Brown (2010) offers some properties of play which help define it. Play is 'apparently purposeless (done for its own sake)' – that is, there is no practical goal when playing as there might be when we seek food, clothing or shelter. Play is also 'voluntary'; play can't be forced or required of someone and still be real play. Play has 'inherent attraction' that not only keeps one from boredom but is enjoyable to its participants. Players find themselves losing track of time, so there is some freedom from the clock, as well as freedom from our own self-image or self-consciousness about how we might look to others while engaging in play. Play is improvisational, because you never know what will happen, and if you're ready for anything, it may take you to some unexpected places. Finally, play has 'continuation desire': we want to keep doing it and do it again (Brown 2010, pp.16–17). These properties of play help us to know what it is when we see it, even if we can't exactly say what it is without limiting it in some way.

Play has a deeply spiritual component as well. Play between two or more people can be an act of creation, just as play between people and God can be an act of creation. Prayer or worship can be play. Silence, laughter or casual conversation can be play. The challenge is to learn to see the Transcendent in even the most mundane things and learn to play with even the most threatening of limits. This is how we can wonder about and create something new out of even the most serious of situations. But how do we rise to this challenge when caring for children in such a scary and serious place as a hospital? How do we do this without becoming so scared or serious that we aren't able to find our way to play in the first place?

Being ready

> ### PRACTICE EXAMPLE 6.2: JANNA'S DOLL
>
> Last year, a newly diagnosed leukaemia patient, five-year-old Janna, was admitted. Her opinions and language skills are both above those of your average five-year-old. The clinic uses dolls that are bald. Upon being presented with them, most of our little girls, already bald from their chemo treatments, are immediately in love, exclaiming over the doll's being 'just like me!' So one day when Janna was in for treatment, I found her playing with a bald Barbie. Since many of our patients want to talk about their bald dolls, my conversation began with 'What happened to your doll's hair?' No answer. I must have been off my game that day, because I didn't pick up that Janna didn't deem the question worthy of a response. So with different words, I asked again essentially the same question. To

which, with a sigh and an eye roll, Janna replied, 'She doesn't have cancer. She's just a doll.' Oh. All righty then! Ouch. A minute later the physician came in; while examining Janna, he too asked if the doll was bald due to chemo. A pause, then before Janna could repeat the exasperated answer she'd given me, her mother said, 'No, but if she did need chemo, her shirt is perfect for easy access to a port!' With a tone that indicated how unbelievably lame grown-ups are, Janna responded, 'She don't got a port; she only got boobs.'

Chaplain Marty Koontz, East Tennessee Children's Hospital, USA

This story is a playful example of what happens when we enter the world of a child with expectations about what is most important to the child at that time. Here we see the chaplain assuming that the child is identifying with the doll (as does the doctor), and when it is clear that she is not, Mom jumps in to save the day with a 'no, but...' to keep things on course. Janna, the patient of five years old, is clear with everyone that whatever game the adults in the room seem to want her to be playing is very much their own – she is playing a different game altogether! What we learn from this light-hearted account is that, sometimes, we as adults can use play to assume a child is making meaning that they aren't necessarily making (or that they are making the same kind of meaning that we are). Other times, adults seem to use play to keep things light and approachable and accessible when what is happening might be better contained in the more serious side of play. Certainly, we know from child development theory that young children think in the concrete, and sometimes they are thought to lack the imaginative flexibility of mind to think more abstractly, but perhaps we might be called to be more open to other possibilities. The story ends with the child correcting the adults' concrete assumptions, but what if that was just the beginning of the story? What if, at that point, the adults were able to stop, breathe and get ready by being fully present to what Janna was creating in that moment? What could we wonder about with Janna, about who this doll is that she holds in her hands? What kind of meaning was she making at that moment and what would happen if we let her do the meaning-making, rather than the adults in the room? If we really engaged in play, what mysterious creation might come from a question like 'I wonder about the doll that you're holding?' rather than focusing on the doll's hair and moving the meaning-making in a specific direction?

Caring at the limits

Children deal with the existential limits of death, freedom, meaning-making and aloneness just as much as adults do (Berryman 2017, p.100). These limits can raise a child's anxiety, particularly in a setting like a hospital where they are much more tangible and on the surface than usually. Children, just like adults, don't know what happens beyond death, feel the limitation of freedom or the responsibilities of freedom when choices can or cannot be made, search for meaning and the answer to the question 'Why?' when often there doesn't seem to be one, and struggle with the aloneness that is a part of human subjectivity. These limits to being and knowing frame each and every human life. Spiritual carers of children need to be ready to allow that these limits are known and made known to children through symbols that may not make any logical 'sense' to us, but that nevertheless hold deep significance for those who experience them. Something as simple as a doll with no hair can hold many possibilities beyond the obvious and concrete – we as adults need to be ready to meet those possibilities, to hold them gently and reverently, and to allow them to become whatever the child needs them to become at that time.

Such care begins with an open heart, perhaps a few deep breaths and the willingness to simply be present with that child in whatever way that child needs us to be. We often presume that children's needs are the same as ours (or we confuse the two unknowingly), but what children really need from us is the presence to be able to identify their needs without requiring them to express those needs through vocabulary that they don't possess or that is simply insufficient. Some of this is more intuitive than anything else, and intuition requires a very ready presence. Experience at Dallas with therapeutic clowning and chaplaincy draws on the work of Madson (2005):

- **Don't prepare.** Sometimes getting ready means being ready for anything.
- **Just show up.** You have to be with those you serve to offer the presents that presence can bring.
- **Start anywhere.** Let the relationship frame itself – sometimes card games turn into deep conversation and sometimes a doll's boobs may be a frame for deep meaning-making.
- **Pay attention.** Not only to words but to body language – reading the room is an incredibly important skill to have.

- **Face the facts.** Work with what you have. Wishing things were different doesn't change anything.

- **Stay on course.** Don't change the subject or move to a more comfortable topic when the difficult realities make their appearance in the interaction. What's hardest to face may be just the place where the sacred is found. Then again, it may also be that this is just a time to play – don't force an interaction to be 'spiritual' by one definition (through the content of the interaction, for example). It may be that the 'spiritual' interaction at the moment is about play, not piety. Let the child set the course and enjoy the ride.

These maxims can help us to get ready to be with children as we walk with them through difficult circumstances.

Godly Play

Godly Play is an approach to sacred storytelling that was created by Jerome and Thea Berryman. Based on Montessori education and most often used in churches, it has been adapted for clinical use. Godly Play is an imaginative approach to sacred storytelling. Through story, wonder, play and art, people are invited to discover their own meaning and find their own ways of expressing what's most important to them. Many people find their own stories in the midst of the stories that are told. These stories can be provided one-on-one at the bedside, in a special place set aside, in groups, with patients and their siblings and extended families, in psychiatric units – even with the staff themselves who care for children and youth in the hospital. This methodology utilises the theoretical frameworks and principles above to give children and youth (and adults, too) a way to engage the deep spiritual work that is often being done internally by providing an external 'third thing' that children and participants can project on to: a shared narrative and 'field of play' that exists between the storyteller and those hearing the story. The story itself is comprised of material placed on the floor (or bed, or whatever 'field of play' is handy) between the storyteller and the 'circle' (participants). An act of creation takes place as the story unfolds, whereby the circle and storyteller witness the discovery of meaning through wondering about the story together. 'I wonder' precedes every open-ended question that is asked in regard to the carefully scripted story, and there are no right or wrong answers. These stories are intentionally scripted in published volumes and are then memorized by storytellers to open up the possibilities for meaning-making, giving the existential limits some attention within the safety of a narrative, and allowing for relational consciousness to find expression. Usually, after the wondering about the story, space and time are provided for children to do their 'work', most often a kind of artistic response to the story that may include drawing, writing, crafts, poetry or some other tactile or creative way of expressing one's response to the story and wondering just encountered. Often, the activities and art responses are as rich in relational consciousness and existential awareness as the wondering. The power of being present and observing what happens in a circle cannot be fully communicated. In an article regarding its use in a paediatric psychiatry unit, the authors make note:

> Our belief is that facilitating these spiritual expressions through these relational dynamics, and within the context of their existential limits, does indeed lead to spiritual and emotional well-being, and that allowing paediatric psychiatry patients the opportunity to do so within the confines of a safe group and an intentional narrative (the Godly Play method) allows them to carry these expressions with them beyond the group process so that they can access them whenever they need to during the course of their admission and well after discharge. (Minor and Campbell 2016, p.41)

Of course, Godly Play is not the only methodology for creating a safe, sacred, shared space between spiritual guides and the children and youth they serve. Discerning the quality of available resources in supporting children spiritually is especially important. Our hope is that this chapter will help that discernment as you apply the techniques you develop or discover to the principles, theories and practices contained herein.

Youth work principles

Youth workers (a recognised profession in the UK with undergraduate and postgraduate qualifications) 'create a kind of sacred circle…in which youth worker and young person work together to heal hurts, to repair damage, to grow into responsibility, and to promote new ways of being' (Sercombe 2010, p.11). The principles which underpin youth work in a UK context have resonances with chaplaincy (O'Connell 2013).

Voluntary participation

In youth work, young people are encouraged to be participants rather than consumers: they co-create experience and have choice. Youth workers meet young people where they are at and young people have complete autonomy as to whether to engage or not. In a hospital context, that is true of very few other professionals apart from a chaplain. Voluntary participation also infers that we are clear about what will be involved in an activity, so consent to engage is informed.

Equal opportunities

Equality of opportunity is about equal access to opportunities rather than everyone being treated the same. It is about challenging the impact of inequalities and seeking to identify interventions which support young people in doing this themselves. Equal opportunities also involve supporting young people to celebrate diversity and recognise the strength in differences of culture, race, language, sexual identity, gender, disability, age, religion and class.

PRACTICE EXAMPLE 6.3: ELLIE'S PICTURE

One morning the class was decorating/painting/sticking artwork for Easter. The teaching staff had placed all the children around the table. While the class worked, Ellie just watched from her wheelchair. I decided to make a change. She was paralysed from the neck down but was able to move her head from side to side. After chatting to her I gathered the colours and equipment she desired. Using a large clipboard, I held her sheet of paper and after her choosing her paint colours, I placed the paint brush in her mouth and held the paper close enough so that she could reach. I will never forget the sparkle in her eyes! Without words, I understood her sense of pride and accomplishment. This was echoed in her need to call her mum at break time to boast about her amazing art work.

Jodie Cotterrell, Chaplaincy Youth Worker, Birmingham Women's and Children's Hospital, UK

Empowerment

Empowerment of young people is about supporting them to understand and act on the personal, social and political issues which affect their own lives, the lives of others and the communities of which they are a part. Youth workers believe that they can learn as much from the young person as the young person might learn from them. Again, in a context where usually it is the professional who is offering the answer or solution to the young person, an element of autonomy and reciprocity can offer a welcome respite. Knight (2008, p.228) talks about a fourfold process which begins with listening and then moves to:

- understanding (thinking critically about particular themes and discovering their root causes)

- dreaming (reflecting on the resources of one's faith tradition and discovering a word of hope and guidance about how to address the theme from a faith perspective)

- acting (planning and implementing an action project to address the theme).

One of my most precious memories is of a mental health hospital youth group who made a giant Pudsey Bear as part of a plan to raise money for a charity, Children in Need (www.bbcchildreninneed.co.uk).

Being an informal educator

Informal education is 'the wise, respectful and spontaneous process of cultivating learning' (Jeffs and Smith 2012). It takes place anywhere, any time or anyhow. Young describes the process as 'a reflective exercise which enables young people to learn from their experience, develop their capacity to think critically and engage in "sense-making" as a process of continuous self-discovery and re-creation' (1999, p.81). I have used the metaphor of an odyssey guide to describe this journeying with dimension of being an informal educator (Nash and Palmer 2011). If an odyssey is a long, eventful, adventurous journey, then this is surely what a sick young person embarks on, and having someone alongside them to help them learn can make a significant difference as to how they overcome some of the challenges of the journey.

Future development and research needs

- Wider application and synergy of worldwide professional principles and good practice of relating to babies, children and young people in multifaith and cultural religious, spiritual and pastoral care.

- Standards and guidelines to ensure spiritual and religious abuse does not happen.

- Efficacy and reliability testing of Godly Play and Spiritual Play as screening, assessment and intervention tools.

Summary

- How we relate is more important than what we do.

- Play and informal education are core skills to use with paediatric patients.

- We need to create safe and sacred spaces where we engage with children and young people on their terms and timing.

- Honouring the agency and choice of the patient is one of the differences in engaging with a chaplain compared with other healthcare professionals.

Questions for reflection

- In what ways can we mitigate against the possibility of spiritual abuse occurring in our institutions?

- Are there issues or experiences from my own childhood which impact my approach to chaplaincy?

- Critique and apply to your context the four professional youth work principles. How might your practice be changed in the light of these principles?

References

Berryman, J. (2013) *The Spiritual Guidance of Children*. Denver, CO: Moorehouse Publishing.
Berryman, J. (2017) *Becoming Like a Child: The Curiosity of Maturity Beyond the Norm*. New York, NY: Church Publishing.

Brown, S. (2010) *Play: How it Shapes the Brain, Opens the Imagination, and Invigorates the Soul.* New York, NY: Avery Publishing.

Doehring, C. (2006) *The Practice of Pastoral Care.* Louisville, KY: Westminster John Knox.

General Synod of the Anglican Church of Australia (2016) *Faithfulness in Service.* Sydney: The Anglican Church of Australia Trust Corporation.

Harris, B. (2011) *Working with Distressed Young People.* Exeter: Learning Matters.

Jeffs, T. and Smith, M.K. (2012) 'What is informal education?' infed.org. Accessed on 22/11/2017 at http://infed.org/mobi/what-is-informal-education.

Knight, J.S. (2008) 'Transformative Listening.' In M.E. Moore and A.M. Wright (eds) *Children, Youth and Spirituality in a Troubling World.* St Louis, MO: Chalice Press.

Lewis, T. Amini, F. and Lannon, R. (2000) *A General Theory of Love.* New York, NY: Random House.

Madson, P. (2005) *Improv Wisdom: Don't Prepare, Just Show Up.* New York, NY: Random House.

Minor, C. and Campbell, R. (2016) 'The Parable of the Sower: A case study examining the use of the Godly Play® method as a spiritual intervention on a psychiatric unit of a major children's hospital.' *International Journal of Children's Spirituality 21,* 1, 38–51.

Nash, S. and Palmer, B. (2011) 'Odyssey Guide.' In S. Nash (ed.) *Youth Ministry: A Multifaceted Approach.* London: SPCK.

O'Connell, D. (2013) *Working with Children and Young People: Good Practice Guidelines for Healthcare Chaplains.* Birmingham: Red Balloon Resources.

Richards, S. (2014) 'Appropriate Relationships: "Like a friend".' In S. Nash and J. Whitehead (eds) *Christian Youth Work in Theory and Practice.* London: SCM Press.

Sercombe, H. (2010) *Youth Work Ethics.* London: Sage.

Young, K. (1999) *The Art of Youth Work.* Lyme Regis: Russell House Publishing.

Chapter 7
Working with Families
Krista Gregory

Why explore family systems in pediatric chaplaincy?

During my first week of working as a pediatric chaplain, I remember saying to my supervisor, 'I had no idea that being assigned to care for 50 children would mean that I would need to multiply my patient assignment by at least three.' I had worked in an adult hospital for over ten years, and I thought I was reasonably prepared for the new venture into the world of pediatrics. What I had not fully anticipated was the complexity of each visit as I would always encounter a family. Families are less defined by biology and more defined by intention, but each patient had a caregiver – a mother or father or grandparent or aunt or village of aunts. Some had two or three who considered themselves significant decision-makers in the child's life. Many had siblings or cousins or very close friends who also wished to be considered as nuclear family. Each individual was at a different developmental stage; each was dealing with the illness or the accident or diagnosis through a unique lens of experience; each would express a distinct spiritual interpretation of its meaning, no matter his/her chronological age.

More importantly, they would be interconnected. I could no longer focus on just the patient or the significant other but had to be mindful of every person who showed up at the child's bedside and even the ones who did not. Perhaps it was at that moment that I realized that I would be drawn into an even more meaningful work of chaplaincy as I dove deeper into my understanding of the family system.

Researched approaches to family systems

In its simplest definition, a system is 'a set of things working together as parts of a mechanism or an interconnecting network' (Simpson, Weiner and Proffitt 1993). A family system is one in which the system refers to biological or sociological connections formed by blood or common mission. The traditional view of family systems would consider the genealogy in the formation of connections. However, family systems can include groups with fewer biological connections and more connections of intention.

Dr Murray Bowen, considered the father of family systems theory, views the family as an 'emotional unit' and asserts that individuals cannot be considered in isolation from one another (Bowen 1993). While some individuals might claim that they have no connection to their family because of distance or choice or even removal by the law (such as in the case of child abuse), that is not to say that they are not still very influenced by the thoughts, feelings and actions of family. The bonds of connection result in reactive behaviors which indicate an interdependent relationship. To be clear, reactive behaviors are not always negative and are not always unconscious, but they are related to systemic relationships that affect the functioning of the individual.

My favorite illustration of this interconnectedness is the *mobile*, a kinetic sculpture of objects often linked by wire or string or rods. When one object in the mobile moves, the entire mobile moves in order to regain equilibrium since all the objects are interconnected. One object cannot stubbornly decide not to move because it wants to remain stable or static. The nature of the structure, of the system, is such that regardless of the intention or wish of a singular object, the structure is universally affected by the movement of the one.

PRACTICE EXAMPLE 7.1: A NEW EQUILIBRIUM

A young teenager with autism suffered a brain injury through a tragic accident. His family system included two parents and three older siblings. Besides the compromised functioning of the teenager after the injury, the mother's functioning changed too as she now devoted all of her time to keeping the injured teenager alive, clean, fed and out of pain. The father became more absent as he was now the sole breadwinner of the family after the mother had to quit her job to care for her child. With this significant change in the family 'mobile', the older siblings faced the emotional and societal struggle of late adolescence without significant involvement from their parents. Over the next several years, two of the siblings began to exhibit strong behavioral reactions, facing challenges in their coping and unconscious resentment about the absence of their parents.

> With intentional pastoral support from the chaplain, the family was able to work together to find a new equilibrium based on the new paradigm of functioning in their family.

As pediatric chaplains, we need to recognize the moving parts of the family system, particularly when illness, accident or disease shifts the mobile. Our work cannot be in isolation with the patient or even just the patient and parent. Every part of the family system experiences the disequilibrium whether expressed in real time or years later.

Relationship agreements and family rules

In order to mitigate the movement of the mobile and thus increase the potential for the stability of the family unit, family systems inherently develop relationship agreements, sometimes known as family rules. While some rules or agreements are spoken and clear, others remain assumed or implied. Some are even passed down from generation to generation. Relationship agreements can be based on many factors such as roles in the family, gender identity, generational mores, religion and sibling order. Here are some examples of some family rules or agreements:

- Our family does not express anger and avoids conflict at all costs.
- Girls wash dishes, boys mow the lawn.
- Children are expected to keep quiet.
- Crying is not tolerated by men and is expected from women.
- When mother is not happy, no one is happy.
- We do not speak to anyone outside of our family about our family problems.
- No one is allowed to express doubt about their faith.
- We do not draw attention to ourselves or outshine others in the family.
- Whoever yells the loudest will win.
- Final decisions are always made by _____.

The effective pediatric chaplain assesses for the unspoken rules which are attempting to keep the family mobile stable, especially in times of illness or trauma or crisis. While the family may or may not be able to articulate such agreements, the influence of these rules cannot be underestimated. Notably, some family rules are also exaggerated or brought to bear only in times of crisis. The desire for homeostasis, to do things as they have always been done, is strong. An illness or a trauma, a diagnosis or accident challenges the homeostasis of the family in that things cannot always be done the same way. For example, previous beliefs do not always correspond to a new set of circumstances and can bring unexpected faith challenges.

PRACTICE EXAMPLE 7.2: ASKING THE QUESTIONS

The patient was approximately two years old and had been previously diagnosed with progeria, the rare genetic disorder that causes premature aging. The child was admitted with cardiac concerns which normally would have been manifest in an older adult. She appeared much older than two. Her mother was at her bedside and appeared distraught. When I introduced myself as the chaplain, she shifted her demeanor and began talking about how 'OK' she was, how much faith she had in God, stating how much she believed in healing. When I did not display a complementary response, but simply listened calmly to what she chose to express, she began to question what I believed about healing. As a good chaplain, I turned the question back on her: 'What do you believe about healing?' She began to tell me about her family system. Her husband was a pastor, her children very involved in church, her community all members of their faith tradition, a tradition that believed in miraculous healing if you have enough faith. Her family agreement, her family rule, embodied the belief that healing would always come if you had enough faith, yet her daughter had not been healed despite being taken to many faith healers across the country over the last two years. As this desperate mother began to trust me and share with me that she was not so sure anymore that this 'family rule' was accurate, she appeared to become very anxious. 'What if all that I have ever believed about God turns out to be wrong? What if God is someone very different than I thought? And if I allow myself to go there, my friends and family will no longer accept me in their community.'

Family rules and agreements are often such a part of the structure of the family system that for a family member, a parent or even a child not to agree, to believe differently, to challenge the accepted truth, results in a big movement of the mobile and instability in the family system. As a pediatric chaplain, sometimes we are there to support individuals coming to their own revelations about these agreements. Other times we are the ones to become aware of the unspoken agreements by which a family operates. Either way, we become key members of the interdisciplinary medical team in serving as interpreters of the family system to the other staff, helping them become aware of the 'rules' by which a family strives to maintain equilibrium in a changing system. This can be particularly important when difficult medical decisions need to be made.

The chaplain can also remind the medical team that they themselves can become part of a larger 'hospital family system'. In *The Private Worlds of Dying Children*, Myra Bluebond-Langner (1980) offers a description of how the child, parents, family and medical team can function when cancer becomes terminal. She describes the often unspoken hospital family rule of 'mutual pretense' in which everyone avoids the topic of approaching death in order to maintain the mobile equilibrium of each person's role in this system. The doctor's role is to heal children, the nurses' roles are to comfort and heal, the parents' roles are to protect and raise their child to adulthood, and the child's role is to grow up to be a healthy, happy adult. The equilibrium of all of these deep, core roles in this larger family system is threatened by the child's terminal prognosis.

Murray Bowen's eight interlocking concepts of family systems

In his family systems theory, Murray Bowen identifies eight possible links or rods or interconnections in this mobile called a family (Kerr 2000).

We will explore only two of these concepts in more depth in how they directly relate to the work of the pediatric chaplain with families in the healthcare setting: (1) triangles and (2) multigenerational transmission process. A reference is included for a deeper examination of each of these concepts as they all have applicability in the work.

Triangles in families and triangles involving the pediatric chaplain
A triangle is a relationship with three persons. Although triangles have the reputation of being a difficult system, they are considered the most stable type of relationship system. When two people disagree, they usually

involve a third person in order to regain equilibrium. When three people disagree or are 'unstable', they can rotate the tension around the triangle, thus potentially finding more stability in the relationship system.

Even while that is true, sometimes the third person pulled into the dyad will align with one person opposed to the other. When two sides of a triangle are in harmony, the third side can then feel like an outsider. This is what we know as 'triangulation' and is often present in the healthcare setting.

> ### PRACTICE EXAMPLE 7.3: ABSENCE AND PRESENCE
>
> I was responding to a complaint by a parent about a chaplain in the pediatric intensive care unit, and when I arrived, the parent met me at the door and asked to take a walk. She explained that the chaplain who had visited was about her mother's age and that as she had talked about her relationship with her mother to the chaplain, the chaplain appeared to defend her mother. She felt alienated and angry at the chaplain and expressed that she just did not listen to her. She also stated that she did not want her to visit again. The mother felt like the outsider in the relationship. Whereas the chaplain could have offered some balance in the relationship between mother and daughter, she instead inadvertently aligned with the mother's mother, creating more distrust and disequilibrium. In this case, the mother's mother was not even present at the hospital but was definitely 'present' in the conversation.

Another example of a triangle is in medical decision-making. Whether the physician and nurse are in agreement about the care of the patient and the parents share an opposing view, or whether one parent wants treatment and another parent does not, the pediatric chaplain will do very well to be aware of the dynamics of the family system and the triangles forming. To align with one side of the triangle or to appear to carry the agenda of the medical team will only serve to create more distress in the family system. Awareness is the key to avoiding unconscious alignment which can disrupt the chaplain's effectiveness.

Multigenerational transmission involving the intergenerational work of the chaplain

The beauty of pediatric chaplaincy is the complexity of the family system. So much is at play at the bedside: past, present and future beliefs; persons alive and dead; concepts about illness and suffering that have passed from generation to generation. All the more reason for the chaplain to explore beyond what is evident in the current circumstance. This concept of Dr Bowen relates to one of his other eight concepts of family systems, differentiation of self. Differentiation is the ability to separate one's own feelings and thoughts from feelings and thoughts of others, particularly family members in family systems theory. In exploring multigenerational transmission, the chaplain assesses the levels of differentiation between family members and the history of differentiation or lack of differentiation through the generations.

How often have we heard language in a family about a child that reminds someone of another relative? 'Little José is just like his Tío Jo. He's slow and not the sharpest crayon in the box.' Whether this assessment is true or not, the multigenerational transmission of a belief about little José can affect who little José becomes. Will it be a self-fulfilling prophecy?

> ### PRACTICE EXAMPLE 7.4: ASSUMPTIONS
>
> One child was diagnosed with what is known as short-gut syndrome – much of her bowel had been removed when she was younger due to medical complications of prematurity. She is now 11 years old and suffers from the result of not being able to digest food normally. The nurses called me in desperation as they considered the patient incorrigible. No matter what techniques they used to help the patient recover from her most recent illness, the patient refused to cooperate. She refused to take her medicines or eat the right diet or exercise with the therapist or basically anything they asked her to do. The mother was infrequently present and, when she was, did not support the nurses either. She let her daughter do whatever she wished. The nurses made many assumptions about the mother and her relationship with her daughter: (1) perhaps the mother did not love her daughter, did not care; (2) perhaps she is simply a bad mother with no parenting skills and no desire to learn them; (3) perhaps she enjoys spoiling her daughter and is benefiting in some way from that behaviour. The cause honestly did not matter to the nurses; they just wanted help.

> The clue to this behavior came several weeks into the case in a lengthy conversation with the mother about her family system. The mother revealed that her brother had died at a fairly young age. She talked about how her brother's death had affected her mother, how her mother talked frequently about her regrets, what she wished she had done or said or not done in caring for her son. Finally, the mother of the patient had her own 'aha' moment as she reflected on the short life that her daughter would probably also have, when she stated, 'Perhaps that is what I am doing with my daughter. I am letting her get away with everything and anything because I don't want to have any regrets like my mother.'

In this multigenerational work of the chaplain, everybody is in the room. The pediatric chaplain must hear the stories of those who are influencing those in the room, whether those stories have been spoken or not spoken, are spiritual or psychological, or are from this generation or many generations before. Thus, a significant question to always ask is 'Who is *not* in the room but still affecting this system?'

Paul Rosenblatt's use of metaphor in family systems

Earlier, we explored the metaphor of the mobile when examining the dysfunctional moments in a family system which can lead to instability. The use of metaphor more acutely in family systems theory has been widely developed by Paul C. Rosenblatt (1997).

Metaphors can be playful yet poignant ways of understanding a family system and can serve the pediatric chaplain in helping the patient and family member articulate their own understanding of their family, no matter what their developmental age. The ways individuals use and reuse metaphors also tell us something about what they value, so the metaphor a family chooses to use to describe itself says something about the deep values and expectations regarding behavior and relationships.

Imagine the family is a house. What might the pediatric patient or family member be implying when choosing this metaphor?

- A stable structure protects, comforts and separates those inside from those outside.

- It stays standing even as individuals come and go from it.

- A person can be locked in or locked out.
- A person can feel contained and safe or confined and imprisoned in a house.

How to use metaphor with children and pediatric patients

While a therapeutic conversation might feel invasive or threatening, children can sometimes access metaphors more easily. An example of this is a class project at School of the Osage, Missouri, where a teacher asked pupils to describe their family as a metaphor. This is one of them:

> *My family is the Solar System.*
> *My younger sister is the sun.*
> *She is very bright, but everything always has to revolve around her.*
> *My stepdad is the moon.*
> *He comes out at night to do his job, but come day he is nowhere to be found.*
> *My mom is the stars.*
> *She is always everywhere; she knows your business front and back.*
> *She also lights up the sky whenever the moon has gone into hiding.*
> *My oldest sister is Pluto.*
> *She stayed around and put up with the other planets for a while, and then she just left.*
> *I, well, I am Neptune.*
> *I am farthest from everyone, and I am usually the little planet who is cold and alone.*

A child's illness can influence the family metaphor as the family may reinterpret the metaphor in light of what has happened or shift it to a completely different metaphor altogether. The child's developmental stage can also be reflected in the metaphor, as can changes in the stability of the family system.

Instead of a dialogical visit to assess the family system, the pediatric chaplain can utilize metaphor by inviting the patient and family to essentially assess themselves indirectly. The chaplain could provide a list of possible metaphors on cards or with pictures such as a rock, a house, the government, a river, a forest, an aquarium, a tapestry. Invite the patient and/or family member to choose which word feels as if it describes their family and why. Each individual would be encouraged to choose what makes sense for them and not assume that everyone in the family would use the same metaphor. The person can then be invited to write it out, to draw it, to talk about it or to use some other medium through which to 'play with' the metaphor.

Future development and research needs

- Understanding how different faith and cultural family systems affect a child's stay in hospital.
- Identifying how family systems theory and training can be integrated into curricula for pediatric chaplaincy and spiritual care.
- Exploring the efficacy of different interventions with families.

Summary

Family systems theory and the use of metaphor can be helpful tools for the pediatric chaplain who wishes to perform a more robust assessment of the patient and family and thus provide worthwhile interventions that go beyond simply listening. Utilizing these tools equips the chaplain to contribute to the larger story of the patient for the other members of the medical team for which the illness may be consuming enough. Additionally, the medical team often fails to recognize their role in the family's larger 'hospital family system'. They are an additional 'system' at work within the patient's family system, one with rules and agreements, triangles and multigenerational transmission. The more aware we are of the larger family in which the patient resides, in which we all reside, the more effective the healing work we provide.

Questions for reflection

- How might the insights and principles of family systems theory shape, influence and improve your practice?
- What are the family systems that you have seen in various cultural and faith contexts?
- What metaphors might you want to use when seeking to explain to families what they might be going through?

References

Bluebond-Langner, M. (1980) *The Private Worlds of Dying Children*. Princeton, NJ: Princeton University Press.

Bowen, M. (1993) *Family Therapy in Clinical Practice*, 1st edition. Lanham, MD: Jason Aronson.

Kerr, M. (2000) *One Family's Story: A Primer on Bowen Theory*. Washington, DC: Bowen Center.

Rosenblatt, P. (1997) *Metaphors of Family Systems Theory*. New York, NY: Guilford Press.

Simpson, J., Weiner, E.S.C. and Proffitt, M. (1993) *Oxford English Dictionary*. Oxford: Clarendon Press.

Chapter 8
Staff Care and Self-Care
Kathryn Darby and Carl Aiken

> PRACTICE EXAMPLE 8.1: CRASH CALL/CODE
>
> Doing a ward round, the crash call suddenly went. Panic and fear was felt by the other patients and families and our team did what they could to support, comfort and reassure people. Half an hour later the emergency was over and our clinicians had stabilised the child. The lead nurse went around our staff to check how they were. I noticed the cleaner in the corner crying and a play specialist cuddling a baby with tears running down her face. This incident made me question where the support was for non-clinical staff. I teamed up with the department's psychologist, and we ran reflective spaces for the non-clinical staff on the unit, later made available to clinical staff. Staff found it a safe, confidential space to share how a situation made them feel. As chaplaincy and psychology, we found the huge benefit of holding the space together as sometimes the issues were psychological, but many spiritual concerns and questions arose too. Another idea birthed from the crash call was to devise some spiritual care training for wards and Trust Induction covering topics such as the difference between spiritual and religious care; being compassionate to ourselves and others; delivering compassionate spiritual care.
>
> *Sister Kathy Green, CA, Chaplaincy Team Leader,*
> *Sheffield Children's Hospital, UK*

Caring for the carers – why is it needed?
Staff care is a distinctiveness of paediatric chaplaincy as noted in the Introduction to this book. What we are seeking to do is to offer strategic support to staff working in a stressful, painful environment. This chapter offers practical suggestions for the support and care of the staff we work

alongside and our own self-care. The practice examples are not exhaustive and you may have creative ways of care that work in your context. Don't forget that the most important resource you have for caring is you. Research suggests that the dangers of compassion fatigue, vicarious trauma and burnout – the combination of emotional exhaustion, depersonalization and lack of personal accomplishment – are real (Berger *et al.* 2015; Wicks 2008). From a spiritual perspective, self-care is grounded in a sense of being valued and nurtured in a source of love outside of ourselves. While supporting staff and caring for ourselves in a secular environment, ideas drawn from spirituality and religious traditions can be adapted to offer nurture and support. Spiritual practices, religious or otherwise, can offer immense resourcing and rootedness for us as we care for others.

> ### PRACTICE EXAMPLE 8.2: PRESSURES OF PAEDIATRIC HEALTHCARE
>
> People choose careers in medicine for many reasons. Experience tells us that a sense of calling, of vocation, rather than of just a job is part of the package. We staff come into the world of a busy children's hospital believing that we are functioning on the high level of what Abraham Maslow called 'self-actualization' – fulfilment of a long-held dream, perhaps. But in the murky world of real human beings interacting, things do not remain on that lofty level. The context of suffering, children dying, parents who actually harm their child, creates a burden of stress that can overload idealism quickly. While our brains engage in strategizing and delivering care, our emotions, buried as they may be, run amok. Our accomplished adult self is not as fully in charge as we would like to believe, and we are bounced back to more basic levels of concern – Maslow's first three levels in the 'hierarchy of needs' – needs for physiological comfort and safety, for a sense of belonging and for affection from others (Maslow 1943).
>
> One can observe how many staff members struggle with overeating, how often alcohol is turned to as a stress reliever, how many folks tell the chaplain about poor choices in personal relationships. We, like many of our patients' families, are triggered back to unmet needs from our own childhoods and to unfinished emotional work.
>
> *Alice A. Hildebrand, former Chaplain, Barbara Bush Children's Hospital at Maine Medical Center, Portland, Maine, USA*

How might it be expressed?

One of the ways to develop staff support is to have Chaplaincy provision integrated into the wider staff support policy and structure of the institution. Chaplains may well be some of the best-trained pastoral care staff and perhaps the only ones on site. We can have a quiet confidence in the transferable skills and knowledge that we sometimes take for granted and what we therefore bring to the table. As with patients and families, when life's worst is thrown at staff at work, it can affect and overflow into the whole of their lives, and this is when we can be available.

Much of our strategy and work will be around:

- religious, spiritual and pastoral care
- training and modelling
- crisis and preventative support
- one-to-one encounters
- small group non-clinical supervision and support
- formal processes such as Schwartz Rounds
- activities and events.

Complex issues

There are several issues to be aware of in staff support and self-care. These are some of the key ones:

- **re-traumatisation:** understanding the impact of revisiting traumatic events
- **resilience and wellbeing:** that staff can be and learn to be more resilient but our institutions also have a duty of care for the wellbeing of staff
- **showing emotions in front of families:** having criteria of good practice – for example, that the focus of care does not move from the family to you
- **boundaries and safety around exploring what works best for you:** what drains and recharges you.

It is also important that our strategy, values, objectives and principles are to be both proactive and reactive as well as consulting and partnering with other disciplines. Much appreciated and significant support can be offered when we communicate we are both able and available.

When one chaplaincy team discussed what type of relationships might be helpful to have (mentor, best friend, soul friend, non-clinical supervision, counsellor, etc.) to feel supported and have someone with whom to talk about very sensitive and complex issues, almost the whole group said they only had one of their parents to fulfil all these functions.

Spirituality

Underpinning chaplaincy staff support and self-care is the concept of spirituality. We understand spirituality to encompass a person's search for, and experience of, meaning and purpose, and the sense of relatedness or connection to self, to others, to nature, and to the wider world. Spirituality may include a sense of the sacred, transcendence, or Otherness, that which cannot be fully fathomed. Spirituality may be communal or individual, and experienced in significant moments such as birth or death, climbing a mountain, crossing a desert, listening to music, watching a sunset or being still. Spiritual practice includes making safe spaces for significant conversations. Its focus is on making sense of life, a situation, an event. This work of meaning-making and connection is an important health-giving activity for ourselves and those we care for (Gordon, Kelly and Mitchell 2011). It is an inner exercise, much the same as the physical activity we engage in to keep fit. Our spiritual practice may be grounded in a religious or faith tradition, or it may not. As chaplains and spiritual carers, we are heart specialists, taking the pulse of hopes and dreams, fears and uncertainties, and the longings of the heart.

Principles of self-care

Developing a list of principles that guides your practice and can be offered to others is a very helpful way to communicate what we are seeking to do alongside individual staff and management. Birmingham Women's and Children's Hospital (BWC) chaplains have created an illustrated postcard with a list of principles they have formulated about self-care to stimulate reflection:

- Identify the care you need – think 'I'm worth it'.
- Understand what sustains you – nurture body, mind and spirit.
- Be aware of your own rhythms and how you work best.

- Identify and establish your marker posts and shelters.
- Make time and space for reflection and learning.
- Nurture positive identity and self-image.
- Process negative events and emotions – love and forgive yourself.
- Be mindful, enjoy the moment, express gratitude.
- Be brave enough to change practice and attitudes.
- Ensure you are rooted both professionally and personally.
- Cultivate resilience and the capacity to flourish in desert and oasis.
- Seek to create an environment in which you and others flourish.

PRACTICE EXAMPLE 8.3: MARKER POSTS AND SHELTERS

To cross safely by foot to the tidal island of Lindisfarne in the UK, people can follow the Pilgrim's Way, identified by a series of marker posts and shelters or towers which exist along the sands. The marker posts guide the way and the shelters offer refuge for those caught by the rapidly rising tide. The metaphor can guide our thinking about our own set of marker posts and shelters or self-care resources which help us to remain on course and keep safe. Examples include taking regular holidays and retreats, study, leisure, building relationships, personal interests, receiving supervision. A picture of the Pilgrim's Way of posts and shelters has been printed on to a long sheet as a linear labyrinth which people can walk, reflecting on the existing support in their lives.

The Revd Paul and the Revd Dr Sally Nash, Birmingham Women's and Children's Hospital, UK

Collaborating: multifaith and multidisciplinary

Working across disciplines builds stronger and more effective approaches to supporting families and staff. These are some approaches.

Defuse or debrief groups

Debrief or defuse groups offer one platform for working together with other disciplines. Often staff need to understand what has occurred from a medical perspective. Staff may also need permission and help to articulate their emotions. Being heard and validated in feelings, whatever they may be, is often enough to bring some balance and healing, particularly when this is done in a semi-formal way with others who have experienced the loss. Stating boundaries of confidentiality and process at the start of the session helps people to make the most of the opportunity and feel safe in the group. Unfortunately, the tempo of acute care means that staff may be required to move on immediately from one situation to the next. Shorter, impromptu defuse groups offer a briefer version of a full debrief group meeting, as staff gather to check in emotionally before leaving for the day. Otherwise, the cumulative effect of such an unrelenting pace can contribute to high levels of staff illness and turnover, which, in the end, is neither caring nor economical.

Keep it bite-sized

Time and availability for staff to engage in self-care reflection and practice can be limited, and therefore bite-sized, easily accessible, easily digestible ideas and strategies are effective. Being present and alongside is an important reminder to staff that they are not alone and their burden is shared, making the most of conversations in the corridor or the café. Consider a mobile trolley to take resources to staff to promote self-care and signal support, creating opportunities for conversation and relationship-building.

Drop-in sessions on the ward, using a few simple props and resources, can be offered for staff so that in the midst of a busy day they can take some time out and be recharged. Using music, subdued lighting, soft textiles and aromatherapy, hand massage, self-care handouts and refreshments, a staff room can be transformed into a resting place of care and unexpected delight. In such sessions, staff have shared concerns ranging from bereavement, stress at work, domestic violence, to personal illness, family concerns, relationship difficulties. One-to-one support and signposting to other services may also result.

In many US hospitals, they have a 'Code Lavender' (a pastoral equivalent to a heart attack, code red team) which is a formalized rapid-response programme which dispatches a team with a 'to go trolley', to provide support for individual or teams of staff, during times of high stress (e.g. after the death of a patient). It is a rapid response called to resuscitate the emotional and spiritual wellbeing of health care staff – to optimize healing of mind, body and spirit – and can offer comfort in terms of food and drink treats or a brief massage, as well as human presence. Some hospitals also offer this service to all caregivers.

PRACTICE EXAMPLE 8.4: MAKING SPIRITUAL CONNECTIONS

Staff and patients are seeking a connection that is real and spiritual. Prayers, anointing and other rituals are embraced by them when they are offered as a relational response to a situation but vigorously avoided when they are simply a rote religious response. Chaplains are tapping into the whisper in the mind and the shy hope in the heart.

I have used the practice of sprinkling water on the doors of units within the hospital that have been refurbished or to bless the hands of the staff with the reminder that their hands touch with care and healing. Recently, we had three visiting surgeons who were in Australia as part of an exchange programme. I was invited at the beginning of the proceedings to offer a blessing on those gathered. This I saw as a deeply religious act and I used hand anointing as part of the ritual.

The Revd Carl Aiken, Women's and Children's Hospital, North Adelaide, Australia

---

Mindfulness

Mindfulness is the practice of becoming aware of the sensations and feelings experienced in the present moment, simply noticing, accepting how things are, and enjoying a place of non-striving (Kabat-Zinn 1990). Much of our focus in the day can be about chasing goals and thinking about the future, analysing, sorting, planning or reflecting on the past, sometimes dwelling in regret or self-criticism. We can become fixed in our reactions and inner attitudes, becoming over-critical and negative, at times wounded by the events and interactions of the day. Mindfulness brings our attention into the present: how things are and our response to them. Becoming aware and letting go, particularly of judgements, negativity, worry and accumulated stress, allows the space within us to become more expansive, flexible and compassionate towards ourselves and others. Regular practice of mindfulness can help to reduce stress, manage pain resulting from illness and/or stress-related disorders, reduce anxiety and feelings of panic, and enhance wellbeing (Williams and Penman 2012).

Staff can be taught mindfulness strategies for easing tension, which in turn help to cultivate a compassionate awareness and contribute to a healthy work environment for others. Mindfulness can be introduced at away days, training sessions and lunchtime sessions, generating discussion and changing culture.

Complementary therapies

At University Hospital in San Antonio, over and above the care the staff chaplains and spiritual care volunteers provide for staff, there is a Center for Caring. This provides stress management tools such as reflexology, reiki, hypnotherapy, aromatherapy, critical incident debriefing sessions, and an annual retreat open to all hospital staff.

Retreats

The annual retreat run by BWC Chaplaincy is an off-site day for staff to explore strategies for wellbeing and resilience. Themes can be around regenerative and sustaining practices, art, relationships, etc. A spacious room and extensive grounds lend themselves to this day, which includes group reflection, mindfulness, reflection exercises, art materials, a central reflection focus (using textiles, flowers, candles, stones or other decorative symbols and objects), books and some group discussion on the subject of self-care, and plenty of individual space.

'A moment of insight is a fortune, transporting us beyond the confines of measured time. Spiritual life begins to decay when we fail to sense the grandeur of what is eternal in time' (Heschel 1979, p.6). Given time and support, those on retreat can come to a renewed sense of self-awareness and priorities.

Bereavement support: shock absorbers

Supporting people in grief is a significant part of a chaplain's role and can sap energy and do us harm. Strong bonds of affection develop between staff members and the children and families in their care, and the death of a beloved child can usher in immense sadness and grief. Chaplains, along with other health professionals, often function as 'shock absorbers', carrying the pain and distress of others, which in turn they will need to find ways to unload. In these critical times, support for staff can have multiple facets such as memorials, de-briefing, rituals and supervision.

MEMORIALS

When a child or colleague dies, staff members may wish to gather for a memorial service or communal time of marking, remembering and recognising the significance of relationships in a 'holy space', lighting candles, for instance, or writing messages on prayer leaves for a memory tree.

WHEN A CHILD DIES

There are many ideas that can be incorporated in a service remembering a child who has died. At times it might be appropriate to hold a parallel memorial service for staff who cannot attend the funeral. Offer everyone in the service a chance to write a message on a paper butterfly which can later be stuck or sewn on to a mounted, painted sheet of canvas to create a memorial picture. Departments, particularly those who experience multiple losses, may welcome an occasional memorial reflection service which can begin with a corporate act of remembrance, lighting a candle (electric if appropriate) for each child and saying their name, reading a poem, brief tributes, music, prayers and space to remember, with the aid of interactive stations.

WHEN A COLLEAGUE DIES

Opportunities to remember and celebrate the lives of colleagues who have died, especially for staff members who were not able to attend the funeral, are important for the hospital community. Friends and colleagues can prepare tributes, gather stories, pictures, choose special music, readings, poems, write messages for a prayer tree. In a multifaith context, look for ways that people can feel at ease in coming together and remaining faithful to their own traditions.

PRACTICE EXAMPLE 8.5: A BUTTERFLY BUSH

Recently, a nurse died and this was traumatic for her colleagues, even though they regularly deal with complicated losses of patients. We held a memorial service at our hospital and dedicated a butterfly bush to her memory. This nurse loved nature and it was a fitting tribute to her: this bush will be part of an ecosystem that brings

> nourishment to the patients, families and colleagues that she loved so dearly. Considering the impact she made on the junior nurses she trained so effectively and the challenging patients that she cared for with determination and gladness led others to reflect on their own legacy. Walking with these nurses through the 'valley of the shadow of death', both with patient losses and now a colleague's death, has certainly deepened relationships.
>
> *Jessica Bratt Carle, Chaplain, St. Jude Children's Research Hospital, Memphis, Tennessee, USA*

Remembering and rituals

When there has been a loss of life, create a 'sacred space' in a staff room for a small group of staff, using simple visual aids such as a piece of gold cloth, artificial rose petals or confetti, glass beads or hearts representing love and care, a battery-operated candle to 'light' as the session is introduced, in these ways demonstrating respect towards and a cherishing of the child being remembered. Ending the session with an affirmation of the staff, celebrating their contribution to the life of the child and family, giving a small gift such as an inspirational card with an encouraging message or a small gold cloth heart as a memento can be restorative.

Non-managerial supervision

Supervision is essential for the wellbeing of chaplains and other staff (Gopee 2011; Oelofsen 2012). Supervision is confidential and individual (or in small groups) and addresses the personal and work issues of the practitioner. Issues addressed in supervision might include models of practice, team dynamics, psychological models (e.g. drama triangle) and reflective practice. Such conversations remind us of the importance of staying human; recognising, valuing and expressing the raw emotions we can have, recognising we are not alone.

Corridors and coffee

Supervision may also be informal, taking place in corridors, cafeterias or wards. The corridor is more than a thoroughfare – it is a people place where lives are lived out. A corridor can be called the hospital street, an image of the traffic it carries. At any time there are people moving around: staff delivering supplies or mail, cleaners working through an area, staff members going to and from meetings, and others moving between patient care jobs or breaks. There are also families – some moving with purpose, others lost and trying to find their way around. People will ask, 'Did you know about patient Smith?' or 'Are you in the loop about...?' The information exchange is rich, often spontaneous, and may also be a two-way street. Corridor and coffee conversations vary from the superficial to the significant, leading to sacred moments, at times, when mystery is evident and the thin places are experienced.

Without trying to overstate things, at times it is more than simply the chaplain present. The conversation and sharing takes on a sacramental role. The chaplain represents God in a secular place, hearing stories and offering care.

PRACTICE EXAMPLE 8.6: COFFEE IS OFTEN CODE FOR CARE

Intentionally, I have a coffee with any of my team who are in for the day. It helps me to keep abreast of what they are doing and able to support them in their work. At a recent morning tea, there was one biscuit left and the Catholic priest offered to share it. As he prepared to break it in half, his hands assumed the position of breaking the wafer at the Mass. We have a very positive relationship, so I teased him about how he was about to share the biscuit. When I was a new army chaplain, a senior colleague suggested it was always wise for the padre to carry a mug with them. His reasoning was that the soldiers would make coffee at every opportunity and that to share in that was important. He said it is a communion moment. I believe he is right and that the coffee and the deep conversations that take place there are a sacrament, as with the breaking of a biscuit.

The Revd Carl Aiken, Women's and Children's Hospital, North Adelaide, Australia

---

Wellbeing and resilience building

Life inevitably holds challenges, pain and loss, and working within paediatric health care brings people into the foreground of traumatic experience daily. In a training context, self-care is best explored in an experiential way. For example:

- noticing the particular pressures faced by a ward and the distinctive contribution of staff groups
- identifying sources of gratitude
- managing breaks and feedback
- processing bereavement and loss
- ideas about 'failure' and 'success'
- supervision and peer support.

Knowing when to refer

Most of us will be part of a wider staff support structure and it is important that we do not over-stretch our competence and know the other resources available to staff. As well as the obvious counselling services, this can also include suggestions that we might want to refer the issue to the clinical ethics group or patient safety processes. For many staff, to feel empowered to be able to do something with what is weighing them down will be very liberating.

Enhancing self-care for chaplains and staff – hospital choirs

BWC chaplaincy established a staff choir to sing at key events in the life of the hospital including the Annual Memorial Service and Christmas. The health and wellbeing benefits of singing give staff a boost in their day (Clift and Hancox 2010). Staff meet across disciplines for fun and relaxation, and connection, possibly sorting through difficulties at a less conscious level. Their music is shared, bringing pleasure to others and building community in the hospital. Some hospital staff and chaplaincy volunteers come in to practise even if they are not on shift.

Care for yourself as chaplain

Life wisdom tells us that we cannot effectively care for others unless we attend to our own health and wellbeing socially, physically and spiritually. Although this section appears last in this chapter, our own self-care needs and reflection go hand in hand with what we offer as we face the same issues as the staff we are seeking to support. All these principles and practices for wellbeing, flourishing and finding a best fit will apply to us as chaplains. As Thomas Merton (2013) suggests, we will never be able to give to others what we do not possess ourselves. Foundational beliefs, values and learned ways of caring may need to be critiqued. For instance, guilt can be a stumbling block and we may lose a sense of our own needs in the rush to help others. Having a clear idea of our role and self-expectations as well as educating others about their expectations may help to restore our equilibrium. When do we have to say yes and when can we say no?

Faith traditions have a long and rich history of resources and practices for healthy spiritualty, including the rule and rhythm of life, spiritual directors, soul friends, the *examen*, a daily reflection of Ignatian spirituality (see Linn, Fabricant Linn and Linn 1995), the centring prayer of the mystics (see Keating 2007), Celtic practices of engaging with nature, daily reflection with sacred texts and prayer. What is important is what works for you, and this may shape and change over time.

Core skills

- Active listening and counselling skills.
- Person-centred approach, hospitality, inclusion.
- Skills in framing, facilitating and holding safe spaces for others.

Recommended resources

- Self-care cards with inspirational pictures or quotations.
- Heart badges as a reminder to self-care.
- Beautiful textiles and objects that can create an instant self-care focus.
- Small gifts.
- Worksheets for reflection.
- 'Thought for the week' sent through the institution's email.

Future development and research needs

- Effectiveness of our staff support interventions: moral, wellbeing, employment satisfaction, less sickness/cost saving.

- Helping staff process trauma.
- Spirituality as a resource for self-care.

Summary

Make the most of bite-sized and accessible staff support. Non-managerial supervision or its equivalent is important for reflection and balance. Spirituality is to be explored. Explanations are not always necessary.

Questions for reflection

- Do you have good resources for the difficult parts of your life journey?
- Professional supervision is important in stressful and traumatic work environments, assisting with our reflective practice and keeping us safe. Do you intentionally engage in supervision? Is your safety net in place?
- What additional elements of staff support could you consider offering?

References

Berger, J., Polivka, B., Smoot, E.A. and Owens, H. (2015) 'Compassion fatigue in pediatric nurses.' *Journal of Pediatric Nursing 30*, 6, e11–e17.

Clift, S. and Hancox, G. (2010) 'The significance of choral singing for sustaining psychological wellbeing: Findings from a survey of choristers in England, Australia and Germany.' *Music Performance Research 3*, 1, 79–96.

Gopee, N. (2011) *Mentoring and Supervision in Healthcare*, 2nd edition. London: Sage.

Gordon, T., Kelly, E. and Mitchell, D. (2011) *Spiritual Care for Healthcare Professionals*. London: Radcliffe.

Heschel, A.J. (1979) *The Sabbath*. New York, NY: Farrar, Straus and Giroux.

Kabat-Zinn, J. (1990) *Full Catastrophe Living: Using the Wisdom of Your Body and Mind to Face Stress, Pain, and Illness*, 15th anniversary edition. New York: Bantam Dell.

Keating, T. (2007) *Open Heart, Open Mind*, 20th anniversary edition. New York, NY: Continuum.

Linn, D., Fabricant Linn, S. and Linn, M. (1995) *Sleeping with Bread*. New York, NY: Paulist Press.

Maslow, A.H. (1943) 'A theory of human motivation.' *Psychological Review 50*, 4, 370.

Merton, T. (2013) *Spiritual Direction and Meditation*. Mansfield Centre, CT: Martino.

Oelofsen, N. (2012) *Developing Reflective Practice*. Banbury: Lantern Publishing.

Williams, M. and Penman, D. (2012) *Mindfulness: A Practical Guide to Finding Peace in a Frantic World*. London: Piatkus.

Wicks, R. (2008) *The Resilient Clinician*. Oxford: Oxford University Press.

Chapter 9
Chaplain to the Institution
Jim Linthicum

> ### PRACTICE EXAMPLE 9.1: SPEAKING THE SAME WAY
>
> As a healthcare chaplain, it is so important for our co-workers in the Trust to feel empowered and valued. A fundamental value of mine is to treat all as equals, irrespective of role. I love this quote from Albert Einstein:
>
> > I speak to everyone the same way whether he is the garbage man or the president of the university.
>
> The joy of my job starts as I walk into Accident and Emergency and say good morning to the ward clerks, I then continue my good mornings all the way up to the office; sometimes it can take me half an hour to get there! On the wards the cleaners really appreciate me talking to them and asking how they are; I always get a laugh when I bow down to them, saying we couldn't do what the hospital needs to do without them, but it's true. This level of care stepped up when I found the courage to go on the Executive Corridor of the hospital to ask a member of staff there how they were; I'd seen them earlier on in the canteen not looking quite right. It took all the nerve I had, but the encounter was fruitful. Even the execs need care too.
>
> *Sister Kathy Green, CA, Chaplaincy Team Leader, Sheffield Children's Hospital, UK*

As Sister Kathy so accurately writes, 'sometimes it can take [the chaplain] half an hour to get to the office', if the chaplain is seen as a significant part of the institution. Others, however, might envy the privileged opportunity to be so well known by the staff within the institution. They may feel 'in' the institution, but not 'of' it. This speaks to some of the difficulties of trying to describe chaplaincy to the institution. In the research and literature regarding healthcare chaplaincy, much is sometimes made of, in some cases, being oppositional to parts of the institution and 'powers that be'. Yet there is also a case to be made for the effectiveness and value that chaplaincy has to the institution. The work of this chapter is to highlight and look at ways of building upon and/or developing that relationship.

While there is an increasing amount of research being done on the role of the healthcare chaplain, both specifically and in general, little truly reflects what it means to be a chaplain to the whole institution in practical terms (Nash 2014). The organisation and institution are mentioned as fertile places in which chaplaincy can become situated. In fact, as Kevern and McSherry write, 'chaplaincy is usually conducted within or answerable to an organisational structure which imposes its own criteria and values' (2016, p.50). However, particular procedures are often left to local arrangements. Part of this is because of the variety of chaplaincy structures both within the NHS and around the world. The APC 'Standards of Practice for Professional Chaplains' locates 'Chaplaincy Care for the Organisation' in its second section. Here connections are made not only with patients, families and staff, but consistently 'working with the organization's values and mission statement' (Association of Professional Chaplains 2015). Equally, Section 4 of the 2015 NHS UK Chaplaincy Guidelines speaks of 'Staff and Organisational Support [as] informed, competent, critical' (Department of Health 2015, p.11). In so many cases, though, the guidance stops short of defining the terms 'institution' and 'support'.

Perhaps there is so much that needs to be done to locate chaplaincy within smaller spaces that, once the location has been accomplished, a bigger picture will emerge. Here an attempt will be made to define and locate the terms, followed by suggestions on how location within the larger institution or organisation can add value to both spiritual care and that which surrounds it.

VALUE

VALUE is an acronym I have developed which embraces both what spiritual care seeks to bring and possible approaches for implementation.

V = Visibility

Little formal research has been done on the role that the visibility of spiritual care provides. There is much that is anecdotal, however, and this offers a good place to begin, at the very least, a pilot study. At Great Ormond Street Hospital work has begun on looking at how presence at ward psychosocial meetings tends to increase referrals and interface with other professionals as well as family and staff. Professionals within the institution speak of how seeing spiritual caregivers around reminds them of the availability of this service – both night and day within many institutions. For those Trusts and hospitals with smaller spiritual care teams, the opportunities for visibility could rest in taking advantage of awareness-raising opportunities such as festival celebrations, contributions to any 'in house' publications and strategically placed notices about the presence of the team and what they do (pictures of staff and activities do help as well).

A = Accessibility

Knowing that a service exists, however, is only as good as the opportunities to access it. The 2015 NHS Chaplaincy Guidelines stress '[e]nsuring staff awareness of how to access chaplaincy services which includes the availability of non-religious pastoral and spiritual support' (Department of Health 2015, p.9). Analysis of on-call figures, both during the workday and out of hours, offers an opportunity to see both how often the service is being accessed and the reasons for it. They can also inform methods of access. Having some type of regular hours during which the chaplaincy 'centre' will be staffed can also ease access to spiritual care services. In work done at Great Ormond Street Hospital, it is found that chapel chaplaincy is a part of the service in and of itself. Part of this reflects the unique nature of the space, but, once again, location is important, as a place not only for people to go to find increased 'liminality' (for example, the sacred space between two worlds) but for the contact which follows upon visibility.

L = Love

While this word is often considered overused and underlived, it nevertheless still contains meaning. In fact, if one were to look for a locus for theological reflection on chaplaincy to the institution, this would be the place. Even within those communities without a sense of *theos*, the role of compassion and commitment to others is contained within the term. To return to the example that opened this chapter, a quality of relationship highlights the narrative of Sister Green's greetings to the staff. Sometimes this relationship is understood more locally and personally, and, at other times, within the wider sense of community. What engenders this love is the theological work of the spiritual care service. Living it out is the practice, and a sense of a role of chaplaincy to the institution is the result.

U = Understanding/Uniqueness

This letter serves two roles at once. Questions are asked about the reason spiritual care needs to be under the aegis of the healthcare institution. 'Why not just use their local minister?' These arguments go on to suggest that external religio-spiritual agents related directly to the patient, family or staff would be more appropriate to serve their religious and spiritual needs. While this argument has its strengths based on the role of normalisation within an existing community, what is lost is the sense of understanding. Spiritual caregivers located within the institution itself have an understanding of the intricacies and systems within the healthcare institution. Some of these may be able to be described. However, not everyone outside the institution may be aware of the non-religious and spiritual rituals that are a sometimes more hidden part of the bigger institution (cf. Nash, Darby and Nash 2015, pp.145ff.). At other times, the institution may request rituals both appropriate and responsive to its needs that can best be offered by those who understand the context.

At the same time, however, chaplaincy to the institution brings its own uniqueness that is important and distinctive and could not be supplied by any other provider located within the system. Early on in this chapter, the call to be challenging was found in many of the chaplaincy and spiritual care supporting documents. Challenge is a unique embodiment of chaplaincy. In fact, the more that chaplaincy to the institution is recognised, the more challenge can be expected. Once again, there is very little research evidence on this, and therefore this is another area for further study, albeit one that is already rich with anecdotes. This uniqueness carries into other areas as well, including methods of working, role perceptions by others within the institution, expectations, and the fact that it is one of the few disciplines based entirely on patient, family or staff choice.

E = Engagement/Embeddedness

Even when the institution is aware of the work of chaplaincy, the only way to continue to interact is through engagement.

> ### PRACTICE EXAMPLE 9.2: REFLECTING BACK
>
> Our hospital has been undergoing an extensive remodeling. The chaplaincy department is at most 'tables' in the discussions for the plans and excitement. One plan seemed to slip by and caught our attention – signs had gone up announcing the 'motherhood/ maternity' unit! In an age where nearly weekly a story in the news highlighted abuse of newborns at the hands of their mother's boyfriends, and the hospital's own focus on family-centered care, this limited naming seemed antiquated and disjointed. Standing up at the next leadership meeting and asking that this be reconsidered was not a popular stand; significant marketing and research, competitor's usage of the terminology and conventional physician comfort with the phrasing were challenges returned. We sow seeds when we can, and make time to serve on more committees.
>
> *Mary D. Davis, Regional Director, Spiritual Care and Education, CHRISTUS Santa Rosa Health System, San Antonio, Texas, USA*

Mary's example highlights the importance of sitting at 'tables' and contributing to the work of the institution, even when that comes across as challenge. Even more telling is the idea of 'mak[ing] time to serve on more committees'. Some might say that this impacts on time spent visiting patients and families and supporting staff. Although there is some truth to this, another view would be that of ministering to more patients, families and staff by being involved in the macroscopic. It is also a question of balance in which the chaplaincy to the institution touches individuals, groups and all points in between. Priorities, of course, are regularly maintained and adjusted, but the opportunities do abound. It must be highlighted that this engagement is just not for the sake of 'being seen', but has an important dimension of making a difference. This feature can also be of use in determining with which parts of the institution chaplaincy can most beneficially engage. The question 'What effect would it have on the care of patients, families and staff if chaplaincy were not involved?' can help with decision-making in the use of valuable time and human resources.

At the same time, the more engaged the chaplaincy is in the institution, the more embedded it becomes. Cadge mentions one chaplain working with and being influenced by the 'spirit of the institution' (2012, p.119). Using a Christian scriptural metaphor, the idea of leaven in the loaf comes to mind. A chaplaincy embedded within the ethos, values and decision-making of the institution has in many ways reached the point of being chaplaincy *to* the institution.

EVER Institutional Engagement and Opportunity Instrument

This model I developed can be used to evaluate current levels of engagement and identify future opportunities (Table 10.1).

TABLE 10.1: EVER MODEL

Institutional location and values	Opportunity	Engagement	Rationale	Result
Equality and diversity *Understanding/ Uniqueness/ Engagement*	Teaching related to practices of different cultures, religions and philosophies. Awareness-raising of festivals and celebrations within particular faiths and philosophies. Representations and advocacy for patients, families and staff from the entire spectrum of faiths and philosophies.	Participation in institutional events and courses on equality and diversity. Hosting and publicising festivals and celebrations throughout the institution in order to raise awareness. Becoming a resource for patient advice and liaison services as well as human resources and complaints departments when issues related to equality and diversity (particularly spiritual, religious and philosophical) arise.	Chaplaincy sits within the institution as a service comprised of representatives of a variety of faith and philosophical communities. Both external relationships and internal skill sets allow the service to be ideally placed for negotiation, reconciliation and representation.	Chaplaincy and spiritual care become known as one of the 'go to' areas in looking at equality and diversity.

Institutional location and values	Opportunity	Engagement	Rationale	Result
Values and meaning-making, including development of institutional and departmental mission statements

Engagement/ Uniqueness | Being a part of ethics committees and subcommittees including both clinical and research ethics (UK) and institutional review boards (US). Participating in listening exercises and groups developing values at both institutional and departmental (including ward) level. | The chaplaincy and spiritual care service participates in institutional ethics committees and groups. The chaplaincy and spiritual care service is represented at listening events and, at the very least, submits feedback on proposals to establish values and policy based thereon. | The chaplaincy and spiritual care service concerns itself with issues of values and meaning. Access to and availability of resources, both written and human, place it in an ideal context to engage and negotiate within this area. | The chaplaincy and spiritual care service has adequate access to the diversity of viewpoints represented within the institution and becomes a 'key player' in values establishment and ethical conversation (Kevern and McSherry 2016). |
| Education and training

Uniqueness/ Engagement | Offers training, both targeted and institution-wide, in aspects of religio-spiritual care. Availability for debriefs in which cultural/religio-spiritual issues are a factor. Training provision in values-based planning and decision-making (see above). | While the chaplaincy/spiritual care department is not seen as the sole source of spiritual care (this can be provided throughout the institution through a number of providers), it can use expertise from within the department or external links to offer specialised training and may be seen as the gatekeeper. | There is often found both interest and need within an institution to know more about the spiritual/religious needs of patients, staff and families. The chaplaincy to the institution provides resources in this area, both written and human. | The chaplaincy and spiritual care team becomes the 'go to' group for issues in this area with an eye to empowering rather than just presenting didactic material. |

Resources for institution including end-of-life care and staff support *Visibility/ Accessibility/ Love/ Understanding/ Engagement/ Embeddedness*	An amalgamation of all of the provision listed above including those areas that cannot be categorised anywhere else and particularly focusing on end-of-life care and staff support.	Spiritual care department holds texts, religious articles and contact list for faith and philosophy spiritual care providers. Spiritual care department available for end-of-life care rituals, information and support. Spiritual care department is part of larger institutional staff support structures including availability for 1:1 and group debriefs. The department can be a 'clearing house' for most staff support opportunities throughout the institution.	The spiritual care department is seen as a 'non-medical' and non-managerial resource available for needs, information, resources and support that cannot be found elsewhere within the institution.	The spiritual care team is embedded within the institution to provide 'lived-out' values and activities.

> ### PRACTICE EXAMPLE 9.3: RESPONDING TO RELIGIOUS SENSITIVITIES
>
> Several Muslim families at our Women's and Babies' Hospital requested that no male physicians ever enter the patient room. This request for modesty caused concern among the staff and leadership. What if a medical crisis arose in the middle of the night? What if a female doctor was not immediately available?
>
> Our Muslim chaplain sat down with me and our administration to work out the best way to respond. Fortunately, many obstetricians are now female, so this scenario is unlikely. Still, he advised us in

> preparing a religiously sensitive letter to assure these families that we understand their request, that we will do our best to assign female physicians to them, but that in a medical emergency, if a female physician is not present, then a male physician will be entering the room and caring for the patient. As soon as the crisis is past or her female physician arrives, our policy reverts to the patient's requested gender-sensitive staff assignment.
>
> *Chaplain Mark Bartel, Manager of Spiritual Care, Arnold Palmer Medical Center, Orlando, Florida, USA*

Paediatric distinctiveness

The question now arises: what, if any of this, speaks specifically to paediatric chaplaincy? Reflecting on Nash, Darby and Nash's (2015) distinctives of paediatric chaplaincy, several key elements appear:

- **Space creation:** As Mary Davis writes above, chaplaincy and spiritual care representatives often 'sit at the table' of decisions made on use of space. Recognition of the uniqueness of space requirements for the paediatric patient in general and their spiritual needs in particular can be articulated by these representatives working out of their own unique knowledge and skill base.

- **Working within the wider relational context:** As the distinctiveness of paediatric chaplaincy often features working within wider group settings, a different skill set is needed in terms of both general care and spiritual/religious care. While, again, little research appears in this area, there is much anecdotal evidence of bonds created between patients, families and staff – heightened by the overt and covert implications of working with children and vulnerability. At times of crisis needs arise including general questioning unique to these situations and working within prescribed boundaries. A chaplain/spiritual caregiver who is considered a part of the institution will often have awareness of these needs through visibility and understanding, allowing them to be approached to offer support through accessibility.

- **Developmental stages:** Paediatric spiritual care obviously entails the ability to relate and resource at a variety of ages and stages. Nash, Darby and Nash's book clearly illustrates the variety of activities available for children and young people to articulate their spirituality. Within these opportunities are understandings of metaphor and meaning unique to children and young people for understanding issues of faith, religion and spirituality.

Even within this distinctiveness are a variety of options that can be used by chaplains to the institution in different settings. However, the above represent absolutely essential requirements and gifts that a paediatric chaplain can bring and make use of to the degree that s/he is seen as an integral part of the institution.

Contribution to the institution

Obviously, most understandings of chaplaincy to the institution are anecdotal, local and needing research. Most chaplaincies, however, are already collecting data that could be helpful in analysing this work and providing, at the very least, practice-based evidence. Some of this data includes:

- referrals received, including source
- referrals made, including source
- institutional meetings attended
- worship and liturgical services performed, with description (including services in the community and institutional services)
- teaching within the institution
- teaching external to the institution
- research done by spiritual care service
- research done in partnership with other parts of the institution
- publications.

It is suspected, however, that most chaplaincy and spiritual care departments are already contributing a great deal to the institution. The opportunities are clearly available, so understanding and recording can supply a platform from which to build.

Future development and research needs

- Formalising the reporting of spiritual care and applying the results to both existing work and new policies, recommendations and guidelines.

- Developing data sets which offer evidence of the scope of spiritual care (similar to EVER instrument).

- Finding creative ways of recording and disseminating the work of chaplaincy within the institution.

Summary

This chapter has reflected on the vast amount of spiritual care that is supplied to the institution, the expectations that much international chaplaincy guidance has for such relationships and some practical ways to build upon and articulate what is on offer. In order to standardise some of these understandings, one implementation framework (VALUE) and one measurement instrument (EVER) have been suggested as models for moving the evidence of these relationships from anecdotal to useful data. Spiritual care to the institution exists. It now needs to move into an arena where it can be more fully appreciated and built upon.

Questions for reflection

- How can spiritual care be given to the institution and, at times, challenge it? How does this describe the fundamental roles of spiritual care in a 'secular' institutional setting?

- How might your chaplaincy department and your personal practice add value to your institution?

- Using the EVER instrument or creating one that seeks to record similar themes, evaluate your spiritual care department in light of these themes. What does this say about your spiritual care to the institution? What areas of growth and opportunity does this show?

References

Association of Professional Chaplains (2015) *Standards of Practice for Professional Chaplains.* Accessed on 22/11/2017 at www.professionalchaplains.org.

Cadge, W. (2012) *Paging God*. Chicago, IL: University of Chicago Press.
Department of Health (2015) *NHS Chaplaincy Guidelines*. Leeds: NHS England.
Kevern, P. and McSherry, W. (2016) 'The Study of Chaplaincy: Methods and Materials.' In C. Swift, M. Cobb and A. Todd (eds) *A Handbook of Chaplaincy Studies*. London: Routledge.
Nash, P. (2014) 'What is the Distinctiveness of Paediatric Chaplaincy and What are the Implications of this for Training and Development?' Unpublished Masters Thesis, University of Gloucestershire.
Nash, P., Darby, K. and Nash, S. (2015) *Spiritual Care with Sick Children and Young People*. London: Jessica Kingsley Publishers.

Chapter 10
Managing and Developing the Chaplaincy Provision and Team
Paul Nash

> **PRACTICE EXAMPLE 10.1: CREATIVE CHAPLAINCY**
>
> I believe that what makes pediatric chaplaincy unique are the limitless opportunities for creativity in ministry and practice. One of the ways I get to be creative in my practice is with the use of my four-legged furry companion, Uno. He is a trained and certified service dog, who works full-time alongside me in the hospital. I'll never forget one particular day with a patient. William was a 14-year-old patient in our cardiac ICU waiting for a heart transplant. He was a quiet teenager, and it was difficult to get him to smile or talk in the hospital. However, we discovered early on during the hospitalization that he loved dogs. So, I began making daily visits with Uno. William's mom would say to us every time, 'This is one of the only things that can make him smile.' While William spent time petting Uno, I would engage him and his mom in conversation about how they were coping with the hospitalization and, over time, William began to open up a little more.
>
> It was a Friday afternoon, and Uno and I were making our daily rounds. We stopped by William's bed space, and Uno jumped right into bed with William, which, of course, brought a huge smile to William's face. While we were there, the transplant team stopped by the bedside to inform William and his mom that a heart had become available. What a privilege it was to be at the bedside during this moment with William and his mom. In the hour that followed, Uno stayed in bed as William and his mom made phone calls and began to prepare emotionally for the upcoming surgery. As we prepared to leave for the day, Uno and I offered prayer with William and wished him well.

> Sadly, when we returned to work on Monday we learned that there were complications during surgery, and William did not survive. It was heartbreaking to hear and felt unfair. I decided because of our relationship with William that I would take Uno to attend the funeral, which is not something we typically do. When the funeral was over, Uno and I took our place in line to offer our condolences to William's parents. William's mom burst into tears when she saw Uno and said to me, 'I can't ever thank you enough for being with us on Friday. Uno made William smile one last time, and it is something I will forever be grateful for.' Working with Uno has broadened my practice and given me ways to connect more deeply with patients and their families which I find very sacred. After all, as one five-year-old once pointed out to me, 'Dog is God spelled backwards.'
>
> *Samantha Snellgrove, BCC Staff Chaplain, Sibley Heart Center Children's Healthcare of Atlanta at Egleston, Georgia, USA*

I started with this story to give a flavour of the diversity of issues and provision that chaplaincy team leaders have to manage. There is certainly no one-size-fits-all approach and some will depend on the unique gifts and personality of individual chaplains, but in this chapter we want to explore developing a robust, comprehensive service. Much of the history of healthcare chaplaincy has been to fill in where there are gaps. It is a compliment in some ways, but, in others, problematic. What happens when another discipline also tries to fill that gap or it is no longer perceived to be a gap?

Self-audit

In Chapter 1 we identified some of the distinctiveness of paediatric chaplaincy and presented a model as well as some standards (Pediatric Chaplains Network 2018). These can all be resources to help us in a self-audit, as can exploring presenting needs. There are some simple questions that we can ask in our chaplaincy teams and across our organisations that will help us articulate what it is we could and should be doing:

- What is your organisation not doing so well or could do better, and is this an area where chaplaincy can facilitate improvement?
- What are staff less confident in doing?

- What can your team offer to add value to or contribute to patient satisfaction?
- What do we do well/not so well/not at all?
- What are the presented and real needs of my organisation?
- Where are the complaints?
- Has the patient profile changed? What difference does this make?

It was in asking and positively answering some of these questions that we found the evidence for a large-scale development proposal. As the Muslim population of our city and therefore our hospital grew, we needed a more fit-for-purpose prayer room and raised funds to establish this as well as for Islamic-specific paediatric bereavement resources. Evidence-based approaches are particularly important in health care and exploring how we gather evidence is an important dimension of managing and developing the provision.

PRACTICE EXAMPLE 10.2: ORGAN DONATIONS – JUST NOT ENOUGH

Being on the transplant and organ donation working group, I knew first-hand we were not having many donations from certain cultural and religious groups. We also knew this was a national not just a local issue. So I proposed to one of our funding streams that we explore with the community to discover how we might better engage and support the possibility of offers of donation. We now have a separately funded project to try to do this. In this way I can offer additional work to existing part-time or honorary staff. Also, having some project work helps with the rhythm of my day and week as there are times when continually being on a ward is not helpful.

Failure is not failing…it is not having a go

Running a pilot is one of the main ways to try something new that gives us the security of a set endpoint if it does not work. We have trialled many ideas, and a high percentage still continue:

- participation day of activities with patients and families (now once or twice a year with external visitors who come to see our spiritual play approach)

- memorial service (now in its 13th year)
- chaplaincy choir – now seen as the hospital choir and invited to perform at key events throughout the year
- hospitality team in chapel
- volunteer training with other hospitals
- multifaith celebration events (now over ten years old)
- volunteer administrative support (works well when we have them)
- spiritual care modules for multidisciplinary staff (full recruitment)
- residential hospital staff retreat (low recruitment so did not repeat)
- day retreat (now once or twice a year with waiting lists sometimes)
- staff support events away from the wards (staff too busy to attend, so we now offer them on the wards)
- chapel by candlelight, early evening before Christmas (now three nights every year)
- prayer tree now seasonal, managed by an honorary chaplain
- memorial picnic and walk (now in its 12th year)
- social care provision (raise money to give to financially struggling families: we wait and see, but someone not knowing our plans just offered our families £20,000; we also partner with the local Salvation Army food bank).

So, as you can see, some work, others do not, and some do to a certain extent. We have only gained experience and knowledge through these experiments. When we put time frames around them and set them up as 'let's try it and see', the personal and departmental sense of fear of failure is diminished. We have also tried some short-term or time-limited projects:

- test paediatric taxonomy
- trial spiritual care activities
- snapshot of recording chaplaincy activity.

These projects have the advantage of being high energy for a short period of time and produce quality data for analysis.

Not always how we think: new resources

We designed postcards as a way of trialling new resources before we put them all together in a book. Not only did the activities work well but so did the format of postcards. So now we design lots of new individual postcards and worksheets and don't have to worry about wasting a lot of money if they don't work.

Start from our strengths: what do we bring to the party?

It's important to realise what we do well and not to put ourselves down. We need to start from a self-belief that we do a great job and bring a lot to our organisations. We are highly skilled and knowledgeable in our areas of expertise – for example, multifaith care and bereavement, self-care, services and rituals, doing a lot with very little. Many of our organisation's staff are having to deal with situations that are either not what they have had much training in (multifaith) or not what they signed up for (bereavement). We have hypothesised that if staff wanted to do dying and death, they would work in a hospice! If there is any truth in this hypothesis, then this is where we come into our own; this is what we bring as our contribution, our strength, our skill set. Also, we know that dealing with complex patients, difficult families and fallout between staff members all add to an already difficult role and therefore this is already an environment where chaplaincy is a resource to help.

PRACTICE EXAMPLE 10.3: THE CONTRIBUTION OF CHAPLAINCY

Our paediatric hospital is a part of a major healthcare centre. While the paediatric unit has been included in chaplains' rounds for a long time, my intention to focus solely on the children's ward was new to the paediatric medical team. I feel we have accomplished a lot during those six years of learning to work together.

My contributions are most welcome in end-of-life situations. Once, a dying girl was brought in after an accident. I was not called, but, as many times before, God led me to that unit at the right time.

> I saw the crying parents first and in the next room I saw for the first time how a child was being resuscitated. I saw the desperate effort to revive her and felt the helplessness of the staff that they were not able. I thought I would be asked to leave, but I wasn't. I returned to the crying parents, offering them an active presence: watching mom as dad left to inform family and offering tissues and water. In cooperation with the staff, I also attended to the family of another patient wanting to see their toddler. Giving them attention made it easier for them to accept that they would not be able to return to their toddler today due to the emergency situation. Then I accompanied the physician telling the family that the patient died. After checking with the staff I led family members to the bedside and stayed nearby as the staff requested. When they left, I talked the case through with the physician. He reflected on my contributions: 'My colleagues do not even know how many ways they could use you and what a burden you could take off their shoulders. You help not only the parents but you also help us emotionally.'
>
> The Revd Dr Edina Farkas, Paediatric Chaplain, Velkey László Center for Child Health, Miskolc, Hungary

Principles for developing provision

Altrupreneurial chaplaincy

This is a way of working that combines altruistic and entrepreneurial approaches – a sacrificial service with a creative development approach. Altruism is a concern or regard for the needs of others which does not have an ulterior motive. Being entrepreneurial involves exercising initiative, being willing to take risks, seeing and making the most of opportunities. I describe altrupreneurial (AP) chaplaincy thus:

- is a creative and service-centred, *kenotic* approach to our ministry and identity as chaplains
- seeks to develop our work, pushing boundaries, not looking for glory or credit
- takes assessed risks in the development of our work for the sake of and in response to the needs of others.

When change is desired but we are not doing anything differently to achieve it, I find myself drawing on the often quoted definition of madness: 'to do the same thing over and over and expect different results'.

AP chaplaincy gives us an approach to save us from this, to ensure we are not stagnating, being debilitated by obstacles. It involves having audacious goals and seeking to be the best service we can be as well as being good stewards of the resources we do have.

PRACTICE EXAMPLE 10.4: A RELIGIOUS, SPIRITUAL AND PASTORAL BEREAVEMENT CARE PATHWAY

This piece of work is a good example of many of our principles. At the time, we had 200 patient deaths a year. Some were offered a chaplain around the time of death, but there was no system or a consistent service. This was also an area in which the hospital was keen to improve its provision of support and care. So we used the hospital model of a pathway and researched what families would like and what others hospital/hospices did (see Nash 2013 for full details). We ended up with this:

1. Condolence card (Muslim only)
2. Belief-specific booklet: sent around two weeks after death
3. Invitation for inscription in Remembrance Book
4. Invitation to annual memorial service
5. Invitation to annual memorial walk and picnic
6. Anniversary card for two years, since families told us everyone remembers the first year.

Don't offer, don't know

This is a slightly more gentle version of 'don't ask, don't get'! I used to be reluctant to apply for grants and ask for money, but no longer. Because I truly believe in the unique contribution of chaplaincy to our organisation, I now apply almost every time the invitations come around. We have been successful many times. One senior chaplain asked individual departments for small amounts of money so they could have a named or assigned chaplain.

Pro- and reactive

To be AP is to both react to opportunities and invitations but also to make offers. When someone once asked about my leadership and management style, I said I seemed to respond to opportunities with 'Why not?' rather than 'Why?' Becoming a 'can do' person is crucial, in developing our service. Yes, we do need to be mindful of individual and departmental limitations and not becoming overstretched, but being passive doesn't lead to development.

Patient and family led

The reason we ended up with an annual memorial service at Birmingham Women's and Children's Hospital (BWC) is because a family asked why we did not have one. Sometimes the way we develop our provision will be in response to feedback we get which may be verbal or come out in discussion, but can also be discovered through small-scale pieces of research or audit.

Build up a track record of delivering

I think we have been given additional money because we have delivered in the past. We applied for our first pot of money with others more experienced in how funding bids worked. It was the refurbishment of the chapel and was delivered on time and to specification. The second was a bereavement book for Muslim families, which again was completed to time and budget and was picked up by a major Islamic publisher. This was a small yet significant start to our now regular bids for small pots of money to enhance our work. We know we have only limited time and energy, but in wanting to develop our provision we need to push boundaries. One of the ways we have gone about identifying projects is to think about where the need is or what might add value or what helps the organization to look good. Our CEO has copies of our new resources to show visitors. We have also sought to always have evidence to demonstrate the need for what we are proposing.

Cultivating people of peace

'People of peace' is a term found in the Bible in Luke 10. At BWC we have found lots of other employees who are pro-chaplaincy and/or religious or spiritual care. I did some hospital-wide consultations on how staff thought chaplaincy might be delivered, which included a potential development list just to get the conversation started. More multifaith staff and bereavement care was near the top, and at the bottom was refurbishment of the chapel. It is a 150-year-old traditional building with pews and was in some, but not urgent, need of modernisation. Two of the members of staff who came to consultations said that the chapel should be a priority. I responded, not wanting to push a Christian-centric position, that it was on the list, but perhaps there were more pressing needs and gaps. The two members of staff disagreed and said they felt so strongly that they would raise the money and oversee the work. They were senior staff in facilities management. This they did and all the chaplaincy team had to do was to tell them what we wanted! We now have a versatile area with a children's spiritual play area, sofa for family, prayer tree, public address system and recording equipment, and a small group meeting space as well as heating! A senior consultant had seen the value of chaplaincy since her training and, although of no particular faith, helped Paul write a business plan to expand the chaplaincy team in line with how much the PICU unit grew. We received the equivalent of one full-time member of staff, adding 30% to our work force. Another example is that when our Muslim prayer room was in need of refurbishment, one of our lead consultants complained to the hospital executive about what an embarrassment it was. The money was then found.

Political awareness

All organisations are by their very nature political environments. Agendas are pushed, sides are taken, games are played, won and lost. We are a part of this culture but we need to work towards being politicians of integrity: political awareness without the game playing, point scoring or favouritism.

4 Rs of healthcare chaplaincy

At BWC we have framed some of our development around four key areas – what we call the 4 Rs:

1. Relationships

Relationships are key in paediatric chaplaincy. They are the foundations of our work; they are both the object and the method of our work. Learning to make, build and sustain relationships is core to our practice.

2. Resources

We need context-specific resources for our patients, families and staff across the wide spectrum of contexts and illnesses. We have the knowledge in our team and the heart to share, so perhaps we could be more proactive in formally producing and disseminating our resources. The Pediatric Chaplains Network (USA) is particularly good at sharing ideas, and the Centre for Paediatric Spiritual Care (UK) is good at helping us produce them.

3. Rituals

Rituals are at the heart of most world religions and are still desired by those of no particular faith. We can rise to the challenge to design activities creatively for everyone to join in with. Our use of gold hearts for family members to both leave and take, which we use in end-of-life blessings and prayers, is one that continues to be very well received and meets a need for people to do something.

4. Research

Research has not been at the foundation of paediatric chaplaincy, but this is beginning to change. Several research projects have now taken place and more are underway. The UK Board of Healthcare Chaplaincy has research literacy as one of its core competencies, and both the Association of Professional Chaplains (USA) and the Health Care Chaplaincy Network (USA) have led the way in raising funding and encouraging research in our field.

External expertise

One of the ways to build up our work is to bring in external experts to help us with projects. At BWC we have found this invaluable as we knew we did not know what we needed to know about our areas of development. We have brought in professional youth and children's workers who produced a good practice manual for work with young people and their families, a psychotherapist to help us understand staff support needs and be available to us as a team and individuals, and an international specialist in children's spirituality to help us develop our spiritual play activities.

Volunteers or not

Whether to use volunteer visitors is an emotive subject in many paediatric chaplaincy contexts, and not many of us are neutral or ambivalent about it. In our own work, we did not have any volunteers when we arrived due to the lack of staff to do supervision. We have also recruited lots of volunteers who do not do any visiting. They can do:

- administration – draft rotas and prepare bereavement mailings
- make blankets, prayer ropes, teddy angels, etc.
- prayer and chapel hospitality teams
- lead mindfulness or other activities with staff.

The benefits have been extra visiting that costs little financially and freeing up paid chaplains from some of the administrative tasks they would have done, as well as including a wide spectrum of people in our work. The disadvantages have been the time given to supervision, a risk to standards and a potential undermining of professional chaplaincy.

Our essential components for volunteer training are:

- a rigorous recruitment and selection process
- shadowing and classroom training
- a daily debrief and regular supervision
- a clear referral system.

When is a volunteer not a volunteer? When they are an honorary chaplain. In some of our contexts, an honorary chaplain is someone who is already recognised and endorsed by their faith or belief group. They are classified as volunteers because they are not paid, but to us they are much more because they bring with them a standard of practice and external oversight. These people can be a wonderful enriching resource, and being an honorary chaplain also offers some ministers the opportunity to engage in a field more closely aligned to their passion and calling.

Deeper integration

There are many ways in which chaplaincy and spiritual care have helped develop its organisation and added value to its overall image. This is a list of some of the ideas that have been tried and tested to further develop and integrate paediatric chaplaincy in varied contexts, to share about our work and seek advice.

Glad and sad days: celebrations and memorials

One of the core skills most of us bring with us is the ability to organise and lead a service. These are invariably appreciated by staff as we gather together to put words, actions and rituals to unspoken feelings and public joy and tragedy. Many of us have taken our own tradition and widened it to include other faiths and cultural events. Some types of events that we can offer to our institutions and individual wards/units are:

- religious festivals
- cultural festivals
- memorials for staff and patients
- healthcare days: St Luke's Day (UK).

Ownership and leadership of some of these events are an issue in some contexts, but if you do not already have them, get a few people of peace around you and start one.

Multidisciplinary working

Groups you could seek to join (or start one if it does not exist):

- ward multidisciplinary teams (MDT)
- clinical ethics advisory group
- research ethics group
- organ donation committees
- bereavement and palliative care review
- staff health and wellbeing
- diversity
- allied health professionals
- senior nurses group (occasionally, as appropriate).

You may already do some of these but you could try and start a:

- multifaith and cultural advisory group
- multifaith celebration programme of events
- spiritual care working group

- spiritual care journal club
- participation project exploring the spiritual needs of patient and families
- staff support groups: choir, mindfulness, retreat day
- staff training programme on multifaith, spiritual care and self-care
- MDT project group to write a new resource
- religious and spiritual bereavement support programme
- grand round presentation on an aspect of your best practice.

Chaplaincy team and individual support

By the nature of our work, it is important we get this right. As well as facilitating regular supervision and personal development plans, we need to ensure that we are aware of factors that need to be taken into account around such things as personality, leadership and team role styles, external pressures or responsibilities, preferred communication styles, etc. Some of the best practice that happens in our networks includes:

- monthly team meetings
- regular lunches together
- paid-for non-clinical supervision in work time
- regular team reflection time and space.

Continuing professional development

High-quality continuing professional development is vital for the development of chaplaincy, including the opportunity to study for further qualifications as appropriate in different contexts.

These are some of the ideas which work in practice:

- all staff have a development project
- access to appropriate training
- encourage staff to write up case studies of their work and discuss them in your team meetings
- have research as a normative part of the department's programme

- multidisciplinary spiritual care journal club
- publish your own resource once a year
- attend grand rounds
- attend MDT conferences
- publish your case study with the Paediatric Chaplaincy Network
- attendance at annual paediatric chaplaincy networks
- in the US, attendance at the Pediatric Chaplains Institute
- apply for opportunities – I joined a NICE guidelines group seeking to define the NHS end-of-life guidelines for children and young people as a spiritual care specialist.

Responsibilities individual team members can have

There are many ways team members can be developed without spending lots of money on external training. Having an area of responsibility to develop is one way. It is important to find a good fit, where the individual is interested and it is a priority and need of the service. This should not be a problem as we have so much to develop and so few staff to do it! Examples include staff support, diversity/multifaith celebrations, staff training, volunteer supervision, community liaison, social care, palliative and bereavement care, mental health, spiritual play, research.

Pros and cons of rotation

Most of our children's hospitals, where there is not denominational visiting, would have allocated staff to particular units and wards. Advantages are that it helps build up long-term relationships of trust and we can become familiar with the medical condition. However, in some contexts we may become over-exposed to the pain, perhaps lose our edge or experience a lack of personal development. One of the tests may be when staff have their annual reviews and their work responsibilities are discussed and planned for the forthcoming year.

Development of the children's wards in a general hospital

We know this is an issue because it is raised at almost every one of our gatherings; feelings of not being welcomed or needed are experienced. See Appendix 1 for one person's perspective.

Development of senior chaplains

This is a difficult issue to address as we are in so many different situations. I have found much of my development has had to come from my own suggestions because many of our line managers do not fully understand chaplaincy. I have identified major development projects, joined regional and national groups, organized working groups and actively worked for the development of the profession through accredited study, research, writing and developing resources. Most if not all of these will be win–win as the chaplain gets developed and the organisation gets a higher profile.

Support for paediatric chaplains

Both the Pediatric Chaplains' Network (USA) and the Paediatric Chaplaincy Network (UK) have websites with resources and ways of being in touch with others in the field. They also signpost to other useful lists and networks.

Future development and research needs

- Chaplaincy managers network to discuss and support each other.
- A sharing site for project and idea planning, briefings, etc.
- Further specific training in paediatric chaplaincy including master's-level courses.

Summary

- Individual team members' areas of responsibilities.
- Lots of applications for additional money.

- Multiple ways for reflection.
- Research as a normative part of our work.
- Regularly rotate roles and responsibilities.
- Cultivate people of peace.
- Be altrupreneurial and have audacious goals.

Questions for reflection

- Where do you think your department and team could grow in its 4 Rs of relationships, resources, rituals and research?
- How could you support and facilitate your chaplaincy department to be more 'altruperneurial'?
- What internal and external people, skills and knowledge would it be helpful to bring in to support your development?

References

Pediatric Chaplains Network (2018) Competencies. Accessed on 9/2/2018 at http://pediatricchaplains.org/about/professional-standards.

Nash, P. (2013) 'Birmingham Children's Hospital: Paediatric End of Life Care and Bereavement Pathway.' In P. Gilbert (ed.) *Spirituality and End of Life Care.* Brighton: Pavilion.

Chapter 11

Medical Ethics
Practice and Decision-Making
Mark Bartel

> **PRACTICE EXAMPLE 11.1A: GREGORY'S HEART – PART 1**
>
> Lyman and Frances Glidden carried their infant son Gregory through the cold winter wind into the Variety Heart Club Hospital in Minneapolis, Minnesota, one day late in December 1953. Dr C. Walton Lillehei introduced himself to these parents and listened to them tell the story of their son's heart defect. Their eleventh child was suffering from a ventricular septal defect (VSD), a hole between the lower chambers in his heart, just as an older sister had and from which she had died three years earlier. They were there to ask Dr Lillehei about his new 'artificial heart' which offered the promise of more time to operate, hopeful that it would save the life of their son. Dr. Lillehei had to explain to them that his untested 'artificial heart' was actually a human – one of the young patient's own parents used as a heart–lung bypass 'machine'. Gregory's dad turned out to be an O+ blood type match, and if they so decided, his heart and lungs could cross-circulate blood so that baby Gregory's heart could be slowed and cleared in order to see and close his VSD.
>
> But would it be ethical to use a child's parent to serve as the heart–lung bypass for open heart surgery? This would create a surgical situation that threatened 200% mortality – the death of two patients at once. To ask parents to put their own lives at risk for a child would be to play upon their love and self-sacrificial, parental tendencies. And would it be right to perform an experimental surgery on a child who at the moment was playing and laughing, eating and sleeping well, and might have many good years still left to him without surgery? (Miller 2000)

No one will deny that the decisions faced within current medical practice are daunting. Along with each life-saving breakthrough we celebrate, it seems that a new medical dilemma arises. Parents are given heartbreaking, tangled decisions to make for their children, and as parents they suffer the weight of this responsibility with deep worry and dread. Should we continue to treat? Should we try this new procedure? If we don't, are we 'giving up' too soon? Gregory's parents in the example above are representative of a frightening spectrum of choices still faced by families of sick children today. How did modern medicine bring us to this point?

History

The medical ethics from the era of Hippocrates sufficed to guide medical decision-making for two millennia. In Decorum 4 in the Hippocratic Corpus, ethical issues of beneficence, non-maleficence, virtue and confidentiality are described which have been followed ever since (it is noteworthy, however, that patient autonomy was not just ignored but prohibited).

Since the late 1800s, social trends and new technology have changed the landscape such that we face wrenching new decisions never before imagined. Some of the main sources of these ethical challenges include new worldviews, World Wars, new medical machinery and surgeries, efforts to save the lives of newborns and the advent of genetic modifications.

New worldviews, which included biological evolution and its possible corollaries such as eugenics, were faced and debated within Western society as the twentieth century began. Questions of which lives are worth living and worth medical care demanded to be re-answered by society. Two World Wars challenged core notions such as individual worth and the ethics of medical research.

There were also many new medical machines, techniques and technology. It is not hyperbole to say that the humble mechanical ventilator is at the root of more ethical dilemmas than any other piece of modern technology in our medical centers. Thanks to our ventilators, we can keep people 'breathing' far past any historical boundary lines, and we can perform surgeries long thought impossible. But where is the boundary line between supporting someone toward recovery and merely keeping them oxygenated with no hope of further recovery? Am I always alive if my chest goes up and down and air goes in and out of my lungs? Is it killing to discontinue use of a ventilator knowing that without it the patient will die? In the mid-1970s, the case of Karen Ann Quinlan made Americans face these questions when her family requested permission to remove the ventilator from this 23-year-old vegetative patient (McFadden 1985). Ventilators are a valuable tool when there is hope for improvement and recovery; the difficulty is in the ethical process of deciding when to continue and when to stop.

In the field of surgery, two frontiers were finally breached during the twentieth century: brain and heart surgeries. Add dialysis and transplantation breakthroughs, and one can find the sources of a significant portion of our current ethical quandaries, whether based in equity, futility or research.

The world of the very low birthweight babies – 'preemies' – is another world with numerous ethical dilemmas facing families and practitioners. Many involve discernment between heroic measures and medically inappropriate treatment plans. Other dilemmas involve cessation of treatment versus 'giving up too soon', such as in the 1969 Johns Hopkins Medical Center Down syndrome case (Rothman 1991, ch.10).

Current advances in genetics promise even more difficult choices for us. In 2001, Adam Nash was genetically selected from among 12 embryos to be his sister's bone marrow donor in the US. More recently, the CRISPR-Cas9 gene editing technique promises to allow the cure of many genetic diseases even as it raises the specter of building the 'perfect' baby. And in the spring of 2016, the first three-parent baby was born in Mexico to a Jordanian couple through the efforts of Dr John Zhang, a New York fertility specialist (Hamzelou 2016). This process is illegal in the USA at the time of writing but was approved in the UK in 2015.

These challenging ethical issues (and more) face us as healthcare research and treatments move forward, and many involve the world of pediatrics.

Terms to know

Beneficence and virtue
Beneficence is the calling to do good, to help others, to heal and to relieve pain. Virtue, in this context, is the personal integrity needed to continue this beneficence over time and across populations. These two terms describe the foundational calling to serve others and relieve suffering, both of which are key to successful health caregiving.

Non-maleficence
The ancient dictum is *Primum non nocere* ('Above all, do no harm'). This is coupled with the wisdom to know when to stop as well as when to

start a medical treatment. When medical treatment crosses the line from helping the patient (with some hurt) into hurting the patient (with little or no help), this principle is set in motion. Albert Jonsen notes that 'do no harm' originally meant not 'subjecting to the rigors of medicine those who have no chance to recover' (Jonsen 2008, commenting on 'Art' and 'Epidemics 1' of the Hippocratic collection).

The rule of double effect

In the 13th century, theologian and philosopher Thomas Aquinas set out this rule for use in complicated situations, when an action will solve one problem but cause another: 'Effects that would be morally wrong if caused intentionally are permissible if foreseen but unintended.' An example would be when administering morphine to calm the air hunger and suffering of a child dying from cystic fibrosis also has the undesired side-effect of dampening the drive to breathe. The patient may die sooner, and one has to acknowledge the two effects and decide the ethical use of the drug.

Autonomy and communitarianism

Autonomy includes the right of individuals to decide which treatments they will accept. This must include full and clear information about the illness and possible treatments. It must also include understandable options, uncoerced choices and the real opportunity to decline.

Communitarianism, on the other hand, refers to the right of a community to be part of the decision process. This is more common in non-Western cultures and we do well to be aware of it.

Justice and utilitarianism

Justice has several aspects in medicine. Distributive justice is spreading the benefits of medical care throughout society fairly, and individual justice is treating each patient equitably.

Utilitarianism refers to the attempt to do the most good for the most people. When some treatments must be rationed, these two ethical principles come into play. In the early 1960s, for example, a shortage of dialysis machines necessitated rationing. In Seattle, the decisions about which patients would receive treatment were made by a special committee faced with extreme justice and utilitarian ethical issues (Alexander 1962).

Competence and assent

Competence is both a legal term and medical term. In medical ethics, it refers to the decision-making ability of a patient to understand fully and decide between treatment (and non-treatment) options. When patients are incompetent to decide (through sedation or mental impairment or young age), then others have to decide for them. Although there is agreement that age is not a good delineator of competence (Bluebond-Langer, Bello Belasco and DeMesquita Wander 2010, p.332; Hein *et al.* 2015), current practice often relies on specific age levels, and there is wide variation around the world for assigning a particular legal age. In the US, the age of 18 is the common dividing line, whereas in Switzerland and in many parts of Canada there is no set age at all. Each child in those countries is evaluated individually for their level of competence. In the world of pediatric medical research, the concept of assent seeks to include the child in the discussion. Children as young as seven years old are asked to assent, meaning to agree with what their parents and doctors are deciding. This does not grant veto power to the child, but is an attempt to include them in the process and help them to understand and agree to what is being planned (Bluebond-Langer *et al.* 2010, pp.338–340; Hein *et al.* 2015). The age of assent continues to be debated, and we do well to be aware of the practices in our location.

Patient's best interest

This is the superior way to decide what to do in cases where the patient is not able to decide or express a decision concerning their medical treatment. Choosing 'what I would do' or 'what most people would do' is not as reliable in cases of ethical decision-making. Such 'substituted judgment' is not as strong as fully weighing the benefits and burdens in each case with a view to the patient's quality of life with each possible choice. Note that the patient's *value* of life is not in question with such discussions (Beauchamp and Childress 2012, in their chapter on non-maleficence).

Futility

'Futility' is more difficult to define usefully than would at first appear. Generally, it has fallen into disuse in the world of medical ethics. Instead, terms such as 'medically inappropriate treatment' are used. However, most families and many medical team members continue to use futility as a word generally understood and helpful. Two types of futility have been identified. A treatment may be seen as futile if:

1. quantitatively, it has a miniscule chance to heal the patient, or
2. qualitatively, it will not treat the larger, persistent problem (Schneiderman, Jecker and Jonson 1990).

Common issues that lead to ethical dilemmas

Perhaps the most common reasons for calling an ethics committee into session are decisions of treatment and non-treatment. Whether the child's family wants to stop sooner or prolong treatment longer than the medical team, these differences of opinion are frequent subjects for ethical deliberation.

Faith and worldview differences can sometimes contribute to the depth of ethical challenges. Among the topics for which faith can offer both guidance and prohibition are those of fertility treatments, genetic selection, abortion, palliative sedation, cessation of hydration/nutrition and physician-assisted suicide. In these cases and others, the chaplain has much to add to all sides of the discussion, for we live in both worlds – the medical and the religious/spiritual. The involvement of the chaplain is critical to understandings and to resolutions that will be acceptable to all.

PRACTICE EXAMPLE 11.2: BRIDGET'S SURGERY

Bridget was born at term and transferred from an outside hospital with concerning seizure-like activity. The EEG monitoring confirmed that these events were seizures and the medical team began trying to determine their cause. One component of this process was genetic testing, which would take six to eight weeks to come back. I met Bridget's mom, Tracy, within a few days of the admission, and recognized that she had a firm grasp on the possible severity of her daughter's condition.

In just two weeks, Bridget's seizures became more frequent and intense. The medical team had been unable to determine a cause and were awaiting the results of the genetic testing. She had not been able to eat by mouth since birth, and the standard practice in the NICU was to recommend that a gastrostomy tube be surgically placed. They presented the idea to Tracy, who consented to the procedure. She later shared she didn't realize she could say 'no'.

> When the genetic testing came back, it indicated a progressive, devastating seizure disorder with no cure. Bridget died before she was two months old. In reviewing this case, the primary ethical question for our team was: Should we have delayed the surgery until the results of the genetic testing came back? Did the benefits provided by the g-tube outweigh the burden of recovering from surgery during such a short life?
>
> *Joshua Andrzejewski, Chaplain for Pediatrics and Women's Health, VCU Health, Richmond, Virginia, USA*

How to decide?

The easy ethical decisions are resolved quickly, often at the bedside. Other dilemmas resist simple answers and need much more focus and deliberation; they are not just medical data sets with percentages to be calculated. And in any case, very often a family will latch on to a 1% chance of success given to them, saying, 'Our child is one in a million!' Percentages are extremely hard to derive and are rarely helpful in making individual ethical decisions. They need careful thought, honesty and clear communication.

It must be remembered that such cases are never simply a matter of what we *can* do medically, for we can do all sorts of things medically. Our values factor in, and our spiritual beliefs create our values. Instead, it's also a matter of what we should do, and what the patient/family chooses to do, and when.

In the case of pediatrics, there is also another key issue. While the rest of the medical world worries about patient autonomy, we who work with children are concerned with parental authority. We inform the child's parents (or legal guardians) and work with them to arrive at the patient's best interests. In this two-way communication, our goal is to sort through many deep feelings and generate options. Parental emotions are many and complex concerning the wellbeing of their child. Feelings of love and protectiveness or guilt and loss can cloud the decision-making process. And as much as we may sometimes wish to lift the burden of some difficult decisions from the shoulders of parents, they remain the primary decision-makers. In the vast majority of cases, loving parents are the best decision-makers. Only in cases of abuse and neglect (and occasionally decisional incapacity) will parental authority be replaced. Each society has legal channels for doing so. If everyone can keep the focus on what is right for the child, we will see more clearly the best paths to take.

Sometimes, a chaplain will need to challenge practice.

> PRACTICE EXAMPLE 11.3: WHAT ARE RULES FOR?
>
> A young toddler, terminally ill and now finding it difficult to breathe, drew little comfort from his crib environment when he was awake. His favorite stuffed animal, an elephant so well loved, was rarely out of his arms – it was nearly threadbare. As his lungs worsened, his physician barked one day, 'There's not much else we can do – clear everything out of the crib – especially that animal – it's shedding constantly – fibers everywhere – no wonder he can't breathe!' and briskly walked off. I was new to chaplaincy, barely 25 years old – the rest of the team looked at each other, clearly cowed by the physician, and one of the nurses worked the elephant free of the sleeping boy, tears in her eyes. I was down the hall when I heard his cries and knew he'd woken up. By noon he was still crying. I saw the doctor in the hall and timidly asked him about his decision; he disdainfully asked who I was and gave me an earful about fibers and congestion and terminal illness. I asked if the boy was dying. 'Of course he is!' the doctor shouted at me. 'Then does it matter if this toy gives him comfort while he dies?' I asked. The doctor stared at me for a full minute. I assumed I would be fired. He then walked to the nurses' station and wrote an order for the elephant to be placed in the boy's bed.
>
> *Mary D. Davis, Regional Director, Spiritual Care and Education, CHRISTUS Santa Rosa Health System, San Antonio, Texas, USA*

Range of (in)tolerable behavior

Inevitably, there will be times when a loving family's choices in such difficult cases will not match our own, and various levels of distress may arise within us. Moral distress may be defined as occurring when a chaplain (or any healthcare provider) feels powerless to effect change when we see another right/moral course of action. We can feel squeezed between medical staff and family views of the question. How can we deal with this moral distress? Stewart (2010) suggests the following (see also Figure 12.1):

> The questions are NOT: Do we agree with this decision? Or, is this a decision we would make for ourselves? Rather, after personal reflection and team processing, does this decision fall within a range of behavior we can accept, or at minimum tolerate?

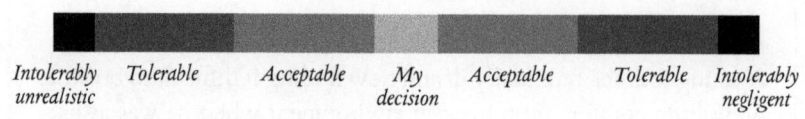

| Intolerably | Tolerable | Acceptable | My | Acceptable | Tolerable | Intolerably |
| unrealistic | | | decision | | | negligent |

Figure 12.1: Decision-making grid

If the family refuses care that the medical team deems necessary, we are tempted to accuse them of medical negligence or call them a 'bad' family. If the family demands care that the medical team deems inappropriate, we are tempted to accuse them of putting their needs ahead of their child's best interests due to unrealistic expectations and call them a 'selfish' family.

Instead, we seek to work together as medical providers and family to reach consensus on what is in this child's best interest.

The ethics committee: decision-making with patient/family/staff

The complex decisions of healthcare are often made within an ethical community called the ethics committee. Present in these discussions are the patient (as possible, based on competency), parents and sometimes extended family, physicians, nurses, social workers, chaplains, ethicists and, in some ethics committees, community members. Once a group with diverse perspectives has been assembled, the greatest need is to build trust within this community. All options must be safe to introduce and discuss, and opposing views must not be seen as adversarial but as beneficial, helpful and as leading creatively to the best interests of the child. From such a healthy exchange of options come the best outcomes. A chaplain may add value to an ethics committee by bringing a particular expertise in faith issues.

The conclusions of the ethics committee are not normally binding upon the physician and family (the Texas Advance Directives Act (1999) is an exception), but are recommendations offered as falling within ethical boundaries and seen as good options by this set of objective experts after a close look at the case.

There are many different forms of hospital ethics committees:

- large multidisciplinary ethics committee (including community members as possible)
- sub-group 'on call' for ethical cases, drawn from a larger standing committee

- ethicist who confers with physician and family as each case arises
- a combination of any of the above.

These committees also may meet at different intervals with different agendas and tasks. The three most common tasks of a hospital ethics committee are:

1. ethics consultations to hear cases and offer recommendations
2. education programs for the larger institution in ethics topics
3. deliberations on ethical issues in current policies and procedures, and assistance in developing new policies and procedures, such as revising a DNR policy or wrestling with medically inappropriate treatment requests.

And finally, while agenda plans for ethics committees will vary, most include some elements of the following:

- medical facts of the case at hand
- clear statement of the ethical issue to be faced
- patient's wishes, parents' wishes (in pediatric cases)
- daily life and social setting, quality-of-life issues
- options for medical treatment, non-treatment or cessation of treatment
- benefits and burdens of each possibility
- religious/spiritual considerations
- community mores, standards and precedents, public health concerns
- any additional issues unique to the case.

For complete models or approaches, see Bresson and Knox (2014), Jonsen, Siegler and Winslade (2015) and https://depts.washington.edu/bioethx/tools/4boxes.html.

Codes of ethics for chaplains

The other important ethical concern of a truly professional chaplain is functioning day to day in an ethical manner. Some of the professional ethics of pediatric chaplaincy include:

- honesty, integrity, veracity, accountability and transparency
- knowledge, experience, professionalism, growth and excellence
- respect, honor and advocacy within diversity
- boundaries (power differentials, self-care, conflicts of interest, non-proselytizing, confidentiality).

Different organizations and institutions may have their own code of ethics for chaplains.

PRACTICE EXAMPLE 11.1B: GREGORY'S HEART – PART 2

Gregory Glidden and his father both survived their pioneering open heart surgery, seemingly healthy and, in Gregory's case, much improved. Unfortunately, pneumonia settled into Gregory's lungs and he died ten days later. Perhaps the infection was inevitable, or perhaps it was encouraged by elevated blood pressure to the lungs during the experimental cross-circulation.

Dr Lillehei performed 45 such cross-circulation surgeries, moving on from VSD repairs to repair atrioventricular canals and ultimately to repair the dreaded Tetralogy of Fallot. In this series of surgeries many of the children died, some misdiagnosed beforehand, others teaching the surgeons valuable lessons by their deaths. But one mother who served as the living bypass suffered brain damage when air got into the circuit through a mistake by the anesthesiologist. The daughter of this woman, Geraldine Thompson, did not have her heart repaired.

Dr Lillehei used cross-circulation from April 1954 until July 1955, when he succeeded in using not a human but a machine for heart–lung bypass, ushering in the modern era of open heart surgery.

Future development and research needs

- Training for pediatric chaplains as experts in clinical ethics common and complex issues, application of principles.
- Writing case studies based on multifaith, spiritual and pastoral issues and ethical principles.

- Reviewing chaplaincy ethical code of practice in the light of working with vulnerable children.

Summary

As current medical ethics are so focused on the worlds of reproduction and children, it is clear that pediatric chaplains are key in the decision-making process. That intersection of child, family system and medical options is precisely where the pediatric chaplain lives and serves. Who better to accompany those involved in such challenges than a medical professional with the dedication to all three? The capacity to advise on multifaith issues and perspectives is also a key role for the expertise of chaplaincy.

Questions for reflection

- Is there a chaplain on your institution's clinical ethics group? If not, consider applying to join it.
- Would you know how to draw upon and apply key ethical principles, such as best interest and futility, and discuss them clearly and compassionately with a family?
- Take a personal ethical code self-audit. How did you do? What do you need to address?

Recommended resources

Association of Muslim Chaplains (USA): www.associationofmuslimchaplains.com/code-ethics-2
Association of Professional Chaplains (USA): www.professionalchaplains.org/files/ professional_ standards/professional_ethics/apc_code_of_ethics.pdf
National Association of Catholic Chaplains (USA): www.nacc.org/docs/certification/NACC%20 Standards%20October%202013.pdf
National Association of Jewish Chaplains (USA): www.najc.org/pdf/NAJC_ethics.pdf
Pediatric Chaplains Network (USA): www.pediatricchaplains.org/about/professional-standards
UK Board of Healthcare Chaplaincy: www.ukbhc.org.uk/publications/code-of-conduct

References

Alexander, S. (1962) 'They Decide Who Lives, Who Dies.' *Life*, 9 November, 102ff.
Beauchamp, T.L. and Childress, J.F. (2012) *Principles of Biomedical Ethics*, 7th edition. Oxford: Oxford University Press,

Bluebond-Langner, M., Bello Belasco, J. and DeMesquita Wander, M. (2010) 'I want to live, until I don't want to live anymore: Involving children with life-threatening and life-shortening illnesses in decision making about care and treatment.' *Nursing Clinics of North America 45*, 329–343.

Bresson, L. and Knox, J. (2014) 'The 4C model: A reflective tool for the analysis of ethical cases at the neonatal intensive-care unit.' *Clinical Ethics 9*, 4, 120–126.

Hamzelou, J. (2016) 'World's first baby born with new "3 parent" technique.' *New Scientist*, 27 September 2016. Accessed on 23/11/2017 at www.newscientist.com/article/2107219-exclusive-worlds-first-baby-born-with-new-3-parent-technique.

Hein, I., Troost, P., Broersma, A., de Vries, M., Daams, J. and Lindauer, R. (2015) 'Why is it hard to make progress in assessing children's decision-making competence?' *BMC Medical Ethics 16*, 1, doi.org/10.1186/1472-6939-16-1.

Jonsen, A.R. (2008) *A Short History of Medical Ethics*. Oxford: Oxford University Press.

Jonsen, A., Siegler, M. and Winslade, W. (2015) *Clinical Ethics*, 8th edition. New York, NY: McGraw-Hill.

McFadden, R.D. (1985) 'Karen Ann Quinlan, 31, dies; Focus of '76 right to die case. *New York Times*, 12 June 1985. Accessed 9/2/2018 at http://www.nytimes.com/1985/06/12/nyregion/karen-ann-quinlan-31-dies-focus-of-76-right-to-die-case.html?pagewanted=all.

Miller, G.W. (2000) *King of Hearts*. New York, NY: Times Books.

Rothman, D.J. (1991) *Strangers at the Bedside: A History of How Law and Bioethics Transformed Medical Decision Making*. New York, NY: Basic Books.

Schneiderman, L.J., Jecker, N.S. and Jonsen, A.R. (1990) Medical Futility: Its Meaning and Ethical Implications. *Annals of Internal Medicine 112*, 12, 949–954.

Stewart, Rev. J. (2010) 'Where Angels Fear to Tread: navigating the mystery of pediatric bioethics.' Unpublished presentation. Used by permission.

The Texas Advance Directives Act (1999) particularly Sec. 166.046. Accessed on 23/11/17 at www.statutes.legis.state.tx.us/Docs/HS/htm/HS.166.htm.

Section 2

Specialisms and Specific Skills

Chapter 12

Giving Voice to the Story

Working with Patients Who Cannot Speak

Daniel Nuzum

Introduction

In this chapter we explore spiritual care with neonates, babies and children who cannot speak. This area of ministry challenges us in how we as chaplains engage in relational spiritual care when words are not utilized by the people we are directly caring for. In the absence of words or in pre-verbal situations, healthcare professionals are called to recognize and nurture spirituality in a multidimensional and multisensory way. Spiritual care in this context raises a number of challenging questions for practice. How do we convey and receive spiritual presence as we embody the sacred or sense of higher power in this context? How do chaplains facilitate the expression of spiritual joy and pain in pre-verbal and non-verbal contexts? How do chaplains foster opportunities for meaning-making and co-construction of meaning with neonates and their loved ones?

There is growing evidence for the role that spiritual care plays not just at times of illness and crisis but also in overall wellbeing. As most babies or children who are receiving healthcare treatment will be in a healthcare facility such as a neonatal or paediatric unit, spiritual care will be provided by the whole multidisciplinary healthcare team in which the healthcare chaplain will have a pivotal role. While overall spiritual care is the business of every healthcare professional, the healthcare chaplain brings distinctive expertise to assess and respond to spiritual need and distress.

Theological and ethical rationale

The care of the most vulnerable goes to the heart of a theology of care. In all faith traditions and in wider societal structures, children are held in particular esteem and by definition are deserving of honour, protection and care. For people of Christian faith, the innate dignity of children is affirmed in Scripture – not least by Jesus who placed children at the centre of the Kingdom of God (cf. Mark 10:13–16). Children in Islam are treated with honour and by virtue of being children were considered worthy of love and compassion by the Prophet Muhammad who himself experienced the death of his sons in infancy. Children, in addition to having a cherished place in faith narrative and secular society, are also by virtue of being human worthy of the highest level of care, and this includes spiritual care. Ethically, as a group that has no voice, babies and non-verbal children depend on the advocacy of their parent(s), carers and society to protect their rights.

As the professional provider of spiritual care, the healthcare chaplain has a particular role to advocate for the spiritual care and values of a baby and a non-verbal child. Taking a lead from the values and beliefs (if any) of parents, the chaplain becomes an advocate for the spiritual environment of care for both the baby or child and his/her loved ones. This could be described as nurturing the 'spiritual community' with the baby or child at the centre. As a child gets older, he/she should be empowered with autonomy to shape his/her spiritual care experience and 'community'.

The chaplain also becomes a link or bridge between this 'spiritual community' of the baby, child and family and the wider healthcare team. This link is important so that everything that is experienced by the baby/child is working towards the nurture and maintenance of this 'spiritual community' of healing, trust and love, especially if a baby or child is approaching end of life (Rosenbaum, Smith and Zollfrank 2011). Awareness of the unique aspects of the life of a baby/child is key to true person-centred care. It is in this context that the story of the baby or child is lived out. The metaphor of 'story' will be used to illustrate a model of spiritual care in this context.

The 'spiritual community' of the baby/child: writing their story

Every baby and child is a unique individual and should be at the centre of his/her care and all decisions concerning him/her. Happily, most babies are born healthy, and there is celebration and joy following their birth. However, a significant number are born prematurely or with health needs requiring support – often intensively – from the healthcare team. When caring for babies in the neonatal period, it most often means that the baby requires support for prematurity or a medical condition, is recovering from neonatal surgery or has a life-limiting condition likely to lead to death. Spiritual care recognizes that for those who are well, this will be a time of great joy and excitement, but for those facing illness, this will be an uncertain, worrying and often frightening time. During this uncertainty, parents and carers may be faced with existential questions and have their meaning structures challenged (Caldeira and Hall 2012; Catlin *et al.* 2001).

A baby by definition is a fully dependent person requiring that all his/her needs are met from those who love and care for them. Children who are non-verbal have varying degrees of dependency. However, common to all babies and children is that their primary carers are in most instances their parent(s). During illness, healthcare professionals become part of the caring team and together with the baby's parent(s) they work in partnership for the wellbeing of the baby in their care. For parents, the healthcare environment can be a very strange and bewildering environment and the presence of technology and medical equipment can be frightening. For babies receiving intensive care, the presence of wires, tubes and other equipment can become a barrier for parents in how they care for and relate to their baby. It is into this caring relationship that spiritual care is offered and experienced, where minutes, hours and days take on enormous significance when time is finite. Good spiritual care helps to affirm the humanity and presence of the baby or child and honours the beauty and dignity of the human person. In addition, good spiritual care for parents fosters confidence and self-belief, which in turn are reflected in the spiritual dynamic between parents, the healthcare team and the baby or child being cared for. Using the metaphor of story, how might spiritual care be provided in these often emotionally charged situations?

Preparing for the story (relationship-building)

Relationship is at the heart of all spiritual care. Building relationships with the baby/child and their family is an essential part of sustaining and supportive spiritual care. The earlier the relationship is established, the better for all concerned. In situations where families have been given a diagnosis antenatally, it is valuable to establish a relationship of trust as early as possible so that the chaplain can accompany a family; in doing so, the chaplain is better able to appreciate the unique life story of this individual family and baby. In other situations, it is often in a crisis moment that a chaplain will meet a family for the first time. In situations such as this, calm, gentleness and support are key to establishing trust and meeting the needs of the baby and his/her family with little notice or preparation.

Hearing and learning the story

Learning the story of the baby/child and his/her family is the first step in building a pastoral relationship of trust. From a stance of respect, the chaplain becomes aware of the unique values and priorities for this baby/child and his/her family. To embrace cultural and spiritual diversity with sensitivity, a chaplain requires a mature sense of personal and professional identity, especially where the values and beliefs of the baby/child and his/her parents differ from those of the chaplain. Acknowledging and affirming the uniqueness of each baby and family, the chaplain is called to enter into the script of this particular story as the chaplain seeks to understand the journey that has brought the baby and family to this particular point.

Creating and telling the story

Every spiritual intervention should aim to allow the story of the baby or child to continue to be told. This gives honour to the life of the baby/child while at the same time giving expression to the value of the baby/child's life. An important practice point while attending to the reality of feelings and fears about uncertainty and powerlessness is also to draw out positives, achievements and strengths, even when life is very fragile. Regardless of the prognosis, the baby being cared for is of infinite value to his/her family; honouring this love is important. At times, parents can also experience ambivalent feelings towards their baby which may manifest as spiritual distress. Attending to these experiences and feelings provides a valuable opportunity to process them safely.

Multisensory life story approaches give expression to experience where words cannot. Telling the story of a baby and family is a 'real-time' activity where memories are being created and meaning is being formed in the present moment. In situations where the future is uncertain, this dimension of spiritual care is building a reservoir of memories to which parents and family will return often as they revisit these days. The story can be told with babies and non-verbal children through touch, music, art/craft and ritual/ceremony.

> ### PRACTICE EXAMPLE 12.1: NEONATAL PARENTING – FROM GRIEVING TO GRATITUDE
>
> A single parent of a 26-week-old baby girl was grieving intensely. With so many wires, tubes and machines connected to her, this mother could not see the beautiful, sweet and precious child she had given birth to. It was important to help her find a way to focus upon her daughter with gratefulness, hopefulness and love. We used breathing as an anchor for her to have a safe place of calm, before visualizing her daughter; seeing beyond the medical equipment and focusing on the child she gave life to. She began a gratitude journal that gave her a place to write down her baby's triumphs, and offered a place to go back, to draw strength from, when there was a difficult day. It turned her NICU experience into a celebration of victories, a source of hope in her journal, and a discipline of prayer and gratitude for the tiniest of miracles experienced each day.
>
> *Peggy Huber, Lead Pediatric Chaplain, The Children's Hospital of San Antonio, Texas, USA*

TOUCH

Touch as a form of expression is a powerful way to connect with a baby/child. Through touch, parents and carers express love, tenderness and security. Touch is also important for older children as they express emotion, most especially love and distress. Spiritual care can be expressed tenderly and evocatively through touch, but it is important to be culturally sensitive and always to operate within the bounds of appropriate touch. The growing awareness of the place of touch in developmental care for neonates provides opportunities for chaplains to use touch in conjunction with other team members in their care of premature babies. The Newborn Individualized Developmental Care and Assessment Program (NIDCAP) is one such example where touch impacts on the parent–infant relationship at the earliest developmental stages (Als and McAnulty 2011).

MUSIC

Music is a valuable medium through which children can express themselves. The provision of various instruments can be a powerful way to facilitate spiritual expression. For younger children and babies, the use of gentle soothing music can help to nurture a spiritual presence of calm, trust and security, although this should be interspersed with times of silence. Music is also an important vehicle of expression both actively and passively for parents as they attend to their own needs while a child is ill.

PRACTICE EXAMPLE 12.2: DRUMS AND BELLS

I use a steel metal drum at the beginning of our worship services as a way to let kids call us to worship. One of our teenage youth comes from a Native American tribe and is wheelchair-bound. He also has limited vision. Over the years I discovered how Native American flute music is soothing for him and often calms him. I had observed that he loves to place toys that make noise up to his right ear.

Now these metal bells are not light – weighing 3.4 pounds. As I placed the bell on his tray he lifted it up and held it to his right ear and began knocking on the bell with his fingers curled. He discovered that if he let his staff or me help him, we could gently tap the different tones of the bell and he would hear soothing sounds and feel the vibration. He was ecstatic and watching his reaction and face laugh with joy was quite amazing. If I stopped drumming for him, he would begin knocking on the bell himself to signal that he wanted more.

Lindy Holt, Chaplain, Anne Carlsen Centre, North Dakota, USA

ART AND CRAFT

Art and craft can be used effectively by children, parents and siblings in the expression of spirituality, to create memories and to express and find meaning in illness. The use of art as therapy has much to offer for both children and parents alike. Examples include the use of paint, clay modelling, textured media such as stones, wood and paper, etc. Working in conjunction with a play specialist or art therapist, spiritual expression can be facilitated in this way. It can also help to express faith and ritual (Nash, Darby and Nash 2015). Examples of this are the use of prayer beads, prayer leaves, expression boards or printed cards. When appropriate, expressions of art can be displayed. In addition to the expressive act in art, the created piece can also be used as a spiritual story-board by the healthcare chaplain or family member to reflect back to the child as part of spiritual care practice.

> ### PRACTICE EXAMPLE 12.3: NON-VERBAL SPIRITUAL CARE – BEYOND WORDS
>
> Mark is severely disabled and unable to talk. He can understand when spoken to but cannot reply verbally. I sat beside Mark and asked him if he would like to do an activity, explaining the spiritual care beading activity as a possibility (making a key ring with coloured beads, there is a sheet with colours and corresponding emotions or qualities). He was immediately nodding his head enthusiastically and seemed pleased to be engaged with someone. Slowly, Mark and I went through the steps to make a bead keyring, looking at the meanings of the different coloured beads. He thought about each bead and nodded or shook his head according to which he wanted: I showed him the options – he chose which he preferred if there were, for example, different shades or shapes. It became apparent that he needed strength and peace, hope for the future, to know he was loved and that he could contribute to the needs of others. I talked to him about the way he hugely contributes to the family and how Mum and Dad value his presence and the courage and strength he offers to them through his determination. I chose this activity because I felt it could engage Mark as fully as possible in decision-making and expressing his feelings and needs without being able to speak or write. I assessed that Mark needed to be reassured of how much he was securely loved by his mum and dad and by God and how he belonged to his family and hospital community. I clearly spoke about this and went over the colours he had chosen for his keyring.
>
> *Liz Bryson, Chaplaincy Volunteer, Birmingham Women's and Children's Hospital, UK*

TOYS

There are several initiatives that seek to take seriously the development of neonates by offering them stimuli and comfort resources. A purposefully designed toy octopus with tentacles is seen to imitate the umbilical cord in the womb. Solid bold colours on mobiles and the offer of a choice of handmade tiny blankets and teddy bears have all been widely appreciated by parents.

> ### PRACTICE EXAMPLE 12.4: PATIENT ON A VENTILATOR
>
> She was a 13-year-old oncology patient spending her last days in our pediatric intensive care unit, on a ventilator but alert. It was difficult to communicate with her because she was too weak to write or use an alphabet board to spell to us. As our focus shifted away from cure and on to comfort and support, she one day made some enigmatic motions with her hands. She tried valiantly to communicate something to us, but we could not decipher it. At last, when I was describing the motions to a relative, she guessed that our patient simply wanted to see outside. Her bed was facing her away from the window, so we rearranged the room so she could look outside. But that wasn't what she had tried to request of us. After more hand signals, we finally realized that she wanted to be outside, physically. This was no simple task, considering all the life-support machines in use, but our PICU staff was enthusiastic. She and her entourage of caretakers were able to go down to the hospital's outdoor playground. Everyone was excited to be a part of fulfilling her wishes, but she motioned again, shaking her head. Had we misunderstood her again? She clearly let us know that we were all chatting too loudly and she motioned for silence – so she could hear the birds singing.
>
> *Chaplain Mark Bartel, Manager of Spiritual Care, Arnold Palmer Medical Center, Orlando, Florida, USA*

RITUAL AND CEREMONY

Ritual and ceremony express our spirituality at a deeper level than words. For parents and siblings, ritual can be very important in marking life stages. Once again, ritual and ceremony should be culturally and spiritually sensitive. Ritual can be used at various life stages and the chaplain should be open to identifying, through gentle enquiry, significant moments in the life story of a baby, child or family member so that it can be marked. In addition, the use of social media, video link-up by mobile phone, etc. should be explored so that others may also share in important ritual, especially in situations where family members are unable to be physically present in some facilities (such as a neonatal unit).

Ritual, while most often associated with religious practice, has a wider application as a vehicle to express feeling and emotion. Ritual is an expression of the story of the individual and therefore chaplains should be open to creatively interpreting the story of each individual family and translating this into gesture, symbol and action. This is ritual at work in a generic and accessible way that is open to all as it reflects, embodies and speaks to the human condition. Examples of generic ritual include acts of love and commitment such as naming, acknowledging particular life moments and stages, transitional moments and achievements in care or also moments when illness progresses or deteriorates. In moments of both joy and sadness, ritual provides a time to acknowledge the present moment and takes on a therapeutic dimension.

RECORDING THE STORY

Recording the story of a baby and family unit is a powerful tool that has both spiritual and therapeutic benefits for all. There are many ways to do this and the chaplain should aim to relate to whatever is most helpful in each situation. Examples of story recording include journaling, art and craft, sound and video. Practice example 12.1 demonstrates how a gratitude journal can become a valuable reservoir of support. Increasingly, the use of multimedia and social media also have a role in recording the story of a baby's or child's life. Good practice indicates that no recording of story should take place without parental consent (even if it is well intentioned on the part of staff). For younger babies, the creation of memories and mementos is a well-established practice. This practice can be used for older babies and children too. It is also worth remembering that creating memories and mementos is a two-way process and so parents/caregivers should also consider making memories to share with their baby/child and his/her wider family. At Orlando Health, music therapists record an infant's heartbeat and create an instrumental song using it as the rhythm track, which is perhaps a different way of articulating a story.

Future development and research needs

- Case studies for work with patients in this category.
- Effectiveness and reliability of a range of religious, spiritual and pastoral assessment tools.
- Further development of resources and rituals for this patient group.

Summary

- Keep the baby or child at the centre and as the focus of care by honouring and nurturing the 'spiritual community' of each baby/child.
- Spiritual care is best provided in an integrated multidisciplinary team approach.
- Caring for and attending to the spiritual needs of the baby's family contributes to the care of a baby/child.
- Be sensitive to the cues/signals from a baby/child in your spiritual care.
- Recognize, interpret, tell and record the story of each child and family.
- The environment of the baby/child's life are expressions of spiritual care.

Questions for reflection

- What religious, spiritual and pastoral assessment tools, resources and rituals do you have for this type of work? What could you trial?
- How might you, as a part of a multidisciplinary team, engage with these issues?
- Do you know some of the common tools used by multidisciplinary teams in communicating with these types of patients?

References

Als, H. and McAnulty, G.B. (2011) 'The Newborn Individualized Developmental Care and Assessment Program (NIDCAP) with Kangaroo Mother Care (KMC): Comprehensive care for preterm infants.' *Current Women's Health Reviews 7*, 3, 288–301.

Caldeira, S. and Hall, J. (2012) 'Spiritual leadership and spiritual care in neonatology.' *Journal of Nursing Management 20*, 8, 1069–1075.

Catlin, E.A., Guillemin, J.H., Thiel, M.M., Hammond, S., Wang, M.L. and O'Donnell, J. (2001) 'Spiritual and religious components of patient care in the neonatal intensive care unit: Sacred themes in a secular setting.' *Journal of Perinatology 21*, 7, 426–430.

Nash, P., Darby, K, and Nash, S. (2015) *Spiritual Care with Sick Children and Young People.* London: Jessica Kingsley Publishers.

Rosenbaum, J.L., Smith, J.R. and Zollfrank, R. (2011) 'Neonatal end-of-life spiritual support care.' *Journal of Perinatal and Neonatal Nursing 25*, 1, 61–69; quiz 70–71.

Chapter 13
Working in Mental Health
Kathryn Darby

> PRACTICE EXAMPLE 13.1: YOU GAVE ME
> JOY AND HELPED ME HOLD ON
>
> Tom (15 years) asked for a visit from a chaplain: at first, Tom was withdrawn, even hostile at times and seemingly disinterested. Bringing activities helped to create a way of being together that was less threatening and opened the conversation. When he was well enough, we went for a short walk in the grounds, and that too eased the flow of being together. Sometimes we talked about faith, and I prayed with Tom, on other occasions we shared a joke or a simple card game, and sometimes he was too ill to talk much and I just sat with him for a while. He appreciated small gifts such as postcards with inspirational readings and a journal for jotting down ideas and pasting in pictures of things that gave him hope and strength. I recorded visits in the multidisciplinary handover book, consulting with other professionals about his progress. There were times when I felt my input was very limited, but I continued to visit as regularly as I could for over a year until Tom was discharged. He gave me an encouraging message: 'You gave me joy and helped me to hold on during the tough times, thank you.'

Brief overview and definitions

Most people in society will have some symptoms of mental distress in their lifetime, perhaps experiencing high or low moods, anxieties that cause insomnia or a crisis of mental stability at times of change, bereavement or loss. In this chapter we are considering the more extreme end of the spectrum of mental illness affecting young people and their families, and the nature of chaplaincy support. But it is important to remember that it is not 'them' and 'us' but requires rather an embrace of our common humanity: it is simply 'us'.

The term 'mental illness' is used to include (Carson 2008; Kinsella and Kinsella 2006; Robinson, Kendrick and Brown 2003):

- experience of hallucinations, visual or auditory ('hearing voices' inaudible to others)
- delusions or bizarre beliefs preoccupying and at odds with a person's cultural experience
- the inability to think in a logical progression
- confused or erratic speech pattern requiring a simple and narrow focus of conversation to maintain some rapport
- anxiety and depression, strong feelings of sadness
- social withdrawal
- persistently negative views of self, the world and the future; facing a meaningless abyss
- feeling abandoned, a failure
- bipolar disorder, which describes the experience of two extreme poles of the mood spectrum, from a low mood or depression to a very high *mania* state; often the first occurrence of the illness happens in late teens or early 20s.

A good place to look for definitions in relation to mental health is www.mind.org.uk – they have an A–Z list which is very comprehensive; www.mentalhealth.gov is a US site with useful material, including for young people.

Medication used to treat mental illness may also result in negative side-effects including social withdrawal, the reduced ability to feel, lack of motivation and apathy, and difficulty concentrating (Carson 2008; Kinsella and Kinsella 2006). While medication can help to quieten hallucinations, reducing anxiety and fear, the young person can also feel lethargic or restless, constantly feel the need to move (known as 'akathisia'), feel thirst, tremors or weight gain (Carson 2008). Eating disorders are also a rising concern in Western societies (Henderson and Ellison 2015). Anorexia nervosa, a condition where a person uses extreme means to lower their weight, and bulimia, the condition of binging and purging, can both be life-threatening.

The stigma of mental illness

Mental disorder can cause stigmatization in the circle of family and friends, among health professionals, in society and even among the patients themselves (Günay *et al.* 2016). One parent writes:

> We have often been lonely through this experience. People draw back not knowing what to say. In our situation, we already had one child with very complex physical problems and then our second child developed mental health problems. In our experience, we found people far less tolerant and accepting about mental illness.

Easing the pain and isolation of young people with mental illness

For young people experiencing mental illness, self-esteem can be extremely low (Carson 2008). Spiritual care activities that help young people to develop their confidence and self-belief can support recovery, such as creating a mobile with inspirational quotations or a keepsake that emphasises themes such as light in darkness or hopes and dreams. Activities may need to require a low level of engagement and effort at a time when the young person's energy and powers of concentration are minimal. Being creative can ease tensions and help a young person to avoid being too caught up in the punishing cycles of worry, confusion or negativity in their own minds. When young people are in an emotionally and psychologically dark place, environment can help to support mental health. Where possible, find a brighter room to meet, or plan activities that involve going outdoors.

Activity ideas

- A prayer tree, with figures representing how you are feeling.
- Make 'comfort boxes' filled with items that bring comfort and solace.
- Decorate a suncatcher as a sign of hope.

(See Nash, Darby and Nash 2015 for further ideas and principles about spiritual care.)

> ### PRACTICE EXAMPLE 13.2: VERTICAL HABITS
>
> Some staff at Cincinnati Children's Hospital can be seen wearing T-shirts with what are called 'vertical habits' on the back and the injunction to make them a habit. They are relational interpretations of concepts that are more usually regarded as Christian practices:
>
> - Love you (praise).
> - I'm sorry (confession).
> - Why? (lament).
> - I'm listening (illumination).
> - Help (petition).
> - Thank you (thanksgiving).
> - What can I do? (service).
> - Bless you (blessing).
>
> *(See www.calvin.edu/cicw/resources/showcases/verticalhabitstemplate.pdf.)*

Creating a safe and undemanding space

Particularly in relation to young people experiencing psychosis, the usual pastoral components of empathy and congruence may not be as relevant as 'loyalty, tolerance and practical caring' (Carson 2008, p.56). Authenticity in listening, telling and reinterpreting stories is also essential (Robinson *et al.* 2003). Psychological and therapeutic approaches require the young person to engage in conversations and group work to explore their feelings, at times within a family meeting. Chaplaincy also aims to offer a space to explore, which can offer a supportive presence, creating a safe space to be together but without mandatory involvement. Young people do not always have vocabulary to explore the difficult territory they are in and may welcome some 'time out' from this kind of recovery work. In such an opt-in or opt-out creative space, young people have an opportunity to be 'normal' and cared for in an atmosphere of acceptance and inclusivity, while being treated with respect, dignity and humanity.

Activities that are too reflective and introspective may not be timely and may trigger symptoms. One parent reflects: 'I thought that Janie would appreciate a creative worship space being offered at church, but she came back disappointed saying – "I just had too much headspace to think and that made me feel low about myself".' Sometimes the simplest activities – a card game or a silly fun game that brings laughter and a joke can offer relief, allowing a shaft of light to come into an otherwise challenging day. At the same time, being 'jollied along' is not desirable. Acknowledging the depth of despair for a young person can be liberating and healing. Simple statements which take the situation seriously will be appreciated: 'I am so sorry you are in so much pain.'

Working safely

While offering activities to celebrate a religious festival, one young person, seeing our bowl of sweets, said, 'Be sensitive! We have eating disorders! Get with the programme!' While we shared a chuckle about this, it also reminded us of the need to work with awareness. When leading an activity, always consider safety, counting any objects such as pens or sharper objects that could be taken and used for self-harm, and taking minimal numbers of scissors, keeping these in the leader's pocket or in sight at all times. Advice from the nursing staff helps minimise risk and develop confidence.

Keepsakes and messages of hope

One parent reflected:

> Maisie experienced a huge loss of hope. She could not imagine getting better and she struggled even to remember what life had been like before she became ill. Small gifts from friends meant a lot. She really appreciated receiving cards – the best ones were those that did not say too much, perhaps simply 'I love you' or a scripture verse, or a short message reminding her that she was valued, while not belittling the enormity of the situation.

Small gifts and tokens may be treasured reminders of hope and happiness. Often those which are home-made or created together with the young person are the most valued. While a young person may be unable to connect with the chaplain during the visit, the card, symbol, picture of hope or inspirational quote might encourage and sustain them at another time.

Religious perspectives

Celebrating festivals and culture

One of the things that 'opened the door' to mental health chaplaincy at the Birmingham Women's and Children's Hospital was introducing the *Celebrate Project* on the three mental health wards to celebrate religious and cultural festivals in the hospital. Each month, the Christian and Hindu chaplains took information, crafts and food to celebrate such festivals as Christmas, Eid, Holi, Easter, Summer Solstice, and Chinese New Year. In a non-threatening and light-touch approach, we brought, for instance, newborn chicks from the local farm at Easter, and the opportunity to 'throw colours' at one another during the Hindu festival of Holi. Gradually, trust with staff was built, and the chaplaincy role was understood more fully. Referrals to visit individuals became more frequent, supporting the principle of Respect (Mental Health Act 2007), which states that:

> the needs and values of each patient should be recognised and respected. This includes their race, religion, culture, gender, age, sexuality and any disability they may have. The patient's views, wishes and feelings should be taken into account and followed where this is possible. (Institute for Mental Health in England 2009, p.5)

The growing rapport with members of the wider team led to improved communication, support and understanding of the religious and spiritual needs of young people.

Working together as members of different faiths communicates respect, acceptance and a common humanity, and builds trust with the young people and staff. Staff may lack confidence and experience relating to the many nuances of a multifaith society and may fear causing offence or distress. The familiar face of a trusted chaplain who is part of the multidisciplinary team can be invaluable. For instance, provision for Muslim prayers was easily arranged with the guidance of the chaplain who was able to ensure that the needs of the family were met.

PRACTICE EXAMPLE 13.3: LIGHT AND DARKNESS

Celebrating Diwali on the mental health wards brought opportunity to explore the theme of light and darkness. The Hindu chaplain led a discussion: 'Everyone is in the dark sometimes. Not only night/darkness, but the darkness of not knowing: will we be welcome today? Will someone show me? Can I find my way through this?' Using the acronym LIGHT he went on to talk with the young

> people about the elements of love (family, caring staff, God), information (We can all say: 'I am human; I have purpose'); God or faith as a centre point; hope and trust. Within Indian culture, Diwali is followed by the New Year when people reflect upon what they can do to improve themselves in the following year. In this way, the chaplain invited discussion about what the young people might do to support their own recovery, using another acronym, SMART: specific, measurable, achievable, reliable, timed. The young people thought of changes in their behaviour and attitudes they could make to increase their own wellbeing and the staff were pleased with the way the chaplain's input complemented their own therapeutic approaches.

The unique contribution of chaplains

Chaplains are uniquely positioned within the multidisciplinary team to work from an appropriate theological or spiritual perspective and can offer meaning, a reason to exist and to 'cling on' (Swinton 2001, p.191), and a framework for exploring the existential questions of life, helping to build resilience and recovery. There are times when using symbols and references from a community's set of beliefs, sacred writings and practices can hold a power and depth that offers perspective, hope and restoration. Looking for ways to humanise the moment and bring a lightness of being will offer support.

Discernment and religious tradition: what helps, what hinders?

Attitudes about mental illness will be shaped and influenced by religious culture. Religion and spirituality can offer resources for coping but may also be a part of the problem (Pargament 1997). Working collaboratively with the psychologists and therapists, a chaplain can help to discern what is helpful within belief systems and practices and what might be causing difficulty or even distress (Bryant-Davis *et al.* 2012). There will be times when the support and expertise of different world faith chaplains can help explain particular needs and contribute to multidisciplinary care. For example, within Islam, it is understood that the 'evil eye' – known in Arabic as *ayn al-husud* or in Urdu as *Boori Nazar* (bad eye/look) – can cause harm or injury and provides an explanation for mental illness (Nash, Parkes and Hussain 2015, p.134). Reciting passages from the Qur'an or charms may be used to protect against the evil eye. Some children being treated for mental illness might be given a black thread to be tied on their limbs for protection. Staff who understand and appreciate the religious value of such practices can support the family in their beliefs and customs which may be providing support in dealing with stress or trauma. Some young people have numinous experiences that draw them closer to God even in the midst of suffering, and a chaplain's discernment can foster growth.

At other times, the chaplain may need to challenge and help dispel potentially harmful beliefs or practices within a family's religious framework. Religious objects or texts may act as a trigger for some abused children (Bryant-Davis *et al.* 2012). Unhelpful and punitive images of God potentially formed within many religions may bring a sense of shame, blame or unworthiness that can be addressed by a chaplain who may bring new theological understanding and communicate being loved, accepted and blessed by God (Bryant-Davis *et al.* 2012; Nash, Parkes and Hussain 2015).

Supporting parents through the storm

Genuine support means walking the long, slow, fragile journey alongside the parents step by step. Regular but short contact with the chaplaincy team can be very helpful. As one parent commented:

> We felt our world came crashing down when our daughter was diagnosed with complex mental health problems which led to a prolonged hospital stay. As parents we felt helpless, frightened and hopeless at times. The road was long, utterly unpredictable and emotionally exhausting. It is difficult to explain the all-encompassing impact on the whole family. To have a chaplain listen, empathise and connect through eye contact, reflection and demonstrating compassion was very healing. Practically, it helped when we knew when the chaplain might come back [knowing we would have another opportunity to talk and reflect with someone who had time for that].

The family may find that their own belief systems need to be reassessed, but this kind of reflection may come later. Practical support may be the most appropriate response, particularly at the shocking and disorienting time of admission and diagnosis. One mum reflects: 'Only now, a year and a half later, I realise that we probably went through the stages of grief over the first few months.' Another parent comments:

> The help we received from chaplains to reflect on the journey and mark milestones in a simple, creative way was important too. A few

simple questions followed by genuine listening were often enough: how are you doing today? What have the last few days felt like? So much of the time as parents we were in complicated meetings with detailed language and concepts. To be in a safe space and able to be open about our own journeys was a lifeline.

Supportive spaces and siblings

Drop-in spaces may be welcome for parents, where they do not feel judged or required to say much but can experience being nurtured and affirmed in a gentle and non-threatening way. Siblings, too, can be given support, acceptance and understanding. Treatment for mental illness will inevitably involve the whole family in assessment and appraisal which can create immense strain. Parents may feel some element of self-blame and will be analysing themselves, trying to understand 'how it all went wrong'. The mental health needs of parents can increase as their child's health crisis extends, paralleling some of their child's sense of isolation, repressed emotions and heartache. Siblings too can be impacted:

> Our younger daughter found the experience of Dave's mental illness very confusing and upsetting. Previously, Dave had been great with Bess, playing and interacting with her. But when Dave became ill, he just switched. We often didn't know if it was the best thing to take Bess to visit him, because Dave could be cruel to her, ignoring her or saying hurtful things. At times, it was so difficult to leave, because Bess was hoping Dave was coming home with her, and she would end up sobbing her eyes out. We wanted to try to normalise things, and maintain some contact for Bess, but often we didn't know what to do for the best.

Expressing lament

Symbolic acts offer ways of contacting the depths of emotional pain in a safe and healing way. For example, in a confidential and protected space, a chaplain can offer a bowl of water to symbolise a bowl of tears. The parent is invited to dip their hand in the water to make contact with their own tears, gently cupping the water and feeling it slide through their fingers, while remaining silent or expressing in words or with their own tears what they are feeling. Prayers by the chaplain offering containment and blessing may also be part of this small ritual.

Returning to the community: being discharged
Recovery from mental illness is often a circular process, with two steps taken forward and one step back, rather than following a linear process. Faith communities might be expecting to hear the news that 'all is well' in answer to prayers, when, in fact, there is rarely a sudden or complete recovery from mental illness. Coming home after a lengthy hospital admission does not signal that all has returned to 'normal'; rather, a family may continue to live with immense pressures and a changed reality that require ongoing resilience, patience, adaptation and support.

Struggles and tensions for the chaplain
At times, contact made with young people will seem fragile, even non-existent. The polite veneer which usually cushions our interactions with others may be in short supply. The role of the chaplain is not to push or cajole, but to journey alongside a young person in the long slow work of giving support, believing in them and their capacity, holding on to hope when the young person feels hopeless. The chaplain walks a fine line between acknowledging how difficult life is and offering symbols of life, love, hope and inner freedom (Swinton 2001). A chaplain needs a robust sense of self and a rootedness in their own spiritual life when visiting someone who is sunk in depression or feeling lost in a place of anguish, despair or alienation (Carson 2008). At times, seeking to travel closely with someone in this kind of pain brings feelings of inadequacy, powerlessness and discomfort, mirroring not only the existential needs of the young person and family, but also, from a Christian perspective, imitating and even sharing in Christ's own brokenness and vulnerability. Yet from this place of risk and trust, the healing gifts of God's Spirit can also spring forth like water from a deep well to grace each person involved. Sharing the pain and struggle will be part of the story of healing. One parent's words gave encouragement in the midst of challenge:

> It was so precious to see you. You have been such a support and strength over so many years and you indeed have that extraordinary gift of walking closely with people in their brokenness.

Supporting staff and ourselves
Being alongside young people experiencing high levels of fear, anxiety and alienation can be disturbing (Carson 2008). Chaplains may have a

role in supporting staff and also need to take care of themselves, receiving regular supervision in a boundaried and disciplined way (Leach and Paterson 2015). Ongoing training in attachment theory, basic counselling theory, creating therapeutic relationships and holding boundaries is also recommended.

One of the main skills is to be aware of our own limits. This is true of all medical paediatric situations but can be especially true of the back story and issues with mental health patients. Good practice would be to ask for any relevant background on an individual before starting a pastoral relationship, then not to overreach and to stay within our role and know when to refer.

> PRACTICE EXAMPLE 13.4: A FINAL NOTE OF HOPE
>
> One Christian parent describes her theological journey when her daughter became ill:
>
>> What was important was assuring Mary that she was loved and held in the everlasting arms of God. Psalm 91 contains these themes and became highly significant. I found my own ideas about 'what is evil?' challenged through the experience, and my strongest sense was that God was just as present with us in the midst of suffering as when Mary wasn't ill. There was no sense of punishment, but the need for compassion and to communicate to our daughter that she was rooted in the love of God. I still puzzle about some of the New Testament stories of healing but my understanding of those stories is much less black and white now. Much remains a mystery and it does not seem important to understand it all, but to be faithful and alongside our daughter in love. I was helped to face some of my fears, realising that I don't need all the answers and that God had not abandoned us.

Future development and research needs

- Spiritual and religious care as a resource for recovery.
- What do young people identify as helping them in times of crisis?
- Spiritual play as a means of finding wholeness.

Summary

- Light-touch activities can offer relief from mental anguish, boredom and isolation.
- Close multidisciplinary working enhances understanding and mutual support, recognising that the chaplain brings something distinctive from a spiritual and religious base.
- Parents and siblings need acceptance, safe spaces to be honest, and long-term support.
- Simple rituals can help parents process grief.
- Mental health chaplains need boundaried, regular supervision.

Questions for reflection

- How did moments of crisis or difficulties/challenges in your own childhood have an impact on your mental health as a child? And how do they continue to affect you now?
- What might you consider saying to a child who is struggling with, or suffering with, their mental health?
- What might you do to help reduce the stigma around mental health in your context? Are there positive steps you could take in your context to develop your service with young people being treated for their mental health?

References

Bryant-Davis, T., Ellis, M.U., Burke-Maynard, E., Moon, N., Counts, P. and Anderson, G. (2012) 'Religiosity, spirituality, and trauma recovery in the lives of children and adolescents.' *Professional Psychology: Research and Practice 43*, 4, 306–314.

Carson, M.L.S., (2008) *The Pastoral Care of People with Mental Health Problems.* London: SPCK.

Günay, S., Bekitkol, T., Beycan Ekitli, G. and Yildirim, S. (2016) 'Determination of the mental disorder beliefs of students in a nursing faculty.' *Journal of Psychiatric Nursing 7*, 3, 129–134.

Henderson, A.K. and Ellison, C.G. (2015) 'My body is a temple: Eating disturbances, religious involvement, and mental health among young adult women.' *Journal of Religious Health 54*, 3, 954–976.

Institute for Mental Health in England (2009) *Mental Health Act: Essential Information for Parents and Carers.* London: Rethink Publication.

Kinsella, C., and Kinsella, C. (2006) *Introducing Mental Health: A Practical Guide.* London: Jessica Kingsley Publishers.

Leach, J. and Paterson, M. (2015) *Pastoral Supervision: A Handbook*, 2nd edition. London: SCM Press.

Nash, P., Darby, K. and Nash, S. (2015) *Spiritual Care with Sick Children and Young People.* London: Jessica Kingsley Publishers.

Nash, P., Parkes, M. and Hussain, Z. (2015) *Multifaith Care for Sick and Dying Children and Their Families.* London: Jessica Kingsley Publishers.

Pargament, K.I. (1997) *The Psychology of Religion and Coping: Theory, Research and Practice.* New York, NY: Guilford Press.

Robinson, S., Kendrick, K. and Brown, A. (2003) *Spirituality and the Practice of Healthcare.* London: Palgrave Macmillan.

Swinton, J. (2001) *Spirituality and Mental Health Care.* London: Jessica Kingsley Publishers.

Chapter 14
Working with Trauma and Abuse
Bob Flory

> **PRACTICE EXAMPLE 14.1: A CAR CRASH**
>
> It was a bright, sunny fall day; the colours were brilliant and the sky blue. Johnny had a day off school, so he and his best friend were playing Frisbee in their adjoining front yards. Emily Thompson had been to a very meaningful Bible study at her church and was going to pick up a friend for lunch. She turned down a quiet residential street. Just as she entered the street, Johnny ran between two parked cars to catch the thrown Frisbee. Emily did not see him appear between the cars and hit him. She stopped and called 911. Johnny was non-responsive as he was transported to a nearby trauma center. Johnny's parents arrived at the hospital separately within minutes. It was after they arrived that the trauma team stopped resuscitation and pronounced Johnny dead. As the chaplain on call, you receive a page to come to the trauma center to support the parents. As you approach the trauma center, you can hear them wailing. You feel your own adrenalin begin to pump as you wonder, 'How do I support these parents?'

Developing a plan to support these parents

As chaplains, we are setting the ground for creating sacred space and relationships to develop our ministry with those we serve. Our goals are to help create physical safety and comfort, listen openly to the story of the family, help provide information and assurance, collaborate with the appropriate professionals and learn how the family taps into their own strength and support.

Upon arriving in the trauma center, seek out others that have been supporting the family already. Look for a social worker, charge nurse, attending physician, someone who can give you an update about the situation and what has happened before your arrival. The information you can gather allows you to prepare your own emotional and spiritual response. The last response you want to provide is a reaction of surprise. If you can enter an emotional situation with information about the event, you can be more present and listen more carefully to the *lament* of the parents.

It is important to be aware of how you plan to support a family living through a trauma. There are various written models and resources for interventions, and you may interview others in your setting about how they approach a trauma and their strategies to provide focused support. Two excellent websites outline steps to consider while working with a family in trauma:

- Substance Abuse and Mental Health Services Administration (www.samhsa.gov)
- Mental Health First Aid (www.mentalhealthfirstaid.org).

SAMHSA identifies the importance of establishing:

- a baseline of safety
- trust
- peer support/mental self-help
- collaboration
- empowering or giving voice to one's experience
- recognizing cultural issues.

Mental Health First Aid identifies five similar steps and uses the acronym ALGEE. They encourage the support person to:

- **A**ssess for harm, create safety.
- **L**isten without judgment.
- **G**ive reassurance and information.
- **E**ncourage appropriate professional help.
- **E**ncourage self-help and other support strategies.

The first goal is to provide a *safe, secure and comfortable space*. Do we need to get water, a chair, a blanket to wrap up in? Is the space clear of sharp objects or dangerous objects in case someone faints or falls to the ground in emotional pain? I feel it is important to always have a door to the room open, so others are able to observe or hear what is going on. If a family member feels you are concerned about their physical comfort, safety and wellbeing, it creates the first step of trust to continue working with them as their chaplain.

Our next goal is to *listen*. We so often want to offer words of encouragement or support, but if that is our first step, there is an assumption that we know what the family needs. It is critical to listen to the story that is being told so the appropriate and relevant support can be offered.

Before the traumatic event occurred, there was a stable and known reality. This reality was interrupted by this traumatic event and now there is a new and unknown reality unfolding. An important role is to help build a bridge between these two realities. What was this child like before the trauma? What known injuries are changing this reality? What unknowns remain?

It is very supportive to encourage parents to tell the story of who their child was. What happened at breakfast this morning? What were the last words said to each other? Only as we listen will we be able to hear the uniqueness of the story interrupted by this trauma.

An important gesture of support is to help family begin to *gather information*. Denial and shock keep us frozen and closer to the known reality. Information gradually helps to inform the state of shock and begin to soften the denial, so they are able to begin the work of entering this new reality.

We don't do this alone. Is there a child life specialist or local equivalent such as play worker or youth worker available for the siblings, and can the social worker provide resources that the chaplain is unable to offer? Is it necessary for the doctor to review once again the physical injuries caused by the injury? The chaplain can advocate for resources to help the family navigate through this experience. And do not forget to encourage family members in recognizing their own strength and resources to help them navigate through this experience.

What is the spiritual crisis at hand?

It is important for chaplains not to assume they know where the parents are spiritually. It is also important to listen for one's own spiritual response and not confuse it with the family's. An example is in the particular case cited at the beginning of this chapter. The chaplain may have a particular response to the fact that the driver was coming from a Bible study and found herself innocently hitting this young boy. There can be a very different reaction when a driver is drunk, speeding or careless and 'caused' the accident. This case truly is an accident with an innocent driver and innocent child. One might focus on the innocence of the driver, but that is something the parents may not even know or care about. Such a focus might prevent us from seeing the unique grief of the parents.

Listen to the spiritual words coming from the parent(s). Are they in crisis? If so you might hear words like 'Where is God?' or 'Why my child?' or 'How could God allow this to happen?' These questions may express feelings of being lost in their relationship with God, or feelings of abandonment. Conversely, the parents might not be in a place of crisis with God. 'Oh God, give me strength', 'God, I can't do this alone', 'God, you are my strength…you are my courage!' These statements and questions are very different, which emphasizes the importance of listening to the words the parents are saying and not listening for the crisis you think the parents might be in. Listening for the words you want to hear or think you should hear is not ministering from a place of presence. We may also be working with the child who has experienced the trauma and their views are significant as this next story shows.

> ### PRACTICE EXAMPLE 14.2: I DON'T WANT GOD
>
> Following a motor vehicle accident, a four-year-old female was admitted to our trauma service line. Her injuries were orthopedic in nature, and she was neurologically stable. She lived with her parents and other extended family. During her admission, the staff had concerns about potential abuse or neglect in the home; appropriate referrals were made and resources were provided to her mother. The majority of my visits were with the patient (whom I'll call Sophia) and her mother. They identified Christianity as their faith background.
>
> Sophia's family would often request prayer and talk about the accident being a 'wake-up call'. Many families make statements like this in their search for meaning following a traumatic event and they are often motivated to return to the faith of their families of origin. Although her parents and other family members expressed relational consciousness with a transcendent presence, Sophia did not. Sophia expressed her own relational consciousness by saying, 'God is not with me' and 'I can't feel God', and even at times yelling, 'I DON'T WANT GOD!' In my time with Sophia I

> honored her statements while still providing her avenues like Godly Play, conversation, and games to explore her innate spirituality and relational consciousness with herself, others, and her environment. I wondered if Sophia's resistance was due to a lack of understanding, but even when I wondered with her about her understanding of God and prayer, she still did not desire to participate. After that visit, when her parents asked for prayer, we negotiated with Sophia who agreed we could pray without naming God. In my care of Sophia, I heard and validated her voice while affirming the faith expressions of her family. As a result, we developed a trusting relationship with healthy boundaries that lasted throughout her admission.
>
> The Revd Janette Platter, Chaplain, Children's
Health System of Texas, USA

When the child dies: short-term crisis ministry

This is a unique and difficult kind of ministry in which there will not be a long-term relationship as during an inpatient experience. Instead, it is a relationship to help the family be as present as they can, and to say goodbye to their child and to leave the body behind. The chaplain can help create this space by making the parents as comfortable and safe as possible: chairs to sit in, a blanket to warm them, and water and food to keep them hydrated and nourished.

Learn what your hospital has to offer in terms of memory-making activities so you can provide them alongside the appropriate professionals. Are you able to take a lock of hair, create prints of the hands or feet? Do you have a prayer quilt to put over the child's body? Is the family able to bathe the body? All of these activities have to be coordinated and approved by the coroner/medical examiner when a death occurs in the emergency center and an investigation is planned.

If the coroner/medical examiner gives permission to touch their child, then help the family touch and hold their child's hand and, as appropriate, hold the body. Encouraging contact with their child's body is essential to help them accept the reality of their child's death and begin their grieving process. If there are siblings, refer a child life specialist to assist in helping them experience their sibling's death. If they do not have a faith leader coming into the emergency center to support them, explore ways you can offer support in their absence.

Do not be afraid to think creatively. Is there a night-time ritual of putting their child to bed that might be meaningful at this moment?

Examples are tucking them into bed, saying goodnight prayers, singing a lullaby or nursery rhyme. Parents may not think of using a night-time ritual but it can become very healing and comforting to help them leave their child's body. Most children's hospitals do not have a set limit on the amount of time that the family may stay with the body. It is important to support them in taking their time and being with their child as long as they need. This was the last moment their child was alive; it is the closest moment they have to when they were living. Once they leave the room, the death becomes more real and they have begun the journey of grief. For this reason it can be very difficult for a family to leave the room, and the chaplain can be of great help.

Different types of traumas create different personal responses in the chaplain

It is important to be aware of our own responses so that we do not interfere with the support we need to offer. If our emotions take over, we can end up reacting to the trauma as opposed to being present, creating the sacred space to wholly minister in the trauma at hand. Traumas may be caused by innocent events that are truly accidents. An example might be a skiing accident where one hits a patch of ice, loses control and collides with a tree which results in a head trauma. The initial case example in this chapter was a trauma caused by the coming together of two innocent acts resulting in an accident that caused death. In this case, Emily Thompson was not speeding and was not drunk. She was innocently driving down a residential street when Johnny accidentally ran out between cars into the path of Ms Thompson's car.

Cases of child abuse

Non-accidental trauma (NAT), sometimes called abusive head trauma (AHT), is another kind of trauma that presents itself in many of our hospitals. NAT is injury to a child that was inflicted purposefully, also called child abuse. For most people, the NAT is very difficult to minister to without including our own responses or judgment. As one child protection physician once had to remind a healthcare team, 'Never forget you are not serving on the jury.' Chaplains are members of the healthcare team providing support to the patient and family, and helping them navigate this medical crisis. It is not ours to pronounce judgment or be the investigator. As chaplains, it is very important to be aware of our reactive emotions and behavior as we approach these situations. In the long-term relationship with a family and patient affected by an NAT, it is important to keep an attitude of openness and acceptance, to build trust and to create a safe place for families to talk about their journey. It is not to pronounce a verdict or join one family member in judgment towards another family member.

> ### PRACTICE EXAMPLE 14.3: A BAPTISM SHELL
>
> Some years ago, a child was brought in who had been hurt by a boyfriend of the mother. The families of both the mother and father were in conflict with each other, reacting in judgment and protection towards the little boy. We had to separate the families, create different visiting schedules and manage the numbers of family visitors gathering at the hospital. The atmosphere around this patient's bedside was extremely tense, but ultimately his parents came to an agreement on wanting to have the child baptized before he was taken off life support. I spoke with the physician, nurses and social worker about how best to navigate the hostility of the family members towards each other. I advocated for trying to have both families allowed around the bedside for the baptism. Reluctantly, the team agreed to this request, and we invited the entire family to gather around the bedside for the baptism. This represented about 30 family members.
>
> I incorporated the symbol of a shell for the baptism. The shells used were given to me through the years by various people, so I proposed to those gathered that the shells symbolized the larger community surrounding these two families and the child. I reminded them that a shell provides protection for life under the ocean that we cannot see. Thus, I suggested the shells symbolized the promise of life beyond what we know on earth, and that love and support would follow this little boy in his death. I used one shell for the actual baptism, asking that we pass the shell around to each family member and they share a blessing or prayer for this little boy preceding the baptism. At one point I looked out beyond the patient's room and saw the staff standing at a distance, weeping. As I offered the sacrament of baptism, the staff watched from a place of heart, not from a place of mind and professionalism. It was from this place that the staff could feel their own emotional selves and let some healing begin.

> As I listened to each prayer and blessing in the room, I was aware it was the first time that love and family had surrounded this little boy in the hospital. No hostility, no judgment; everyone gathered in love, prayer and blessing for this little boy's baptism. As I finished the sacrament, family members hugged and shook hands. I re-entered the hall, and the social worker and physician both came up to me in tears and said they had never witnessed the dissolving of hostility and the gathering of love that they had just witnessed, and thanked me for advocating for both families to be together for this baptism. As chaplain, I had reminded this family of the meaning of the sacrament and created sacred ground for them to put their hostility towards each other aside and stand in love for this little boy minutes before life support was withdrawn. It was truly a remarkable experience.

Not all patients die from a trauma

In fact, only about 2.5% of children die when brought to a trauma center (Burd 2006; Oliver *et al.* 2001). When the child does not die from the trauma and is admitted into the hospital as an inpatient, there are still many levels of spiritual care to be considered. The most important thought to remember is that the family is grieving who the child was before the trauma. Often the trauma injury creates long-term effects that the child and family will need to learn how to live with. While families are happy and relieved their child is living, the child's personality, physical abilities or mental abilities may be altered. A significant dimension is grieving the child that was and embracing the child that is now emerging.

> ### PRACTICE EXAMPLE 14.4: THE BEFORE AND AFTER SON
>
> I remember working with a family and their 12-year-old boy. The son had been struck by lightning while the family was having their family portrait taken. He had just won a talent show at his school the previous weekend as an Elvis Presley impersonator. The family was very proud of his performance. They had it on a DVD and played it a lot. The boy could no longer talk, was paralyzed on his left side and vision was now compromised. It was important for this family to share with us who their son was just a few days ago. Watching the video helped us realize who they were grieving and

> helped us better support this family during this transition of loving their son in this new physical condition. As I ministered to this family, it was important for me to refer to their son as he was before the accident and after. The healing for this family would come in learning to integrate the 'before and after son' as a whole person.

Another spiritual dimension of healing after a trauma is acceptance and/or forgiveness. The chaplain can assist the family as they work through their reactions. Was the trauma caused by a drunk driver, a driver running a red light, a ski accident as result of bad snow conditions? Was the accident caused by an impersonal force? Often these kinds of traumas shatter the innocence of a child doing what comes naturally for a child. In these situations it is not uncommon for a parent to feel somehow responsible or fearful of leaving their child alone and being very protective and guarded. A goal in this situation is to help recover a basic level of trust in life.

Two other support roles of the chaplain

Every one of us has an emotional response to the trauma event. As healthcare providers, we are driven by our profession to support the family and patient. We often put our own emotional and human needs aside to care for others. As chaplains, one of our roles is to help the team recognize their emotional response and to provide healing and support for them. The chaplain is often the neutral person between the medical interventions, which allows us to walk next to a care provider and help them reconnect with their heart, their spirit and their emotional being.

It may be important to gather the team together for a moment of silence around the patient's bed (Bartels 2014), or a debriefing about the trauma event for them to talk to each other to share how this event is affecting them emotionally. In talking with others, we realize we are not alone in our responses to this event and therefore can receive strength from knowing others care as deeply as we do. Offering support to staff members is just as important as supporting families.

And finally, remember to take care of yourself

Traumas are very difficult situations for everyone to experience, including the chaplain. Please take time to refer to Chapter 8 in this book about self-care. Your ongoing ability to care for fellow staff members and future children and their families depends on your practice of renewing your own spirit after caring for others in trauma.

Future development and research needs

- How chaplains add value and have a distinct role in trauma situations.
- How to be personally, spiritually and emotionally prepared to go empty-handed into trauma situations.
- Are there universal spiritual care approaches and resources that can prepare and equip us for traumatic events?

Summary

- The important of silence and presence.
- Lament.
- Listening and availability.
- Don't take anger personally.
- No simplistic answers.
- Be emotionally and resourcefully prepared: have a 'go bag' of resources.
- Accusations of abuse: if it's true, they need help; if it's not true, they need help.
- Staff support trolley and self-care.

Questions for reflection

- How and when do you get support when you have been affected by trauma?
- Do you know how to process a suspected child abuse situation?
- Are you prepared to be on the receiving end of anger, distress, despair, without the need to offer quick-fix answers?

Recommended resources

Mental Health First Aid: www.mentalhealthfirstaid.org.
Safe Kids Worldwide: www.safekids.org.
Substance Abuse and Mental Health Services Administration: www.samhsa.gov.

References

Bartels, J.R. (2014) 'The pause.' *Critical Care Nurse 34*, 1, 74–75. Accessed on 24/11/2017 at http://ccn.aacnjournals.org/content/34/1/74.full.

Burd, R.S. (2006) 'Predicting hospital mortality among injured children using a national trauma database.' *Journal of Trauma-Injury Infection & Critical Care 60*, 4, 792–801.

Oliver, R.C., Sturtevant, J.P., Scheetz, J.P., Fallat, M.E. (2001) Beneficial effects of a hospital bereavement intervention program after traumatic childhood death, Journal of Trauma-Injury Infection & Critical Care, 50(3), pp.440–446.

Chapter 15

Major Incidents

Naomi Kalish

> **PRACTICE EXAMPLE 15.1: HURRICANE SANDY**
>
> Healthcare chaplains in the New York City area closely watched weather reports of the impending Hurricane Sandy in late October 2012. Hospitals began their preparedness process by encouraging their staffs to develop Personal Preparedness Plans to ensure both their wellbeing and their availability to work through the storm. Hospitals canceled non-urgent surgeries. Many families of pediatric patients flocked to the hospital so that the entire family would be together throughout the storm. With unexpected and unprecedented flooding, major disruption to transportation including to emergency vehicles, and a gasoline shortage in the area, some hospitals evacuated before or during the storm. They discharged the patients they could and transferred the others to hospitals that were still functional. The staff at these facilities experienced a surge of patients from the transfers and in their emergency departments. Chaplains joined as general members of the interdisciplinary team and as spiritual care specialists at every step of preparation, throughout the duration of the storm, and in recovery afterwards.

Hospital chaplains play a critical role in the care team when their hospitals respond to major incidents. These incidents, though rare, require a specialized response from the institution as a whole and from all disciplines, including chaplaincy. This chapter addresses the experience, roles and skills of chaplains during the extenuating situations when the regular hospital system is disrupted and the regular procedures are overridden. Terminology varies by region and institution, with terms such as 'emergency', 'disaster', 'major incidents' and 'code reds'. For the sake of simplicity, this chapter uses the term 'major incidents'.

What to expect in the system?

Despite the rarity of events that would precipitate a major incident such as natural disaster, mass trauma and mass violence against children, the experience of being a healthcare provider often has a profound impact on the caregiver's professional and sometimes personal life. Sometimes the chaplain him- or herself is part of the directly affected population (such as chaplains whose personal lives were disrupted by Hurricane Sandy). Sometimes the chaplain is exposed to disturbing images, sounds and smells, or the chaplain might suffer from feelings of uselessness and helplessness.

During a major incident, the hospital setting can feel chaotic. The needs of the situation extend beyond the normal functioning of the healthcare system, leading it to implement its disaster plan (which may be known by different names in different institutions). After the September 11, 2001 terrorist attack, it has become commonplace for US organizations to have disaster plans that describe chains of command, roles and responsibilities. In the major incident mode, the hospital leadership establishes a command center or major incident control room. The hospital may need to make arrangements for staff to sleep over and eat if travel is impeded, such as through inclement weather or a lockdown. Hospitals in New York City provided accommodations for hundreds of staff during Hurricane Sandy in 2012. During the Boston Marathon bombing, the entire city was put on lockdown and hospital chaplains were among those whose travel was impeded.

With mass victims, multiple hospitals may be involved. The hospital prepares not only to receive an influx of trauma patients, but also for the arrival of irregular and sometimes surprising members to the team and the hospital community. The care team expands and can include law enforcement, firefighters, the FBI, community clergy and staff (including chaplains) from other institutions. Public figures and politicians may become involved and offer words of comfort and condolences, such as mayors, governors, state representatives and even heads of state and major celebrities. The hospital may experience a surge of worried relatives and friends descending on the hospital as they anxiously await information. Critical incidents also become news items. Hospitals are likely to have protocols regarding communication with the press and posting on social media; chaplains should know these guidelines and review them with staff, students and volunteers in anticipation of any critical incident.

> PRACTICE EXAMPLE 15.2: EVACUATING PATIENTS
>
> The Revd David Fleenor, a chaplain at NYU Langone Medical Center, helped nurses process their experience of evacuating patients during Hurricane Sandy after the hospital lost power and then its generator and back-up generator were flooded. He recalled that:
>
>> A pediatric intensive care unit nurse had to put two babies in the pockets of her scrubs in order to continue 'bagging' them [keeping the babies well-aerated and oxygenated] while scurrying down nine flights of stairs in the dark. The Registered Nurse (RN) who told me this said all the nurses were creative and heroic during that harrowing time and are now, understandably, traumatized.

What to expect: the chaplain's roles before and during an incident

Advance planning

Just as disaster plans are developed on larger national, state, city and institutional levels, it is incumbent on each department also to develop its own plan. Core components of a Pastoral Care Emergency Preparedness Plan are:

- **Setting attendance expectations:** A statement of work expectations for every role in the department (leadership, staff chaplains, administrative assistant, Clinical Pastoral Education students, volunteers, per diem chaplains, etc.). It will be important for team members to know if they are expected to work, if the department will seek to run with full or reduced staffing, and what the hospital compensation policy is if they are unable to work or if they come late.

- **Scheduling:** At the earliest point, chaplain leaders should write to their team and ask each member to check in regarding his/her ability to work and, if needed, to stay over at the hospital.

- **Coverage:** A critical incident may call for a revised form of chaplaincy coverage, such as deploying chaplains for continuous coverage in the emergency department as well as a rotation of chaplains to all areas of the hospital for 'check-ins'.

- **Debriefing the chaplains team:** Establish a structure of regular debriefing with your spiritual care team. A best practice in the disaster chaplaincy field is that every team member debriefs with a supervisor or colleague at the conclusion of every shift.

- **Review policies:** Chaplains can also do advance preparation by regularly reviewing the hospital's procedures and pursuing specialized training (in areas including disaster chaplaincy and active shooter situations).

The chaplain's place on the multidisciplinary team

The paradigm of the generalist and specialist is especially helpful for chaplains and other hospital staff during a major incident. While chaplains are spiritual care specialists, they are also general members of the healthcare team who can contribute to the larger response effort in the following ways.

Report to the command centre and be present with hospital leadership:

- The designated leader of the chaplaincy team should report to the command center about the availability of chaplains for the incident. The chaplaincy leader should find out the schedule of leadership meetings and be present at them, serving as an important vehicle for communication between the chaplaincy team and the hospital leadership. As electronic communication may be limited during an incident, it is important to be physically present at these leadership check-ins.

As general members of the healthcare team, hospital chaplains may be called upon to:

- keep track of names and locations of patients and/or family members as they arrive
- provide emotional and spiritual care for the family members and the worried wounded as they arrive at the hospital and await further information
- help connect families or be present when patients and their family members are reunited
- perform administrative tasks (such as coordinating shifts for the labor pool, organizing supplies, distributing food, etc.)
- communicate with the media: sometimes chaplains are tasked with speaking with the media in concert and coordination with

the hospital's media relations team and security (approval from the hospital's administration and/or media relations is necessary).

Strategically assess the situation, keeping an eye out specifically for the emotional needs of the patients and families:

- Review the hospital's plan and consider what scenarios might not yet be addressed and offer recommendations.

- Examine what spaces are required for the fulfilment of emotional needs, such as for waiting, receiving news from the medical team, reuniting children and family members, and viewing the deceased.

- Examine the patient and family/visitor flow issues that would affect the patient or family experience, such as providing patients and family members the opportunity to enter and exit the hospital with privacy and to avoid the media. Strategize travel in the case of a lockdown.

- Formulate caring and compassionate language and communication systems for engaging family members, such as finding a neutral way to ask family members to come forward when the medical team is ready to give them news.

Spiritual care during the incident

While hospital administration and the medical team will be primarily focused on the management and response to the immediate physical needs of the situation, hospital chaplains have the opportunity to provide spiritual and emotional care throughout the incident and proactively visit with patients, families and staff (a more intense variety of our usual spiritual care).

- Be present and provide in-the-moment emotional support.

- Invite people to tell their stories of the incident. When did they find out about the situation? How is this affecting them personally, their families, their homes and their pets?

- Tend to patients and staff who are not part of the incident. The hospital is still filled with patients, family members and staff addressing the ongoing needs of illness, hospitalization and possibly surgery. Not being part of the response to the critical incident can create feelings of guilt and helplessness for some.

- Provide mechanisms for coping with stress, such as coloring, meditation and prayer services.
- Lead staff in in-the-moment memorials if a patient dies after arrival to the hospital, such as through inviting staff to take a moment to remember the patient and the steps taken in their care. This serves to anchor us in our original calling to serve and in the ultimate value of each of our patients (Bartels 2014).
- Minister to the first responders who bring patients to the hospital if they do not have a chaplain assigned to that role.
- Be part of the reunion process between patients and family members.
- Join staff in accompanying family members to view the body after a death.

The chaplain's roles after the incident

The chaplain's expertise in spiritual care can be essential to a hospital system's emotional healing and resiliency after a major incident. Chaplains know that coping and developing resiliency are subjective processes that involve relationship and time alone, silence and listening, reflecting and speaking, and formation of language and thoughts, which all need time to do their healing. The following are primary roles a chaplain may play.

Creating space for emotional and spiritual processing

- After major incidences, chaplains create space that holds people emotionally and spiritually. These contexts may include individual relationships or small processing groups. Caregivers have the opportunity to be together in silence when they lack words and to begin shifting from debriefing in the moment of the incident to beginning to give voice to their narratives.
- Major incidents can be demoralizing to healthcare workers' sense of agency. Some may feel helpless as they are on the periphery of the incident, while others in the midst of the active disaster response may feel the haunting, lingering feelings of being in proximity with violence and death. Others may feel a sense of purpose in their contributions to the effort. Through its Rounds, the Schwartz Center for Compassionate Healthcare

provides a model for 'offer[ing] an ideal forum for caregivers to process collectively the complex and challenging feelings and emotions that may arise when caring for the injured and dying in the wake of a traumatic and communal event like a bombing, a school shooting or a natural disaster' (Schwartz Center 2014).

PRACTICE EXAMPLE 15.3: SCHWARTZ ROUNDS

After the 2013 Boston Marathon Bombing, Schwartz Rounds leaders consulted with facilitators who had conducted Rounds after the 2012 Aurora, Colorado theater shooting and the 2013 Asiana Airlines crash in San Francisco. Six months after the Boston Marathon bombing, they sought to create a safe and confidential context for caregivers to:

- share their experiences and the impact of those experiences
- listen, bear witness and offer and receive support
- share coping strategies
- celebrate their strengths as individuals and as a caregiving community.

Dominant themes from the Rounds included feeling continued distress, guilt that they had not done enough, the importance of organizational support (whether it was something they received or something they lacked and yearned for), their experience of and appreciation for collaboration and teamwork. Participants shared ways they healed, from different therapies to feeling the emerging feeling of wanting to move on, to finding meaning in retrospect in the work they did with those directly affected as well as with their typical patients. Some found healing through engaging the Boston Marathon the next year, and some found strength through the resiliency of the survivors (Schwartz Center 2014).

Hospital multifaith services

Services, whether for memorializing or for garnering hope and strength, create a different sort of holding for a community that has been through trauma. Often held shortly after the incident, these services create connection while people may still be feeling the shock of the incident. Through creation of contemplative space, the use of ritual, inclusively weaving together diverse traditions, and comfort with silence, tears and cries, chaplains can play an important role of bringing healthcare workers into relationship with one another after the urgent medical caregiving has ended.

> ### PRACTICE EXAMPLE 15.4: MANCHESTER ARENA TERRORIST ATTACK
>
> After the 2017 terrorist attack at the Ariana Grande concert at the Manchester Arena, the chaplains at Burnley General and Royal Blackburn hospitals – representing the Church of England, Muslim and Catholic faiths – responded by conducting interfaith services in the hospital chapels in memory of the 22 victims, children, teenagers and parents. The service embodied diversity and solidarity, with each chaplain reading from their sacred scriptures and joining together in prayer, a moment of silence and shared grief. The chaplains' embodiment of solidarity provided hope to the filled rooms of distraught hospital employees (Magee 2017).

Providing spiritual and theological language

An aspect of spiritual distress that occurs after an incident is the loss of words and the shattering of meaning. Through providing processing groups and services, chaplains support people during these times and make space for them when they may feel at a loss.

> ### PRACTICE EXAMPLE 15.5: SANDY HOOK
>
> Monsignor Robert Weiss was the pastor of St Rose of Lima Church in Newtown, Connecticut, in December 2012 when a 20-year-old gunman attacked the Sandy Hook Elementary School, killing 20 children between the ages of six and seven years old and six adult staff. Msgr Weiss helped law enforcement officials inform parents that their child had died in the shooting. At least eight of the 20 children and six adults belonged to his parish. Msgr Weiss reflected afterwards, 'There are no words… There was a lot of hugging, a lot of crying, a lot of praying, a lot of just being silent' (Catholic Standard 2012).

In their healing processes, people begin to want language that helps them make sense of what they have been through, but may lack confidence in their own meaning-making; they feel that their faith has been broken. Or they may be specifically seeking out the bedrocks of their faith. People look to chaplains to offer spiritual language for examining their faith as they begin to articulate frameworks for their narratives and reconstruct their sense of meaning. Chaplains are trained to recognize the nuances of how to offer constructive theological language without imposing, blaming or attributing, and they are poised to provide care-receivers with building blocks for them to use in their healing process.

PRACTICE EXAMPLE 15.6: STAFF CARE

After facilitating a processing group for Danbury Hospital staff who cared for victims from the Newtown, Connecticut, shooting, Rabbi Jeffrey Silberman convened a conference call for 175 distressed rabbis across the United States. Clergy, chaplains and communities prayed around the country as their hearts broke for the children and school teachers and administrators and their families, and they turned to their faith communities and to ecumenical communities for their own support and guidance. On the call, Rabbi Silberman comforted these distressed religious leaders by telling them some of the story of Newtown and how 'the entire surrounding area – inside and outside of Newtown – has become filled with love. Love in all forms: letters, calls, gestures, visits, donations, and everything in between.' One participant in the call, Rabbi Elan S. Babchuck, from Providence, RI, drew spiritual strength from this session and was able to process the tragedy and offer comfort to others in his community through connecting it to Jewish customs of mourning and the words of Prophet Isaiah in Isaiah 60.20: 'No more will your sun set, nor your moon be darkened, for God will be an eternal light for you, and your days of mourning shall end' (Babchuck 2012).

Community relations

Any incident with mass victims and mass casualties becomes a community experience. The increase of mass shootings and hate crimes that target specific groups intensifies the already vulnerable experience. It infuses it with fear and potentially damages community relations. The unique amalgam of chaplaincy's explicit diversity and emphatic embrace of shared humanity positions chaplains to play a uniquely qualified role in community healing after these incidences.

> ### PRACTICE EXAMPLE 15.7: PEACE TREES
>
> Chaplain Heather Bumstead was the hospital chaplain at the Froedtert Campus in Milwaukee, to which survivors arrived after the August 2012 mass shooting in the Sikh temple in Oak Creek, Wisconsin. A man entered and began to shoot worshippers just as women and girls had been 'working in the kitchen to prepare a communal meal for the sharing after the second service'. Six people were killed. Bumstead was tasked to serve as a sort of ambassador from the hospital with the Sikh community. The hospital had created 'Peace Trees' – 'branches in pots, whose leaves were hundreds of ribbons with messages of peace, support and goodwill, written by staff, visitors, and even some patients from Froedtert' and Bumstead was to deliver them. Community leaders, expecting her arrival, greeted her and welcomed her in and placed the Peace Trees at the entrance to the worship area. They gave Bumstead a tour of the temple, showed her where they had already plastered over the holes and the one they left remaining. They showed her where they huddled and hid in fear. Bumstead was a chaplain to them, listening to their stories of where they had been, how they learned of the incident, their heartbreak, and how they are healing (Bumstead 2013).

What to expect in the chaplain's personal experience

A distinctive characteristic of major incidents is that the caregivers are often also directly affected by the crisis. Whether worrying about their own home flooding during Hurricane Sandy, or being on a city-wide lockdown during the immediate aftermath of the Boston Marathon bombing, or feeling a less tangible but poignant sense of one's own community being attacked, first responders and caregivers have their own personal experiences as part of the affected population. Chaplains have the additional role of being caregivers not only to identified patients and hospital staff, but to themselves.

Some self-care steps chaplains can take include the following.

Develop your own personal disaster plan

Before a disaster – in fact, today – chaplains can prepare a plan to ensure the safety of themselves, their families, homes and pets. In preparation for a storm, flood, earthquake, etc., it is recommended that everyone assemble an emergency supply kit. Some of the items which should be included are:

- a gallon of drinking water per person per day
- non-perishable, ready-to-eat canned foods and a manual can opener
- first-aid kit
- flashlights/torches/candles and matches
- battery-operated AM/FM radio and extra batteries
- childcare supplies or special care needs, as appropriate.

In addition, in the event that you might need to vacate your home, be sure to have adequate cash on hand, a full tank of gas in the car, any prescription medications, important personal documents and provisions for pet(s). Most importantly, it is essential to establish a personal emergency plan and review it with family members at the earliest possible moment once a major incident is expected. Additional information is available on the websites listed below.

Tend to your own emotional and spiritual distress

The intangible stressors – the horror of the incident, the sense of chaos and helplessness, the heartbreak at seeing friends and colleagues struggle, the uncertainty and insecurity – will surely touch the souls of chaplains. When devising care plans, chaplains should make sure they create a structure for their own self-care. A hospital chaplain who participated in the Boston Marathon Schwartz Rounds spoke of how 'chaplains would check in regularly not only with patients but also with the caregivers…we were also providing spiritual support for staff in the wake of what happened' (Schwartz Centre 2014). It was significant that this chaplain attended the Rounds not as a caregiver but as a participant and recipient of care.

Tend to your psychological needs

Whether through being directly affected or through the caregiving, chaplains can develop emotional distress beyond the hospital and chaplain support session. They might experience secondary traumatic stress, or compassion fatigue, which is 'a state experienced by those helping people in distress [that] is an extreme state of tension and preoccupation with the suffering of those being helped to the degree that it is traumatizing for the helper' (Figley 2005). It is critical that chaplains seek out professional help in order to maintain their own personal wellbeing.

Future development and research needs

- What training and support needs have become evident in the light of previous major incidents?
- Research the ways in which chaplaincies have been effective, appreciated and supportive in previous situations.
- Developing what we need in our team's 'go bag' to be prepared to be effective in this type of situation.

Summary

- It is key to know your system's policies and procedures for major incidents, and your place as chaplain within the system.
- Be prepared for times of chaos and new opportunities and methods of delivering care.
- Be ready to work with new partnering agencies in a major disaster, including law enforcement and government entities.
- Be aware of the media's needs and activities during these events.
- Know the added expectations within your facility, such as collecting patient information, caring for the surge of families arriving, connecting children and their families when separated, and even media relations.
- Have a plan for delivering bad news, including which rooms to use and the exit paths for helping bereaved families to leave.
- Prepare meaningful and timely memorials and self-care exercises for the staff (don't forget the executives) and for yourself.

Questions for reflection

- Do you know your personal and department's role in your institution's major incident plans and response?
- What might be your emotional and spiritual 'tender points' that you need to be aware of when in this type of incident?
- What emergency plan do you have for your own family?

Recommended resources

American Red Cross disaster planning guide – www.redcross.org/get-help/how-to-prepare-for-emergencies/make-a-plan. Also offered as a disaster app for smartphones.

Resources for talking to kids

National Child Traumatic Stress Network website – www.nctsnet.org/

Centers for Disease Control and Prevention, guide to helping children cope with a disaster – https://blogs.cdc.gov/publichealthmatters/2013/09/helping-children-cope-with-a-disaster

PBS: How to help kids feel safe after a tragedy – www.pbs.org/parents/talkingwithkids/news/help-kids-feel-safe.html. Tips for various ages of children (Babies & Toddlers: 0–2; Preschoolers: 3–5; School Age: 6–8; Older Kids: 9–11) – www.pbs.org/parents/talkingwithkids/news/agebyage.html.

How to Talk to Your Kids about the Orlando Shooting – http://time.com/4366400/orlando-shooting-parenting

References

Babchuck, E.S. (2012) 'Eat, Pray, Love: A Jewish Response to Tragedy.' Accessed on 24/11/2017 at http://trymyrabbi.com/current-events/eat-pray-love-a-jewish-response-to-tragedy.

Bartels, J.R. (2014) 'The pause.' *Critical Care Nurse 34*, 1, 74–75. Accessed on 24/11/2017 at http://ccn.aacnjournals.org/content/34/1/74.full.

Bumstead, H (2013) 'The Sikh Temple in Milwaukee: A personal reflection.' Torn Apart: Pastoral Care Responses to Community Violence. *Caring Connections 10*, 3, 11–14. Accessed on 24/11/2017 at www.lutheranservices.org/sites/default/files/images/pdfs-CaringConnections/CaringConnections_vol10no3_2013_Final.pdf.

Catholic Standard (2012) '"No words" can describe shock, sadness after shooting, says priest.' 18 December 2012. Accessed on 24/11/2017 at www.cathstan.org/Content/News/News/Article/-No-words-can-describe-shock-sadness-after-shooting-says-priest/2/2/5426.

Figley, C.R. (2005) 'Compassion Fatigue: An Expert Interview.' *Medscape*. Accessed on 24 November 2017 at www.medscape.com/viewarticle/513615.

Magee, J. (2017) 'Hospitals come together to remember Manchester bombing victims.' *The Clitheroe Advertiser and Times*. Accessed on 24/11/2017 at www.clitheroeadvertiser.co.uk/news/hospitals-come-together-to-remember-manchester-bombing-victims-1-8573329.

Schwartz Center (2014) *Using Schwartz Center Rounds® to Help a Community Recover After Tragedy. A Case Study: The Boston Marathon Bombings*. White Paper, July 2014. Boston, MA: The Schwartz Center for Compassionate Healthcare. Accessed on 24/11/2017 at www.theschwartzcenter.org/media/81BIRIK40MBJ72N.pdf.

Chapter 16
Palliative and End-of-Life Care
M. Karen Ballard

PRACTICE EXAMPLE 16.1: WHAT IS HEAVEN LIKE?

'What is heaven like, Chaplain Karen?' the 12-year-old with progressive ependymoma asked me frantically. 'Mom, it's not fair,' she continued to lament desperately. 'I've never kissed a boy; I've never even been on a date. I'll never go to the prom or get married. My little sister won't remember me!'

There are no answers to such questions, so I usually know better than to attempt it. This conversation, however, was different. She was screaming the questions at her mom and me, so we tried to bring some comfort and peace with the answers she sought. 'She'll remember you because of all the pictures we have,' her mom offered. 'I don't want to be a picture; I want her to remember ME!' When heaven was mentioned, she responded, 'But how do you know it's REAL?'

The goal of pediatric palliative care (PPC) is to 'improve the quality of life of patients and their families who are facing problems associated with life-threatening illness, whether physical, psychosocial or spiritual' (World Health Organization 2015). It is an active approach to care for children and young people that 'includes the management of distressing symptoms, provision of respite, and care through death and bereavement' (Association for Children with Life-Threatening or Terminal Conditions and Their Families and the Royal College of Paediatrics and Child Health 1997).

The essence of the role of a PPC chaplain is to be present to the anguish and witness to the distress; to attempt to provide a healing presence so that one is not alone in shouting and crying and cursing the questions for which there are no answers. Chaplains and others create a healing presence by cleansing their hearts and minds of other thoughts and experiences and by being fully present to the patient/family before them.

PRACTICE EXAMPLE 16.2: CHRISTMAS IN AUGUST

It is Tuesday. It's James's birthday. There are cup cakes with the face of a fox on them. A big birthday cake. Chips, biscuits, slices, and fairy bread. I make the fairy bread. A number of the young nurses haven't made fairy bread; it's the thing mums and dads do. Simple really. Butter the bread, sprinkle the hundreds and thousands on a plate, press the buttered side of the bread on to the coloured sugar spheres and cut the bread in quarters. Aren't you going to cut the crust off? Hell no, says one of the male nurses, that's what you hold it by! I carry the fairy bread out to the table by the bed and am reminded of another offering of bread to remember a significant event a long time ago. I think we call it sacrament.

It's Tuesday, its James's birthday, he is nine months old. James has a big brother. Jack has only ever seen his brother in hospital. With tubes, without them. With machines, without them. Jack does all the things a big four-year-old brother does. Hugs, kisses, questions, boredom. This birthday is a machine day. James's mum is devoted to him. She is quiet, attentive, gentle and stoic. She gets to cuddle James some days when he is well enough. His dad is more outgoing, chatting, engaging, and always wearing an English rugby top. One of the things he talks about is rugby, a conversation somewhat foreign in South Australia. The conversation about James is limited, a good day, a bad day, a better day... James was born broken; he won't be playing rugby. Multiple and complex issues, the docs say knowingly. More simply, his hydraulics and pneumatics are not very good. Heart surgery has helped the first. But he is growing too big for his breathing bits that can't be fixed and he is needing more and more help from the doctors. They have had those 'difficult conversations' with the parents.

It was a long party, as they are in intensive care units, because of course all shifts have to be part of it. The message went out to the night shift team: don't bring anything for nibbles tonight, there is plenty. And there was. It's Tuesday, it's James's birthday, he is nine months old, and we had a party. It will be Christmas on Thursday. It will be James's only Christmas. It is August.

The Revd Carl Aiken, Chaplain, Women's and
Children's Hospital, North Adelaide, Australia

Spiritual care as a domain for palliative care

People of faith have been instrumental from the beginning in establishing and developing the modern hospice and palliative care movement. Cecily Saunders, considered the founder of hospice and palliative care, solidified the role of spiritual care when she identified 'total pain' in the life of a dying patient as including physical, spiritual, psychological and social pain. Illness and dying create questions of meaning, purpose and hope in which the search for answers is a spiritual journey made by the patient and the family and others who love them (Puchalski and Ferrell 2010, p.3).

'Spiritual, Religious and Existential Aspects of Care' is domain #5 in both the National Consensus Project of Quality Palliative Care Guidelines developed in 2004 (revised 2013) and the National Quality Forum developed in 2006. The domain calls for:

- assessing and responding to spiritual, religious and existential concerns which are used to formulate part of the palliative care plan, ongoing assessment and documentation of the concerns

- addressing and documenting spiritual/existential care needs, goals and concerns and support offered for those issues consistent with the patient or family's cultural and religious values

- providing rituals or practices as desired by patient and family, especially at the time of death

- providing specialized palliative and hospice spiritual care professionals who will partner with the patient/family's faith leader.

(Puchalski and Ferrell 2010, pp.17–19)

In the UK, the National Institute for Health and Care Excellence (NICE), the definitive guidelines group, recommends that spiritual and religious beliefs and values are significant in end-of-life pediatric care (NICE 2016). Together for Short Lives (2013), a leading UK charity in the palliative care field, have also developed a core care pathway which integrates spiritual and religious dimensions in all aspects of palliative care.

The chaplain as member of the team

The needs of children with life-threatening illness and their families are best supported by a dedicated interdisciplinary specialty team offering support for physical, psychosocial, emotional, practical and spiritual needs (American Academy of Pediatrics 2013).

While spiritual care is the primary function of the chaplain who is trained and certified in its provision, all members of the interdisciplinary team may participate in offering spiritual care by 'being a compassionate presence, doing a spiritual history and integrating spirituality in the treatment plan' (Puchalski and Ferrell 2010, p.61). In addition to assessing spiritual needs, developing a spiritual care plan and offering ongoing support to the patient and family, the chaplain may:

- seek to relieve spiritual suffering
- play a key role in improving family–team communication about goals of care
- discuss with patient or family their greatest fears and hopes, thus providing information that can be helpful to the team as they have conversations regarding goals of care and end of life
- interpret for the team the families' cultural and religious beliefs, assisting the team in understanding parents' decisions, goals, priorities and values
- offer the team care to enhance resilience
- train team members in the practice of spiritual care and encourage team members to offer spiritual care to the level of their expertise or comfort.

(Fitchett *et al.* 2011)

When working with members of the psychosocial team, there can be a challenge of role overlap or distinction. In addressing this potential overlap, one must recognize and honor that each discipline approaches the same spiritual crisis with a different lens based upon training. For instance, if it is a grief crisis, the chaplain may look for sources of comfort from the griever's belief system or values; the social worker may offer help with the impact on activities of daily living; the bereavement coordinator may help the griever integrate the grief into the context of his/her life journey; the psychologist may encourage ways of coping and assess for depression or anxiety; the child life specialist may seek to normalize the experience for the griever – the same grief but different approaches to care.

Caring for the patient

When a patient/family is referred to palliative care, the chaplain should be included in the consult for an initial spiritual assessment. The chaplain will provide spiritual support throughout the patient's enrolment and even into the family's bereavement. This support is a continuum of care with visits from inpatient to clinic to home settings as resources allow.

When a patient/family presents acutely because of the sudden onset of illness or injury, the crisis requires the chaplain to establish a caring relationship quickly, complete a spiritual assessment and offer appropriate spiritual support. With the family in such shock and grief, it is often difficult to ask the specific questions needed to determine the appropriate support. In these situations, the chaplain's non-anxious presence and skills are applied in order to ascertain the support and rituals that will be meaningful.

When the situation with the patient is chronic and long-term, the chaplain may have the privilege of knowing the patient/family for months or even years. Multiple opportunities to visit, whether in the hospital or at home, give the chaplain insight into the beliefs, values and system of relationships of the patient/family and opportunity to provide care based upon that knowledge.

End-of-life care can be the holiest of times for a chaplain as we journey with a child/adolescent/young adult and their family. Processing the thoughts and emotions of making that journey demands the ultimate presence of peace and hope from the chaplain and all others who share such conversations. The chaplain must be comfortable with the mystery of death and with assuring the thoughts and hopes that patients and parents have about what comes after death. Having the opportunity to offer rituals, religious or non-religious, that are created in the moment for the particular patient/family can bring a sense of wholeness and peace. Creating space where the mystery of death can be experienced with a sense of reverence and awe is the particular domain of the chaplain. The chaplain is uniquely skilled in creating this sacred space whether or not the family is religious.

PRACTICE EXAMPLE 16.3: MEDIATING KIRSTY'S WISHES

Kirsty was a 19-year-old woman who had been fighting ganglioneuroblastoma for half of her young life. Kirsty was well grounded in her Christian faith and had a wonderful support system of family, friends and her faith community. Upon our first meeting, Kirsty told me very politely that she already had a pastor. Still I endeavored to journey alongside her. The role of the hospital chaplain is different from that of a parish pastor, and I knew there would be opportunities for that to be evident. As time passed, we formed a strong and trusting relationship as I became one who lived in both of her worlds. In my role as a faith leader, Kirsty and her family could talk openly about their faith, hopes, prayers and spiritual struggles. As a member of the health care team, I could be present in times of tremendous suffering as an ambassador of comfort and peace.

Even while Kirsty's body was succumbing to the ravages of her persistent cancer, her mind and spirit were as strong as ever. She and her family continued to pray for miraculous healing, even as they prepared for their final goodbyes. As she neared her end of life, conflict arose as the medical team wanted to discuss what she wanted, and Kirsty, who knew the reality of her pending death, resisted conversations about her wishes. She became quite emotional and angry as again and again the questions were raised by the physicians. It was at this point that the team called upon the chaplain. Kirsty agreed to talk to me, and utilizing the 'Voicing My Choices' (Aging with Dignity 2012) planning guide as well as specific questions from her physicians, we were able to work together and alleviate distress for both the patient and medical team. Additionally, the completion of the planning guide was very helpful to Kirsty's family and pastors when the time came to plan her memorial service.

End-of-life care and decision-making can be very stressful for all parties involved. While the medical team wanted to ensure preservation of dignity and humanity for the patient, Kirsty wanted to live each day she had without dwelling on its ending. I was grateful to be trusted enough by both sides to help in this delicate situation.

Matthew Tweddle, Oncology Chaplain, Akron Children's Hospital, Ohio, USA

Caring for the family

Being a parent carries many assumed responsibilities: caring for the child, protecting the child, providing for the child, raising the child to a level of independence. All of those responsibilities are knocked asunder when a chronic/complex/life-threatening condition takes over the world of the child and parent. Issues of grief, guilt, anger and helplessness are experienced by the parent in levels I believe to be unequalled in other relationships.

It is important for the chaplain to determine how parents cope in the midst of a diagnosis of a chronic/complex/life-threatening condition for their child/children. Such an assessment will assist the chaplain in offering appropriate spiritual care and supporting the beliefs and traditions to which the family adheres.

PRACTICE EXAMPLE 16.4: PRAYING TOGETHER

After traveling throughout the world in search of a cure, a 14-year-old boy with a large tumor on his neck arrived at my hospital for treatment. Unfortunately, our medical team had no treatments to offer. As I spoke to the family, they expressed anger with G-D for taking their only son. The father was so hurt that he deserted the mother and child.

I visited them on a regular basis and each time the mother would leave the room and stand outside the door appearing to be very angry. The boy and I would speak about things important to a teenager – girls, sports and life in general – and after each encounter we would pray together. During one visit he became very serious and said, 'Chaplain, I am dying. I can't stand the pain, but I don't want a lot of morphine, because it affects my thinking. I want to be able to make my declaration of faith ('There is no G-D but one and Muhammad is his Prophet') before I die, so that I can go to Paradise. Please help my mother regain her faith in G-D so I can meet her in Paradise.'

Because of his concern for his mother's wellbeing, we began to speak louder so she could hear our conversations. Eventually, she stayed in the room but did not pray with us. On the next visit when we started to pray she raised her hands a little but still did not pray. It wasn't until the following visit that she raised her hands and prayed with us. The boy and I made eye contact, and I saw someone who was healed and happy. A few days later, he died. A month later his mother called from Yemen to say, 'Thank you, Imam. When everyone left me – my husband, the doctors and nurses – you stayed, and now I go to the Masjid and make my prayers and do all the things I did before.'

Imam Yusuf Hassan, Chaplain, HealthCare
Chaplaincy network, New York, USA

The chaplain's role becomes paramount whenever a family speaks of miracles or healing as these concepts are often laden with religious overtones. It is an opportunity to sensitively discuss with families their hopes and goals for the child and to determine their meaning of the concepts. This may mean 'reframing hope, affirming divine agency, or re-defining healing' when the family is praying for a miracle or trusting in faith healing (Hess 2013, pp.188–189). Some families cling to their hope of a miracle as a means of coping with the fear of losing their child, and yet they can hear and trust the medical team's judgment about prognosis and decision-making. When their hope is based in their faith, most often they are able to reframe how the miracle or healing will occur for their child as they begin to express hope in their child's life after death. It becomes a delicate dance for the chaplain and the palliative care team if the family persists in their assertion that a miracle of healing will occur. Continued attempts to explain the reality of the situation from the medical point of view may cause mistrust and suspicion on the part of the family. Doing a careful assessment to understand the family's beliefs, asking families to share experiences of healing and providing non-judgmental listening as they share their beliefs and experiences, inviting their clergy or faith healers into family meetings to offer prayer and the team participating in faith healing prayer services may foster a climate of collaboration and trust and not a breakdown in communication (Hess 2013, pp.188–189). Following the family's lead in this regard will, no doubt, add time to the trajectory and possibly the resolution of the case, but may avoid negative feelings and judgment on the part of both family and staff.

The chaplain plays an important role in communication within the family and between family and the medical team. The chaplain can provide a spiritual presence as the parents reflect on what they have heard, consider different options and struggle with the often harsh realities of their child's condition. The chaplain can ask clarifying questions that can assist the parents in making decisions.

Caring for the team

Working with children with complex medical needs and their families is a source of profound satisfaction, renewal and affirmation (Rushton and Ballard 2011, p.309), but it also challenges one's wellbeing. Professionally, the PPC team is called upon to care for patients and families facing the most challenging situations medically, socially, emotionally and spiritually. The team seeks to assist the family in achieving wholeness and meaning in their lives despite the extreme challenges of an ever-changing medical situation. Beyond the application of professional skill and training, this work demands that the team offer their humanity in order to form deep and meaningful connections. Personally, individual team members are called upon to find ways to replenish themselves in all the same domains. Failure to do so may lead to diminished wellbeing.

Team care is a standard of practice for the certified chaplain (Association of Professional Chaplains 2015). Given the challenge to a team member's wellbeing, it is imperative that chaplains offer support and use their skills to assist individual team members, as well as the team as a whole, through:

- reflecting upon the questions of transcendence
- acknowledging the experiences of suffering
- transforming suffering by creating meaning
- developing forums for discussion and reflection
- creating an environment of respect for patients, families and caregivers
- fostering respectful communication, decision-making and conflict resolution
- creating mechanisms for acknowledging and processing grief and loss
- developing self-care practices
- and cultivating healthy boundaries.

(Rushton and Ballard 2011, pp.329–336)

Equally important is the chaplain's self-care. The calling to pediatric palliative care chaplaincy is the grounding that will enable one to thrive in this intense work. One must, however, be intentional about strategies for reflection and renewal in order to survive and maintain the resources to care for all the others dependent upon the chaplain. Many of the strategies used by any spiritual caregiver work for the palliative care chaplain: prayer, meditation, yoga, journaling, exercise, etc. There are, however, two strategies that I would suggest are absolutely vital for the palliative care chaplain. One is to identify someone (for me, it is the psychologist on our team) who can provide support through regular debriefings and reflection and call you to accountability in caring for yourself. The other important strategy is to memorialize each death and bring closure for yourself. Such memorializing may be lighting a candle or planting a flower or taking a few minutes of reflection in memory of the child or attending the funeral.

Future developments and research needs

Opportunities abound for the chaplain on a PPC team. The needs for growth and development include:

- an increase in dedicated chaplains for PPC teams
- an appropriate, validated spiritual assessment tool for children and research in all areas of PPC chaplaincy to define and measure best practices
- resources for chaplains to offer virtual spiritual support for isolated and/or far-flung families.

Summary

With the recognition of the spiritual care domain, chaplains are valued members in palliative care and hospice settings. The challenge, however, is funding for adequate positions to meet the demands of an institution's census. For those chaplains fortunate enough to have these cherished positions, the work offers great fulfilment and satisfaction.

Questions for reflection

- From breaking bad news through to bereavement care, how can you contribute to a family's palliative journey?
- Are there any areas where chaplaincy might be more integrated into your institution's palliative care structures, policies and practices? What might you be able to do about it?
- How have you theologically prepared to support a dying child and their family? What conclusions did you come to? How resilient do you feel?

References

Aging with Dignity (2012) *Voicing My Choices: A Planning Guide for Adolescents and Young Adults.* Talahassee, FL: Aging with Dignity.

American Academy of Pediatrics (2013) *Pediatric Palliative Care and Hospice Care Commitments, Guidelines, and Recommendations.* Accessed on 14/11/2017 at www.pediatrics.org/cgi/doi/10.1542/peds.2013-2731.

Association for Children with Life-Threatening or Terminal Conditions and Their Families and the Royal College of Paediatrics and Child Health (1997) *A Guide to the Development of Children's Palliative Care Services.* London: RCPCH.

Association of Professional Chaplains (2015) *Standards of Practice for Professional Chaplains.* Accessed on 22/11/2017 at www.professionalchaplains.org/content.asp?pl=200&sl=198&contentid=514.

Fitchett, G., Lyndes, K., Cadge, W., Berlinger, N., Flanagan, E. and Misasi, J. (2011) 'The role of professional chaplains on pediatric palliative care teams: Perspectives from physicians and chaplains.' *Journal of Palliative Medicine 14*, 6, 704–707.

Hess, D. (2013) 'Faith healing and the palliative care team.' *Journal of Social Work in End-of-Life & Palliative Care 9*, 2–3, 180–190.

National Consensus Project for Hospice and Palliative Care (2013) *The National Consensus Project Clinical Practice Guidelines for Quality Palliative Care*, 3rd edition. Accessed on 24/11/2017 at www.nationalcoalitionhpc.org/ncp-guidelines-2013.

National Quality Forum (2006) *A National Framework and Preferred Practices for Palliative and Hospice Care Quality.* Washington, DC: National Quality Forum.

National Institute for Health and Care Excellence (2016) 'End of life care for infants, children and young people with life-limiting conditions: planning and management.' Accessed on 24/11/2017 at www.nice.org.uk/guidance/ng61/chapter/Recommendations.

Puchalski, C. and Ferrell, B. (2010) *Making Health Care Whole.* Philadelphia, PA: Templeton Press.

Rushton, C. and Ballard, M. (2011) 'The Other Side of Caring: Caregiver Suffering.' In B. Carter, M. Levetown and S. Friebert (eds) *Palliative Care for Infants, Children, and Adolescents: A Practical Handbook.* Baltimore, MD: The Johns Hopkins University Press.

Together for Short Lives (2013) *A Core Care Pathway for Children with Life-limiting and Life-threatening Conditions*, 3rd edition. Accessed on 24/11/2017 at www.togetherforshortlives.org.uk/assets/0000/4121/TfSL_A_Core_Care_Pathway__ONLINE_.pdf.

World Health Organization (2015) 'Palliative Care.' Accessed on 14/11/2017 at www.who.int/mediacentre/factsheets/fs402/en.

Chapter 17

Bereavement Care

Edina Farkas and Stephen Harrison

> PRACTICE EXAMPLE 17.1: ANNIVERSARY LAMENT
>
> 'August 2 will be the first anniversary of S's passing away…but the pain has not become less to this day. We have been trying so many things but nothing really helps. I don't know for how long it will hurt this much. Each day I comfort myself by telling myself that for him this is good, that he does not feel any pain any more… but for me it is terribly, almost unbearably painful… Almost a year has passed and we still don't know how to continue…what makes life worth living without S? Each day we go to the cemetery, that's where we find some peace. Almost each time we tell ourselves that we hope to get into our grave too, as soon as possible, and to finally find relief, finally find peace…to finally be with our son again… Pastor Edina! Tell me what to do! What will soothe the pain? … If God truly exists, why does God allow all this suffering? What did these children do to deserve this?'
>
> *The Revd Dr Edina Farkas, Pediatric Chaplain, Velkey László Center for Child Health, Miskolc, Hungary*

While medical care ends when a paediatric patient dies, spiritual and emotional care needs to continue. Many families struggle with the hopelessness, pain and doubt this mother describes for many months or years after losing their child. Bereavement care starts long before death happens. It starts by getting to know the family and the child, and building rapport with them. It continues by following them through medical procedures, the ups and downs of life in the hospital, then receiving the news of the child's impending death. It may include witnessing the moment of the child's death. All these shared experiences provide a foundation for bereavement care after death occurs. Literature lists the advantages of having the same mental health professional provide care for the family from the time diagnosis is given through to the time death occurs (Nyirő *et al.* 2017, p.1180). Families are more open to bereavement care offered by a professional who is involved in the work of the team with the child before the child's life ends. Families form a strong bond with staff who meet their child alive (O'Malley, Barata and Snow 2014, p.e320). As a mother told me once: 'We like our new parish minister, too…but you knew our daughter.'

Hospital chaplains are in the unique role of being able to offer this continuum. According to a survey, chaplains take part in handling all end-of-life situations in the paediatric hospitals of the USA (Thienprayoon, Campbell and Winick 2015, p.49). In the vast majority of these hospitals, providing resources for the bereaved is primarily the responsibility of the pastoral care department (Thienprayoon *et al.* 2015, p.51). Some chaplaincy teams may use the term bereavement care pathway to describe this (see Nash 2013, for example). This chapter will outline some of the ways chaplains may fulfil their unique role in providing spiritual care when a child dies or in the time leading up to their death.

PRACTICE EXAMPLE 17.2: A WEDDING

A more surprising aspect of the work of a hospice chaplain may be to conduct or at least arrange a wedding. Louise and Richard, for example, wanted to get married but felt this was not possible for them. They wanted their sick child, Ella, to be present but needed somebody to look after her. Eventually, we arranged that on an occasion that they were in for respite care they could get married at the local registry office, and a nurse could be present to look after Ella. There would be a blessing of the marriage and a celebration with cake and champagne at the hospice. The presence of the chaplain enabled the conversation to take place and for them to be part of the ritual by blessing the marriage.

The Revd Stephen Harrison, Baptist Minister, former Chaplain,
Helen and Douglas House Hospice, Oxford, UK

Presence

The literature finds presence essential to a chaplain's work (Nuzum, Meaney and O'Donoghue 2016, pp.197–198). In the same study, chaplains describe being present in paediatric end-of-life situations as offering empathetic companionship and holding ceremonies. Presence is defined as bringing peace into a crisis situation, helping to carry someone else's emotional burden and providing space for the expression of feelings; in the case of children, presence is often a physical connection (Farkas 2017, p.10).

> ### PRACTICE EXAMPLE 17.3: PRESENCE AND THE HOSPICE CHAPLAIN
>
> There is a saying, 'don't just sit there, do something', but this needs to be turned on its head for chaplains: 'don't just do something, but sit there'. Torry says: 'we see very clearly that spiritual care is not finally about doing something; it is much more about being, and at that moment it is about being there where the awfulness is happening' (2006, p.179). Presence is a common thread running through all my work at Helen and Douglas House. It is about the family and what they need at a very difficult time. All that is required of the chaplain is presence and a listening ear. I see my role as talking to families about whatever they want or need to at that time, be that football or the death of their child. As Feldstein (2011, p.159) suggests:
>
>> Within each of us, there is a human longing for meaningful connection. We help alleviate suffering when we create the conditions for connection with each other and what we hold sacred. The depth of that connection is made possible by our willingness to be authentic and by focusing on the quality of presence, and the attention and intention we bring to each other.
>
> Ultimately, what presence offers is time and space to be and for connections to be made. These connections facilitate spiritual care, as Pulchalski (2006, pp.39–40) argues:
>
>> The basis of spiritual care is the connection we, the caregivers, form with the dying and their loved ones through the process of illness and death... Spiritual care is the practice of compassionate presence. It is the ability to love... It is the act of sitting with the ill and dying in moments of deep and profound sadness and grief, sharing the pain with them... It is the ability to be fully present – physically, emotionally, and spiritually – with a person in the midst of his or her pain.

> In my time as a chaplain at Helen and Douglas House, these words have fundamentally informed my practice. The hospice is for those children and young adults who have life-limiting and life-shortening conditions, and it would be true to say that much of my time is spent with parents sitting sharing the pain with them. Time with the children is normally spent playing with them or looking after them. Arguably, this also has an element of being with them and offering good spiritual care indirectly, as I also spend time on shift working with the care teams.
>
> *The Revd Stephen Harrison, Baptist Minister, former Chaplain, Helen and Douglas House Hospice, Oxford, UK*

Ritualized presence: funerals

Experience indicates that there is an important role for chaplains after death. Many of the parents are young and have no previous experience of arranging a funeral. They find invaluable the help that a chaplain can offer in guiding them through the process as well as actually officiating at the service. One mother commented that it made it 'something I could cope with and remember fondly', while another said that it 'made a terrible time a little easier'. So what may appear to be simply a practical way of helping in reality can and does have significant impact. It helps families cope in the extremity of grief and creates memories which later bring much-needed comfort.

Ritualized presence: creating memories and memorials

As a part of palliative and end-of-life care, advance care planning may have taken place and remembrance artefacts could have been discussed. This can include such things as taking handprints, footprints, locks of hair, end-of-life blessings and any rites of passage that are associated with death. This reinforces the importance of continuity of care by chaplains. Days of remembrance play an important part in the grieving process for families. The chaplain has an important role not simply in leading the service, whether religious or non-religious, but in holding people's grief in that time and also being present in the time before and after the service. This time offers a shelter in a world that does not feel as it should and helps families continue living in that world on a daily basis. The chaplain's presence is one element in enabling this to happen. Remembrance days act as a safety valve, meeting an almost physical need to share what they are thinking and feeling. Other teams send either religious or spiritual condolence cards, gift booklets for parents and siblings, anniversary cards, first Christmas letters, and make follow-up telephone calls. Memorial events may also be spiritual rather than religious and can include walks, picnics, planting ceremonies, balloon/dove/butterfly releases (although there are ethical issues related to such activities). Many institutions have books of remembrance where families can have the name of their child inscribed.

PRACTICE EXAMPLE 17.4: COMMON BURIALS

Responding to a need to provide a dignified burial for stillborn fetuses, fetal remains and products of conception under 20 weeks' gestation, a monthly Common Burial provides an opportunity for families to complete the holistic nature of grief: the visitation is the social release of the body, the funeral/graveside service is the spiritual release of the body, and the burial is the physical release of the body. A local cemetery has provided burial sites and the spiritual care department has provided a graveside service for over 25 years at these burial sites. A local Threads of Love volunteer group provides satin-lined caskets for these burials. Patients/families are given a Common Burial card after delivery so that they know immediately when their child will be buried, if they opt for the Common Burial service. Families are consistently grateful for the opportunity to honor their child, hear their child's name being proclaimed in the service, and to have a site to return to for visitation.

Mary D. Davis, Regional Director, Spiritual Care and Education, CHRISTUS Santa Rosa Health System, San Antonio, Texas, USA

Another powerful way of remembering is by creating memories. Literature emphasizes the importance of mementos in grief work (Pilling 2003, p.162). The significance of memories comes from the parents' need for a continued connection with their child even after death (Meert, Thurston and Briller 2005, p.422). For many, gravesites can be places of remembrance and healing.

> **PRACTICE EXAMPLE 17.5: CREATING ARTEFACTS**
>
> It can be helpful to have an object prepared by the child nearing death or by the parents facing the loss of their daughter or son. Children and teenagers often respond positively when I invite them to decorate a picture frame, in which a photo can be placed. At times, parents sit quietly by the bedside of their dying child for days. Engaging them in an art activity of creating a memory can ease the heaviness of waiting, give purpose to the time spent and allow for an expression of feelings. Whether it is the patient or the family who creates the frame, the activity provides an opportunity for life review, which is an important part of saying goodbye (Garros 2003, pp.249–250). Other objects that are useful are cards made by a family member or the chaplain for the child and baseball hats decorated by the teen facing death. The idea is to create something resembling their loved one that will stay with the family after he or she passes.
>
> *The Revd Dr Edina Farkas, Pediatric Chaplain, Velkey László Center for Child Health, Miskolc, Hungary*

Drawing on faith

'We know that we could bear all these trials only with God's help. God gave us strength and relief. We see things in life differently now. We have learned that difficulties and problems can be solved sooner or later' (parents of a preschool-age boy, who died of a brain tumour).

Dying is not merely a physical but ultimately a spiritual experience (Balboni and Peteet 2017, p.47), and, as such, it raises fundamental questions about life that can often be addressed through the lenses of faith. Discussing the impact of grief on Christian faith, a well-known Hungarian pastor and grief counsellor, Sára Bodó, argues that grief cannot be separated from faith (Bodó 2013, pp.78–82). She claims that grief triggers a crisis in one's faith, in a sense that it forces one to plead with God for answers. She sees Christian faith as a particular support for the bereaved, as it enables one to step out of one's inner loneliness created by the loss and stay in communication with God even in the midst of one's deepest crisis of faith. In this relationship with God, the grieving person can experience God's empathetic, listening and counselling presence. Staying in relationship with God can help the bereaved accept and find meaning in the loss on the basis of trust. This trust transforms the question of crisis, asking why the loss happened, into the question of faith, asking where it fits in God's order. I find prayer a useful tool in the chaplain's hand to voice the grieving family's questions to God, which often they are unable to do themselves. Asking them what prayer requests they have reveals much about their faith and the stage they are at in their grief journey, and gives them an active role in the prayer, even if it is offered by the chaplain. At times, it is more appropriate to bless the dying child, saying only a one-sentence prayer. Studies also find that the opportunity for prayer is a crucial need for most parents in coping with losing their child (Meert *et al.* 2005, p.423; Robinson *et al.* 2006, p.e721). In my ministry, I often provide prayer blankets. These can be a tangible symbol of prayer, as they are made by church members with prayers for the sick children who will receive them. Although the blanket makers do not know the child the blanket is presented to, most families are very touched by learning that someone prayed for their child and cherish the blanket for many years.

> PRACTICE EXAMPLE 17.6: IN GOD'S EMBRACE
>
> I gave a prayer blanket to the parents of a toddler who was dying. I explained that it was made with prayers for their son and expressed my wish that when they cover him with it, they remember that God covers him with God's love the same way. Mom put the blanket on this little boy right away. Two days later he died. After the funeral, Mom called me and said: 'Edina, he was buried in the blanket you gave us, because you told us it was like God hugging him. I wanted to bury him in God's embrace.'

Being a team member

> When we lose a little patient, we also die a bit. We know we shouldn't but we are also only people. We nurse and heal every given day and still we cannot help everyone. Unfortunately, this is difficult to accept and process. (Paediatric nurse)
>
> When I stand before God, I will have to give an account of this child, too. There are one or two more of these children God will hold me accountable for… And no matter if I do a hundred good deeds, those won't make up for the three bad ones. (Paediatric doctor)

The medical staff often find it very hard to get in touch with their feelings and give words to their sorrow when they lose a little patient. Being a team member often means providing the staff with opportunities to process our common loss. This can happen plainly through listening to what they have to say or helping them express their love for the child in a non-medical way. For example, they can decorate a T-shirt together for a chronically ill patient they have been serving for many years or they can choose to create the page of the deceased child closest to their heart in our memory book. They are also invited to write about their experience to be read anonymously at our annual memorial service.

Chaplains are also called to be team members in their communities. Local churches can offer support for families that hospital chaplaincy alone cannot provide. They can offer prayer support for hospital ministry, make prayer blankets for the seriously ill children and welcome the grieving families after they leave the hospital. Research also points out the importance of community clergy in offering a continuity of care for bereaved families (Robinson *et al.* 2006, p.e724). Once I had the privilege to introduce a couple grieving the loss of their daughter to their new parish minister. Talking with the parents and the pastor separately first, then having a joint meeting where they could each raise questions and concerns, resulted in a good relationship built between them, in which the minister can continue to offer the support I do not have the capacity to provide.

Future developments and research needs

- Developing greater continuity of care for dying paediatric patients and their families both within the hospital and in their local community.

- Researching the efficacy of different interventions and activities in bereavement care.

- Seeking more ways to build connections with local faith communities that can benefit both the faith community and hospital chaplaincy.

Summary

Offering bereavement care to those losing a child (whether family or a medical staff member) is perhaps the most difficult but also the most beautiful part of a hospital chaplain's ministry. Although paediatric death is extremely painful to face, the chaplain's ability to be present through offering time, space, connections and rituals, the chaplain's creativity in providing opportunities to remember, the chaplain's assistance in drawing on one's spiritual resources and the chaplain's willingness to be the bridge between grieving families and their local faith communities can greatly contribute to making the unbearable bearable. Until, finally, new life can grow from death. And seeing that is beautiful.

Questions for reflection

- What does 'presence' mean for you?
- What tools do you use to help families in crisis to connect with their spiritual resources?
- How can you enhance the continuity of care in your context?

References

Balboni, M. and Peteet, J.R. (2017) *Spirituality and Religion within the Culture of Medicine.* New York, NY: Oxford University Press.

Bodó, S. (2013) *Gyászidőben* (In Times of Grief). Budapest: Kálvin Kiadó.

Farkas, E. (2017) 'Spiritual guidance of patients, families and medical staff during paediatric end of life care.' *Health and Social Care Chaplaincy 5*, 1, 9–15.

Feldstein, B.D. (2011) 'Bridging with the sacred: Reflections of an MD chaplain.' *Journal of Pain and Symptom Management 42*, 1, 155–161.

Garros, D. (2003) 'A "good" death in the pediatric ICU: Is it possible?' *Jornal de Pediatria 79*, S243–254.

Meert, K.L., Thurston, C.S. and Briller, H. (2005) 'The spiritual needs of parents at the time of their child's death in the pediatric intensive care unit and during bereavement: A qualitative study.' *Pediatric Critical Care Medicine 6*, 4, 420–427.

Nash, P. (2013) 'Birmingham Children's Hospital: Paediatric end of life care and bereavement pathway.' In P. Gilbert (ed.) *Spirituality and End of Life Care.* Brighton: Pavilion.

Nuzum, D., Meaney, S. and O'Donoghue, K. (2016) 'The provision of spiritual and pastoral care following stillbirth in Ireland: A mixed methods study.' *BMJ Supportive & Palliative Care 6*, 2, 194–200.

Nyirő, J., Hauser, P., Zörgő, Sz. & Hegedűs, K. (2017) 'Difficulties in communication with parents of paediatric cancer patients during the transition to palliative care.' *Orvosi Hetilap 158*, 30, 1175–1181.

O'Malley, P., Barata, I. and Snow, S. (2014) 'Death of a child in the emergency department.' *Pediatrics 134*, 1, e313–330.

Pilling, J. (ed.) (2003) *Gyász* (Grief). Budapest: Medicina Könyvkiadó Rt.

Puchalski, C.M. (2006) *A Time for Listening and Caring.* New York, NY: Oxford University Press.

Robinson, M.R., Thiel, M.M., Backus, M.M. and Meyer, E.C. (2006) 'Matters of spirituality at the end of life in the pediatric intensive care unit.' *Pediatrics 118*, 3, e719–729.

Thienprayoon, R., Campbell, R. and Winick, N. (2015) 'Attitudes and practices in the bereavement care offered by children's hospitals: A survey of the Pediatric Chaplains Network.' *OMEGA – Journal of Death and Dying 71*, 1, 48–59.

Torry, M. (ed.) (2006) *Diverse Gifts.* Norwich: Canterbury Press.

Chapter 18

Transition: Journeying with Pediatric Patients into Adult Care
The Chaplain's Role
Kobena Charm

Introduction

Providing effective spiritual care to pediatric patients requires patience, skill, empathy and compassion in the best of situations. There are added challenges for a chaplain and the interdisciplinary team as they journey with a patient who is transitioning from pediatric care to adult care. These skills are applicable to many chronic diseases, but this will focus on patients who have been diagnosed with chronic or end-stage kidney disease and cystic fibrosis. In this chapter we will discuss the concerns and circumstances of patients we have worked with, examples of cases and ways in which a chaplain may help in the challenging transition from pediatric to adult medical care.

From the outset we must consider the medical, emotional and physical challenges that patients diagnosed with life-limiting, chronic diseases face. Cecil L. Betz asserts that adolescents with health and disability needs face numerous challenges that require understanding, multi-pronged approaches and unique resources to help them transition to adult facilities and care (Betz 1998, pp.97–115). Some pediatric patients struggle with complying with their treatment protocols, which dictate that they take medicines at specific times and in exact dosages. Some have difficulties with dietary restrictions, making them feel deprived of the things that family and peers easily enjoy. Others grapple with keeping medical appointments, even in the most critical cases such as for organ transplant recipients.

Pediatric patients, such as the ones with chronic kidney disease or cystic fibrosis, often struggle with their self-image because of stunted growth or other co-morbidities associated with their primary diagnosis. Self-image problems come with challenges to self-confidence and the struggle to fit in with peers.

This is attested to by Caren Steinway and her team of researchers who state that 62% of youth with special needs transitioning to adult care are challenged by one or more of the following: anxiety, depression, disruptive behavior, physical altercation and poor social skills (Steinway, Gable and Jan 2017).

Chaplains must also be astute and competent with the emotional and spiritual needs of children and adolescents. Pediatric patients with end-stage kidney disease or cystic fibrosis often have long and recurrent hospital admissions and clinical appointments. They need to provide care in a safe, non-intimidating or compromising way. Throughout all these encounters the chaplain's approach should include a combination of medical and clinical understanding, tactful interaction with patients and families, good communication with the multidisciplinary team and the ability to create a long-term approach to developing and fostering trusting and caring relationships with patients (Clark, Drain and Malone 2003).

Providing care to patients in transition to adulthood or adult medical facilities requires an additional set of skills. The spiritual care provider must understand the following crucial dynamics:

- autonomy of the patient
- patients' fears of losing the comfort and support of the pediatric setting
- adolescent sexual relationship pitfalls or struggles with sexual orientation
- dealing with parental or familial non-compliance and dysfunction
- loss or reduction of some medical and social services after transition to adult facilities
- the fear of loss of control by parents and guardians
- coming to terms with one's spirituality and mortality.

Autonomy of the patient

One common aspirational goal of pediatric patients in transition to adulthood is becoming an independent adult. Thus, they often long for the autonomy to make decisions regarding their health, relationships, finances and where and with whom to live. This aspiration for independence and autonomy can create friction with parents or guardians. Typically, the patient is unaware of blind spots in their own thinking about the real world.

PRACTICE EXAMPLE 18.1: NOT ENOUGH

A patient who had just turned 18 years old wanted his mom to give him the $400 Supplemental Security Income (SSI) money the government was giving the family for his upkeep. He thought he could rent an apartment and be able to live on his own. He was naïve in that the cost of rent, utilities, transportation, food and other needs would cost far more than the $400 he was getting for SSI.

Patients' fears of losing the comfort and support of the pediatric setting

For pediatric patients with chronic conditions, familiarity with the hospital and staff can lead to dependence, comfort and complacency. Chronic, long-term patients are often treated in the same hospital setting by the same clinical teams for most of their lives. They become very familiar with the clinical staff and routines. This can lead to potential safety and boundary issues: patients may grow to take for granted the watchful eyes of others and can become non-compliant, disrespectful and buck the system. Here, firm confrontation and setting of boundaries are required.

PRACTICE EXAMPLE 18.2: BEHAVIOR CONTRACTS

A long-term adolescent patient had become non-compliant, disrespectful and abusive to his nurses. The team discussed the challenge and implemented a behavior contract with him, whereby he incurred the loss of some of his privileges at the clinic (phone, TV) for non-compliance, and he gained them back as he cooperated with his caregivers.

As they prepare for their transition to adult care, patients often display a fear of losing the gentle and caring atmosphere of the pediatric setting. They may not acknowledge this fear openly, but they honestly don't know what to expect in the adult world. Through patient and trusting relationship and conversations, the chaplain can help guide patients to identify and overcome their fears and provide insight into the world of adult care.

Fear, complacency and lack of discipline can impede successful treatment. Compliance with medical treatments typically decreases as patients grow older. They may believe they are immune to complications of their disease and rarely think of the potential of death from non-compliance. These times are when they need to be guided by adults and the multidisciplinary care team. Without this guidance, disease complications can be exacerbated and lead to serious consequences later in the adult setting.

It is the chaplain's unique position as facilitator of emotional, spiritual and social discussion to collaborate with the multidisciplinary care team to guide the patient and adult caregivers about these pitfalls and how to navigate them. Betz offers that the role of chaplains and leaders in the religious community is indispensable in paving a seamless transition for these patients (Betz 2007, pp.103–115). It should also be noted, however, that not all patients in transition to adult clinics dread that prospect. Some actually look forward to this transition because they may feel they have outgrown the pediatric setting and would rather be with adults.

PRACTICE EXAMPLE 18.3: TIME TO MOVE ON

There was an 18-year-old dialysis patient who felt he was too mature to be amongst 'kids'. He was becoming increasingly disrespectful to the nurses and engaging in behavior that was detrimental to the clinical atmosphere. Working together with the social worker and medical director of the dialysis unit, a speedier transition was facilitated for him to move ahead to the adult dialysis unit.

Navigating sexual relationships and sexual orientation

Teens have relationship and sexual issues, and chronic teen patients are no exceptions. Autonomy and new freedoms offer young adults new opportunities for exploration. They are biologically developing and having normal urges and sexual needs. But due to their unique conditions, with the aspirational age of 18 and their attendant autonomy beckoning, some adolescent pediatric patients throw caution to the wind and go wild with their relationship choices and sexual explorations. Often this comes with dire and negative disease exposure and relationship stresses. These can be disastrous to the patient's overall social dynamics with family or guardians, and also with the clinical team.

Occasionally, some of these patients may be exploring or coming to terms with their own sexuality or may be having gender-identity confusion. Some may also be caught in deep introspection or encounter deep difficulties as they reconcile their sexual urges, gender-identity confusion, relational euphoria and disappointments with the cultural, religious and peer pressures of those they live with on a daily basis. This can be challenging also for their family and other patients they encounter in the pediatric clinical setting.

After consultation with the social worker, the clinical psychologists and others in the multidisciplinary team, the chaplain can proceed to explore the concerns, fears, religious biases and emotional struggles of these patients and work in a concerted effort to create a safe atmosphere for them to express or explore their emotions, wishes or decisions without shame or disruption to the clinical operation.

PRACTICE EXAMPLE 18.4: GENDER TRANSITION

As a team in the dialysis unit, we had the opportunity to guide a teenage patient to make a gender transition to a female. With empathetic probing about his desire to change his gender and confronting him with possible pitfalls about making rash or irrational decisions, we embraced his decision to become female and began calling her by the female name she had adopted instead of the name that she was previously known by in her medical records.

Parental or familial non-compliance and dysfunction

It must also be noted that families or guardians themselves may be enablers and become co-dependents. Where there is non-adherence to clearly stated medical protocols, the parents or guardians may be culpable for the patient's non-compliance. Absentee parents, foster parenthood, lack of financial resources and emotional or psychological problems with parents can all contribute to dysfunction that can negatively affect the treatment and overall welfare of the patient. Care conferences organized by the multidisciplinary team, with the parents/guardians of the patient and the patient themselves present, can be called to discuss and address issues that are essential to meeting the patient's medical goals and overall emotional, social, educational and vocational wellbeing. Before, during and after these care conferences, the chaplain's role should be to capture the emotional struggles, religious or spiritual concerns and unmentioned fears of the patient/family/guardian, and simplify or expound on the technical jargon of the other disciplines and other nuances of the care conference so all parties in the care conference can comprehend the discussion and the plan of care.

Loss or reduction of some medical and social services after transition to adult facilities

When patients transition from pediatric to adult clinical settings, they may lose some benefits such as closer attention by physicians, lower nurse-to-patient ratio, the nurturing atmosphere of the pediatric setting, the opportunity to be listed higher on the organ transplant list and other social services that accrue to children. Sometimes these benefits are curtailed so much so that patient and their caregivers can be frightened about the transition.

For those families who are poor or show dysfunction, the caregivers may rely upon the social services or other governmental money for the sick or disabled children. Consequently, a child's transition to an adult facility might lead to a loss of those resources (such as SSI). In such scenarios, it can lead to conflict in the relationship between caregiver and patient, especially if the newly adult patient insists on or begins making their own financial decisions when they become adults. The chaplain and social worker can talk with the patient and family about their thoughts, fears and feelings relating to these changes.

Parental or familial loss of control

Some families of children with chronic, long-term health conditions may develop unhealthy emotional and psychological attachments. When a parent/guardian's identity is focused solely on caring for a chronically ill child, the transition to adult treatment facilities can lead to separation anxiety and role loss with parents and caregivers.

The other side of an unhealthy patient-guardian or patient-parent attachment that may lead to separation anxiety is where the parent or guardian does almost everything for the patient thus making him or her ill-equipped to make the transition to adulthood. The chaplain can help reframe these natural changes as positive signs of the growth of the young adult.

> ### PRACTICE EXAMPLE 18.5: ROAD MAP
>
> A 19-year-old dialysis patient was being prepared for transfer to an adult facility. Both Mom and patient were gripped with a crippling fear, because the patient had never had to make decisions or do anything for himself. Working with the social worker, a 'road map' plan of action was created, whereby Mom could gradually let go of some of her roles and duties. This allowed the patient to assume those responsibilities until he felt confident enough to do so without Mom's help.

In both situations it is the role of the chaplain, in communication with the social worker, to decipher latent or unexpressed fears or angst in the patient and family. This can help them to an amicable solution that doesn't impede the treatment of the patient or contribute to further dysfunction at home.

Coming to terms with spirituality and mortality

The chaplain should be abreast of the spiritual needs of the various stages in life of the patient (see Chapters 1 and 2). The chaplain should also be able to decipher hidden emotions, fears and aspirations behind the stories and words patients use to discover the deeper questions that lie within the patient. Some of the common issues for chronic or long-term patients are their own mortality and deeply religious questions about the after-life. While some may not be direct in their articulation, the chaplain or spiritual care provider must be able to listen, ask clarifying questions and understand the nuances and deep emotions associated with those discussions.

Very often questions about sin, judgment and the after-life may come up disguised as innocent inquiries, but these actually may be the patient's own personal quest for answers. Those questions could be used by patients as a window to their own fears. Whether those questions are direct or disguised, the chaplain must be able to talk with the patient in a non-judgmental or non-directive way. The chaplain instead can lead the discussion in such a way as to be pastoral and compassionate. In most cases, the patient isn't looking for answers to doctrine or religious questions, but rather they are searching for meaning for their personal physical and moral struggles as well as answers to questions about their mortality.

> ### PRACTICE EXAMPLE 18.6: ABSOLUTION
>
> A 16-year-old boy who had a very religious mother began asking serious questions about heaven, hell and judgment. He had end-stage cystic fibrosis. As we discussed some of the doctrinal questions he raised, he began to open up about questions of guilt he had about some childhood animal cruelty. He was afraid he might go to hell, because as a kid he had set some cats on fire, and he wanted to know if he could be absolved from every wrongdoing before he died.

> ### PRACTICE EXAMPLE 18.7: EXPLORING SEXUALITY
>
> In another case, a 14-year-old boy asked questions regarding a particular sexual lifestyle and if this could send someone to hell. He used a friend of his who had an alternate sexual preference as an example in asking me those questions. Later, when he came out with his own gender-identity issues, it became apparent that he had been trying to reconcile his own sexual experience with what he had been taught at church. He saw the chaplain as a safe person to talk to about these issues. In both cases, empathy, compassion and pastoral reflection helped him confront his fears and concerns.

Time, trust and relationships

With the above perspectives on some of the emotional, spiritual, familial and social dynamics involved with the care of pediatric patients making the transition to the adult world, there are three additional strategies that are key to the chaplain's work. These are helpful techniques and care paradigms for the pediatric chaplain:

- Trust is the chaplain's stock-in-trade.
- Time is the chaplain's currency.
- Relationships are the chaplain's indispensable assets.

First, for any clinician, and particularly for the chaplain, it is paramount that he or she develops *trust* with patients, family/guardians and other clinicians. It is imperative for the chaplain to work hard at maintaining trust with patients by having open and non-critical conversations with them and interacting with them in an honest and non-judgmental manner. The chaplain must always be ready to discuss religious or spiritual questions without proselytizing and imposing personal views. Where necessary, confronting them with inaccuracies and discrepancies can enlighten the patient. With the trust given, the chaplain may also challenge and reframe unhelpful or damaging thinking and attitudes.

Other noteworthy strategies include assuring patients of confidentiality, using humor to disarm emotional hang-ups or non-compliant behavior, acknowledging patient achievements and celebrating milestones such as graduations and birthdays.

Second, using *time* effectively is essential to providing ministry for chronic and long-term patients who have weekly clinical appointments (such as hemodialysis patients) or those with reoccurring hospital admissions (cystic fibrosis patients). It is important to develop a long-term approach to care instead of adopting a quick-fix approach. This allows trust to build. Time is the chaplain's currency and must be spent wisely. Unlike most other clinicians, the chaplain has time to sit and engage the patient in long and personal conversations. Such time with patients provides a cumulative repertoire of care that is unique to each patient, rather than adopting a quick-fix approach to caring for them.

Finally, *relationships* are an indispensable asset to any clinician. When relationships are genuine, honest, transparent and trusting, they allow the clinician to discuss and develop a plan of care during difficult moments in the care trajectory of the patient, such as questions about transplant, futility of care or end of life.

The chaplain's role in relationship-building with the interdisciplinary team cannot be overemphasized. While developing a quality and trusting relationship with patient and family/guardian, the chaplain must also consult with social work, clinical psychologists, nurses and physicians to provide seamless, unified and consistent communication to patient and family.

With the above three requirements in place – trust, time and relationships – the chaplain must work in tandem with others on the multidisciplinary care team to develop a plan of care and an action plan with the family to help the patient make the transition from the paediatric setting to the adult medical facility. There may well have been strong attachments formed in the pediatric context and attention may need to be given to how these are dealt with in the transition and how to help build healthy new attachments after the transition.

At the LeBonheur Children's Hospital in Memphis, Tennessee, monthly care plan meetings for our hemodialysis patients are key. At such meetings the various disciplines in attendance provide their unique perspectives on patients and address those patients who may be at risk for poor outcomes due to non-compliance with medication, dietary regimen or medical appointments. Such patients are flagged for special attention and intervention. For those on the right treatment trajectory, plans for kidney transplantation are discussed, where applicable.

Where necessary, a patient and family/guardian care conference is convened to address discrepancies, non-compliance or family issues that impinge on the progress of the patient's plan of treatment.

An important role of the chaplain is to develop a positive care environment in which the transition to adult facilities is less frightening and much more patient-friendly.

PRACTICE EXAMPLE 18.8: GRADUATION

A special 'graduation' celebration is provided to honor our patients going to adult medical facilities. At such graduation celebrations, we provide nutritionally appropriate fruits and punch; a cake is cut for the celebration; a DJ (usually a former patient of the unit) is there to play music. With their family, friends and other clinicians on the unit (including physicians, nurses, child life and social work, and nursing assistants), each patient is awarded a certificate of accomplishment by the chaplain.

Creating such a ritual for the patient and family creates an incentive to anticipate adult transitions for our patients who know they must make the journey (Ramshaw 1987). It also creates a celebrative atmosphere for the entire clinical unit – a celebration and honor that many of these patients cannot participate in at their own schools – or do not want to participate in at their schools because they don't feel they fit in or are accepted there. In cooperation with our child life department, we also hold an annual mock prom or middle school and high school graduation parties to celebrate our patients.

Future development and research needs

- Religious, spiritual and pastoral care integrated into transition pathways.
- Chaplaincy departments have a transition lead with links to adult services.
- Departmental policy for continuity of contact and research into benefits of this.

Summary

Providing spiritual care to pediatric patients in transition to adulthood and adult medical facilities requires thoughtful planning. It should begin with diagnosis and be implemented and adjusted to meet the patient/family's emotional and spiritual needs throughout the duration of the patient's treatment, especially as the time grows close to transition to adult facilities. Careful attention must be paid to patients' aspirations for becoming adults and gaining their autonomy. Other social, emotional and physical needs of patients must be addressed as they approach the transition period. It is the chaplain's role to provide spiritual guidance and emotional support, and, in coordination with others in the care team, to assist patients and families with other social, medical, psychological and governmental support for patients to make this important transition successfully.

Questions for reflection

- Is chaplaincy a part of your hospital's transition working group? If not, how might you get involved?
- How have you worked with patients to facilitate a healthy transition?
- Do you know where the contact and referral details are for the normative transfers of your transitioning patients?

References

Betz, C.L. (1998) 'Facilitating the transition of adolescents with chronic conditions from pediatric to adult health care and community setting.' *Issues in Comprehensive Pediatric Nursing 21*, 2, 97–115.

Betz, C.L. (2007) 'Facilitating the transition of adolescents with developmental disabilities: Nursing Practice issues and care.' *Journal of Pediatric Nursing 22*, 2, 103–115.

Clark, P.A., Drain, M. and Malone, M.P. (2003) 'Addressing patients' emotional and spiritual needs.' *Joint Commission Journal on Quality and Safety 29*, 12, 659–670.

Ramshaw, E. (1987) *Ritual and Pastoral Care: Theology and Pastoral Care.* Philadelphia: Fortress Press.

Steinway, C., Gable, J. and Jan, S. (2017) *Transitioning to Adult Care: Supporting Youth with Special Health Care Needs.* Evidence to Action Brief. Philadelphia, PA: PolicyLab.

Chapter 19

Paediatric Spirituality, Space and Environment

Wyatt Butcher and Lindsay B. Carey

Introduction

Traditionally, in the Western world, sacred space in the hospital was the hospital chapel. Hospitals predominantly have their origins in the caring ministry of the Christian Church and were often built with chapels located to serve the religious needs of patients (Risse 1990). In the late twentieth century, the rise of secularism and pluralism challenged the privileged place of Christianity in hospital institutions. As a greater percentage of the population in many Western countries declare to have no religious affiliation (e.g. approximately 22% of Australians (Singleton 2015); approximately 40% of New Zealanders (New Zealand Statistics Department 2014); in May of 2016 the BBC reported that more than half of the people in Scotland say they are not religious (British Broadcasting Corporation 2016). Two months later the Guardian newspaper ran a similar story that people of no religion outnumber Christians in England and Wales (Sherwood 2016). Both articles report from Social Attitude Surveys but are in themselves of limited value except to document social interest in the 'revolution') there has been an increasing questioning of the place of religious observances and related provisions in our public institutions.

New hospitals are now often built without any religiously dedicated space or with small rooms that are designated as quiet rooms/prayer rooms or multifaith rooms that would otherwise be used by those of any or no faith. Many of these spaces are constructed to be empty of any religious symbolism to avoid risk of causing offence or discomfort (Ysseldyk, Haslam and Morton 2016). Consequently, as Cadge notes, 'While multi-faith chapels try to make room for many with their religious symbols, the movement towards neutral chapels shows hospitals and chaplains increasingly opting for new symbols of art and nature rather than those of religious tradition' (2012, p.73).

> ### PRACTICE EXAMPLE 19.1: ROYAL CHILDREN'S HOSPITAL, MELBOURNE
>
> One paediatric hospital that reflects this contemporary change towards neutrality, nature and art is the Royal Children's Hospital Melbourne (RCHM; see www.RCH.org.au/info), Australia. The recent redevelopment of the RCHM included considerable space to recreate (as much as possible) a natural environment to complement a therapeutic relaxing and learning experience for children (and their families) through several ingenious distractions. A permanent open-air nature habitat with five inquisitive meerkats is located in the RCHM specialist clinic waiting area, providing entertainment and educational sessions. A second facet is a 153,000 litre coral-reef cylindrical aquarium that is two storeys high and contains approximately 25 species of fish. The aquarium presents a colourful and tranquil scene for visitors on arrival that is particularly beneficial for those in the emergency department waiting area.
>
> Finally, a sacred space prayer and meditation room (Murrup Biik – Aboriginal for spirit country) has replaced the traditional chapel but continues to 'provide a welcoming sanctuary for silence, prayer, contemplation or meditation for people of all religious traditions or none' (RCH 2016). Rather than any traditional religious symbols displayed on a wall or religiously designed stained-glass windows, the Murrup Biik sacred space is a neutral place with a scenic meditation and peace garden, pool and fountain, plus a statue of a mother nursing her child.

Despite contemporary attempts to be neutral and therefore supposedly more relevant in a secular/pluralistic age, Cadge (2012) noted that multifaith chapels seem to be used *more* often than the empty neutral spaces that are being created within some health care and other organisations. It is possible, of course, that the totally neutral space is historically lacking in any sense of meaning and has yet to be embraced by an emerging culture. It may also be that the more frequent use of the multifaith chapel is a reaction to the secularist dominance of the twentieth century, whereby people are now searching during this twenty-first century for meaning and a contermporary spirituality that is post-secularist (Tacey 2004). Yet often, and more pragmatically, it is not until a room or space has been utilised in a significant way that appreciation for its meaning and purpose is realised.

> ### PRACTICE EXAMPLE 19.2: BEREAVEMENT CARE ROOM
>
> The first time we used a newly created bereavement care room at Boston Children's Hospital was for an otherwise healthy newborn who had suffered irreparable damage at birth. I suggested that the family might benefit from our new bereavement room, a neutral space, in a non-clinical area of the hospital. The next day, when the family was able to gather together, they made themselves comfortable in the new space, which was decorated like a comfortable sitting room, with soft lighting and welcoming furniture. The family was given time with the baby and welcomed my leading of a brief time of prayer and commemoration. Staff who had been nervous about the use of this room agreed that it offered a healing space for this family, especially given the precipitous and chaotic nature of his birth and death.
>
> *Jessica Bratt Carle, St Jude Children's Research Hospital, Memphis, Tennessee, USA*

Physical 'sacred' space in the hospital

The above discussion highlights the changing nature of the physical sacred space in hospitals – changes that are in line with changes in the prevaling culture. In a paediatric hospital the question needs to be asked, 'For whom is the "chapel", "quiet room", "spirit place" (or whatever title it is given) actually for?' Is it for the patients (children) or for the families and staff? We suggest that it is primarily provided for the use of families, as:

- a place to retreat away from the bedside
- a place of quiet, where families can meditate on their pain at the plight of their child
- a place where prayers can be offered and made if desired.

An environment that is hospitable to and supportive of prayer should be created, as prayer is central to coping for many (Robinson *et al.* 2006).

Obviously, such a space will be limited by its location within the hospital and the images that it includes. Religious images – for example, of 'madonna and child' – may not be sensitive to the circumstances of some users. In the USA, which is arguably one of the more religious nations on the planet, there are no best practice standards as to what services should be offered by children's hospitals to grieving families (Thienprayoon, Campbell and Winick 2015). We suspect that no such standards are in place in other systems. There are large variations in the physical spaces and personal spiritual services offered.

Sacred space for the child (ward and bedside)

Space, as a religious concept, is often linked to physicality as in a chapel or a pre-specified prayer room. However, this mirrors the current trend of viewing religion as something that occurs in a place or institution, whereas spirituality, on the other hand, is located with or within the person, based on the concept that space is found internally (as well as externally). Whether spirituality is intrinsic or extrinsic, it is part of the role of a chaplain to ensure 'a safe and hospitable place where people can choose to explore spirituality in a way that suits them best' (Connell and Beardsley 2014, p.71).

Unfortunately, there is a shortage of competent research that considers child spirituality and often children lack the language to adequately describe their spiritual experiences (Hay and Nye 2006). Children often express their spirituality through interaction with the physical environment and the power of their imagination – as such the chaplain/spiritual caregiver must enter into their world and help create within it a sacred dimension. For Leibrich (2015), space is not just the external environment in which we may seek refuge, but also the internal space within one's self and which we create for ourselves by using our creative imagination: 'I want to be able to enter this sacred space at anytime, anywhere in the world, in the face of crowds, noise, rush, complexity and busyness' (Leibrich 2015, p.102). It is important for clinicians, chaplains and health managers to understand the principles and issues relating to sacred space so as to know how to protect it – physically, within one's self and for the benefit of others' wellbeing. These concepts include space, solitude, silence, slowness, stillness and simplicity (Leibrich 2015 pp.101–151, summarised in Table 19.1).

TABLE 19.1: PROTECTING THE SANCTUARY OF SPACE

Concept	Summary
Space	Space includes but is not limited to physical space. Space may also be internal, that place in our soul – a sacred space – where we appreciate that which we value regardless of our physical circumstances or limitations.

Concept	Summary
Solitude	Solitude is associated with peace, quiet, privacy and personal strength but also being cut off, friendless and forlorn. The paradox of solitude is that it allows an individual to explore their inner world, to know and accept themselves and their own soul more deeply – which enriches their ability to appreciate and connect with others.
Silence	Silence can be awkward, fearful and a form of punishment, triggering primitive fears of emptiness, nothingness, isolation. Silence can also be a relief/joy away from the stress of noise and the assault of technology, and allows the peace of mind to meditate more authentically – with one's self and with God.
Slowness	Slowness is often linked to being dull and sluggish or wasteful of time, but it may be associated with being measured, deliberate, considered and unhurried. The joy of slowness is appreciating one's self and respecting others in the moment by pausing to experience the environment, writing, reading, playing, caring/loving another, caring/loving one's self.
Stillness	Stillness can be seen as static, inert, idle and indecisive, but also calm, tranquil and restful. The joy of stillness is that it helps to create and maintain space – both inwardly and outwardly.
Simplicity	Simplicity can be seen as minimalist and trivial, but also as pure, easy and straightforward. The joy of simplicity leads to reciprocity, humility, developing routines, having rituals, appreciating the difference between want and need, and concentrating on what matters most and having fun.

Entering a child's spiritual space

Children can feel particularly vulnerable in hospital. Separated from their usual secure places, surrounded by adult professionals and often talked about and not talked with. Children may or may not have had time to create and imagine their safe space, be it the bed, the room or even an imaginary space in their heads. As the spiritual caregiver/chaplain enters their space, he or she must be aware of the uniqueness of each patient and, through offering loving attention and care, facilitate positive dimensions of identity being discovered and affirmed (Nash, Darby and Nash 2015).

> ### PRACTICE EXAMPLE 19.3: MARY-ANNE'S HOUSE
>
> I was called to the children's ward not knowing what to expect. The nurse told me that they had a five-year-old who wanted a Bible story read to her and demanded it be read by 'God's person'! I was taken to the room in which there were two other patients and was introduced to Mary-Anne and Mum introduced herself to me. I told Mary-Anne I was the God person around the hospital and asked if it was all right to come into her room. She nodded and asked me to read her a story from her book. She looked anxiously at the others in the room. I offered to pull the side curtains, so they became walls and yet she could still see Mum. 'This is pretty special space you have here. Can I call it Mary-Anne's house?' She beamed at me and nodded excitedly. The creation of Mary-Anne's house instilled safety and privacy for her and gave her pride in having her own space to be in rather than just another bed in a room.
>
> *Murray Elliot, Ecumenical Chaplain, Taranaki Base Hospital, New Zealand*

In the story above, Murray uses his own plus Mary-Anne's imagination to create a special space for her. This special place also becomes a place of safety and a place Mary-Anne now owns as sacred with Murray. Imagination and the use of imaginative language is an essential skill or ability in creating an awareness of the sacred in the mundane immediacy of life. Children live in a hybrid world of reality and imagination. The art of being with them is to join and use their innate wonder and awe in life so as to establish connections to the world, people and God.

Use of ritual and resources

In order to establish a safe connection and place of safety and sacredness it is sometimes useful to use physical resources and engage in practical activities with children. Murray, the chaplain at Taranaki Base Hospital, speaks about how he often spends time in the playroom with the children. As they play and imagine together, the children relax and interact as they do what is natural to them. The playroom becomes their own sacred place and specific toys take on the role of ritual that adults find in practices of their spirituality. Chaplain Marino Gray often uses art activities with children to encourage them to express their feelings and thoughts.

> ### PRACTICE EXAMPLE 19.4: TEDDIES AND ANGELS
>
> In Christchurch Women's Hospital (New Zealand) chaplains have two very special resources that they use to facilitate the making of sacred space beside the child's bed which bring comfort and aid in communication. Small knitted teddy bears are offered to all children on the first occasion of being met by a chaplain. Knitted by volunteers in local churches, these teddies not only act as an icebreaker and introduction for the chaplain but they are also a tangible sign of caring and love. The label attached tells that it is lovingly knitted for the child and has a Bible verse as a blessing: 'God bless you and keep you, God smile on you and be gracious to you, God look upon you and give you peace' (Numbers 6:24). Jesse (a volunteer chaplaincy assistant) recounts a story of how, when she first met a particular child, he was silent and unresponsive. When asked if he would like one of her special teddy bears, he nodded. On receiving the bear, the boy then began to talk to the bear and after a couple of minutes the bear talked to Jesse. From this simple beginning a relationship developed that included the boy, the bear, Jesse and eventually their faith in God. Sacred space was facilitated by a knitted bear.
>
> In the same hospital every child gets given an angel to watch over them. Simple bookmark-sized cards with a picture and the words 'God's holy angels watch over you'. These cards are held very dear by parents of sick children. This is very much the case in the neonatal intensive care unit. Parents value the cards so highly they are upset if they get lost and usually take these to hang over baby's bed at home. By using simple resources, the chaplain normalised the environment, and then by presence and language the bedside became a sacred space.

Chaplains/spiritual carers can have a vital role in helping to provide sacred spaces – for collective occasions and for private rituals. Unfortunately, there is very little empirical research regarding this role. One of the earliest studies considering the utility of chaplaincy and its sacred/sacramental role within paediatric hospitals was conducted over 30 years ago at the RCHM (Carey, Aroni and Edwards 1997). Three 'sacred space' chaplaincy roles were considered in the research – namely, the conducting of 'chapel services', 'administering sacraments' and 'praying with/or helping patients and their families to pray'. Of the 390 clinical staff participating in the research, an overwhelming majority (93%) of those surveyed (irrespective of religious/spiritual beliefs) expected chaplains to provide chapel services as a ministry of the hospital. Similar views were also found with regard to chaplains spending time at the bedside administering their denominational 'sacraments' to children if requested and/or 'praying with or helping patients/families to pray'. Subsequent research has also affirmed the ongoing perception about the importance and value of sacred space activities that seem to assist patients and families to cope with their circumstances (e.g. Carey and Cohen 2008).

Although more research is necessary with regard to the role of chaplains/spiritual careers and their use and/or development of sacred space, it is important to acknowledge that creating sacred space for the benefit of children, their families and clinical staff can require considerable time and effort. Some individuals and organisations can be strongly opposed to religious and spiritual support due to their personal or professional experience with former models of care and training that were purely based upon bio-medical or bio-psychosocial paradigms – rather than the more contemporary and fully holistic model of bio-psychosocial-spiritual care (Sulmasy 2002).

Since the advent of the World Health Organization (2002) Pastoral Intervention Codings (now called Spiritual Care Interventions), it has been possible to utilise a universal system to methodically consider and categorise the various roles of chaplains/spiritual carers. Table 19.2 presents a number of useful strategies by Nash *et al.* (2015) according to the World Health Organization codings (i.e. assessment, support, etc.) which provide ideas for helping to create sacred space within paediatric settings.

TABLE 19.2: CREATING SACRED SPACE FOR PAEDIATRIC SPIRITUAL CARE – THE ROLE OF CHAPLAINS

Spiritual care interventions	Strategy/technique
Assessment	Assessing/questioning how to create/ensure a safe space. Assessing how to help rebuild/restore children from emotional and/or spiritual wounds. Undertaking 'active listening'/being attentive, being non-judgemental, accepting, affirming.

Spiritual care interventions	Strategy/technique
Support	Engaging in activities that provide direct interaction, build rapport, relieve stress, provide comfort and encourage sensory stimulation – for example, through interactive games (e.g. chess, snakes and ladders), reading stories, doing art (e.g. painting), designing and creating meaningful artefacts (e.g. craftwork), organising/participating in alternative therapies (e.g. pet therapy).
Counselling	Encouraging and discussing children's exploratory questions and conversations about life and death, loss and grief, etc.; acknowledging spiritual resources already within children and exploring new possibilities; gaining ongoing voluntary informed consent to continue engaging.
Education	Using 'support' techniques/strategies plus 'counselling' to assist the knowledge of children and to improve their spiritual resilience to cope with their circumstances and environment.
Ritual and worship	Creative use/development of chapels or other religious/spiritual rooms or multifaith spaces to provide appropriate space/time for personal or shared religious/spiritual expression – particularly at times of transition.

Conclusion

Despite the secular influence of the twentieth century, it would be fair to say that spiritual and religious influences plus the importance of identity, culture and rituals are slowly regaining traction in the twenty-first century as being integral to providing fully holistic care. Creating and developing sacred space, both internally and externally, is an important element for encouraging a positive and creative environment for children that, amidst the increasing pace and stress of technological society, provides a sanctuary for peace of mind, body and spirit – which benefits not only children but also parents, staff and, ultimately, the wider community. Chaplains/spiritual carers are integral to this sacred space creativity.

Future development and research needs

- Regular audit giving us clear evidence of the use and appreciation of our religious and spiritual care places and services.

- Best practice in involving patients and families in helping design sacred spaces.

- National and international standards for sacred spaces.

Summary

- Increasing secularism, pluralism and declining religious adherence in Western society is being reflected in contemporary healthcare institutions by modifying/creating neutral and/or multifaith spiritual/sacred spaces rather than traditional chapels.

- Contemporary 'sacred spaces', however, have not necessarily achieved greater utility and are unlikely to do so unless they are utilised in a significant way that provides meaning and purpose to a specified space which otherwise is a seemingly neutral, secular and potentially meaningless environment.

- Currently, it would seem that there are no guidelines or standards with regard to 'sacred spaces', leading to considerable variations in practice.

- Sacred space has traditionally been considered in terms of religious physicality. However, spirituality centres more upon the individual – internally. Children value both, and thus it is important to appreciate and engage children in their sacred/spiritual dimension.

- Encouraging and protecting sacred space is important for adults and children. It is important to consider the concepts and issues relating to sacred space and to know how to protect sacred space – both physically and within one's self.

- Ritual and resources are important and creative elements in helping to develop and sustain one's spirituality and sacred space.

- Community, parents and chaplains/spiritual carers have an important role in developing and maintaining sacred space for the wellbeing of children and thus wider society.

Questions for reflection

- What are your positive and negative experiences of sacred spaces in paediatric healthcare?
- How can you use the six elements of space, solitude, silence, slowness, stillness and simplicity to reflect on your practice?
- Are there ideas in this chapter you can adapt in your own setting?

Acknowledgements

The authors would like to thank Dr Bruce Rumbold, OAM (Director of the Palliative Care Unit, La Trobe University, Melbourne, Australia) for his support and encouragement.

References

British Broadcasting Corporation (2016) 'Most people in Scotland "not religious".' Accessed 13/01/18 at www.bbc.com/news/uk-scotland-35953639.

Cadge, W. (2012) *Paging God: Religion in the Halls of Medicine.* Chicago, IL: University of Chicago Press.

Carey, L.B., Aroni, R. and Edwards, A. (1997) 'Health Policy and Well-being: Hospital Chaplaincy.' In Gardner, H. (ed.) *Health Policy in Australia*, 1st edition. South Melbourne: Oxford University Press.

Carey, L.B. and Cohen, J. (2008) 'Religion, spirituality and health care treatment decisions.' *Journal of Health Care Chaplaincy 15*, 1, 25–39.

Connell, S. and Beardsley, C. (2014) 'Hospitality of the heart – hospitality for the human spirit: How healthcare chaplains can discover, create and offer spaces for spiritual care in the hospital setting.' *Health and Social Care Chaplaincy 2*, 1, 65–78.

Hay, D. and Nye, R. (2006) *The Spirit of the Child*, revised edition. London: Jessica Kingsley Publishers.

Leibrich, J. (2015) *Sanctuary: The Discovery of Wonder.* Dunedin: Otago University Press.

Nash, P., Darby, K. and Nash, S., (2015) *Spiritual Care with Sick Children and Young People: A Handbook for Chaplains, Paediatric Health Professionals, Art Therapists and Youth Workers.* London: Jessica Kingsley Publishers.

New Zealand Statistics Department (2014) *2013 Census QuickStats about culture and identity.* Accessed 13/01/18 at http://archive.stats.govt.nz/Census/2013-census/profile-and-summary-reports/quickstats-culture-identity/religion.aspx?url=/Census/2013-census/profile-and-summary-reports/quickstats-culture-identity/religion.aspx.

RCH (2016) 'Pastoral and Spiritual Care – Prayer and Meditation Space.' Royal Children's Hospital Melbourne. Accessed on 24/11/2017 at www.rch.org.au/cpc/prayer_and_meditation_space/Prayer_and_Meditation_Space.

Risse, G.B. (1990) *Mending Bodies, Saving Souls: A History of Hospitals*. Oxford: Oxford University Press.

Robinson, M., Thiel, M., Backus, M. and Meyer, E. (2006) 'Matters of spirituality at the end of life in the pediatrice intensive care unit.' *Pediatrics 118*, 3, e719–e729.

Sherwood, H. (2016) 'People of no religion outnumber Christians in England and Wales.' *The Guardian*, 23 May. Accessed 13/01/18 at www.theguardian.com/world/2016/may/23/no-religion-outnumber-christians-england-wales-study.

Singleton, A. (2015) 'Are religious "nones" secular? The case of the nones in Australia.' *Journal of Beliefs & Values 36*, 2, 239–243.

Sulmasy, D.P. (2002) 'A biopsychosocial–spiritual model for the care of patients at the end of life.' *Gerontologist 42*, Suppl, 3, 24–33.

Tacey, D.J. (2004) *The Spirituality Revolution: The Emergence of Contemporary Spirituality*. London: Routledge.

Thienprayoon, R., Campbell, R. and Winick, N. (2015) 'Attitudes and practices in the bereavement care offered by children's hospitals: A survey of pediatric chaplains network.' *OMEGA–Journal of Death and Dying 7*, 1, 48–59.

World Health Organization (2002) 'Pastoral Intervention Codings.' *ICD-10-AM (International Classification of Diseases and Related Health Problems – Australian Modification)*. Geneva: WHO.

Ysseldyk, R., Haslam, S.A. and Morton, T.A. (2016) 'Stairway to heaven? (Ir)religious identity moderates the effects of immersion in religious spaces on self-esteem and self-perceived physical health.' *Journal of Environmental Psychology 47*, September, 14–21.

Chapter 20
Paediatric Chaplaincy and Research
Daniel H. Grossoehme and Lindsay B. Carey

Introduction

Given the increasing expectation for healthcare professionals to be reliant upon evidence-based practice and that professional practice will be subject to quality assurance, there is a clear need for research to be seen as integral for both the sustainability and the development of any healthcare organisation and its departments – including that of pastoral/spiritual care within paediatric contexts.

At some stage, most pastoral/spiritual care departments within healthcare organisations – particularly those with secular foundations – will be challenged about the empirical evidence (or lack thereof) supporting spiritual care/pastoral care practice and the role of chaplains in supporting paediatric care. Conducting spiritual/pastoral care research within healthcare settings, irrespective of whether it is within adult or paediatric contexts, has frequently produced illuminating results, some of which have highlighted the substantial work and achievements of chaplains (see Practice example 20.1). Nevertheless, there are a number of issues that need to be considered when exploring and engaging in paediatric spirituality and chaplaincy research which will be the focus of this chapter – namely:

- the research process
- uniqueness of paediatric research
- assent and consent
- spiritual screenings and assessments
- research instruments
- participants
- future directions.

The research process

In general terms, although specific research protocols may vary depending on the context and nature of the research, the process of scientific research to acquire empirical data is the same process whether it be in the laboratory, the hospital ward or in the community, and irrespective of whether it be with adults or children, quantitative or qualitative, physical or religious/spiritual. Generally speaking, all research will fundamentally comprise seven stages (depending on the nature of the research) and usually commences with the formulation and refining of research questions to resolve a clinical or broader healthcare/service issue, and concludes with the final dissemination and publication of findings (see Figure 20.1). The process can be quite time demanding and challenging – even for the best of researchers, let alone chaplains, the majority of whom in our experience are not adequately research trained. There are a number of excellent texts which we recommend that explain in more detail the various research techniques (see Bryman 2015; Koenig 2012).

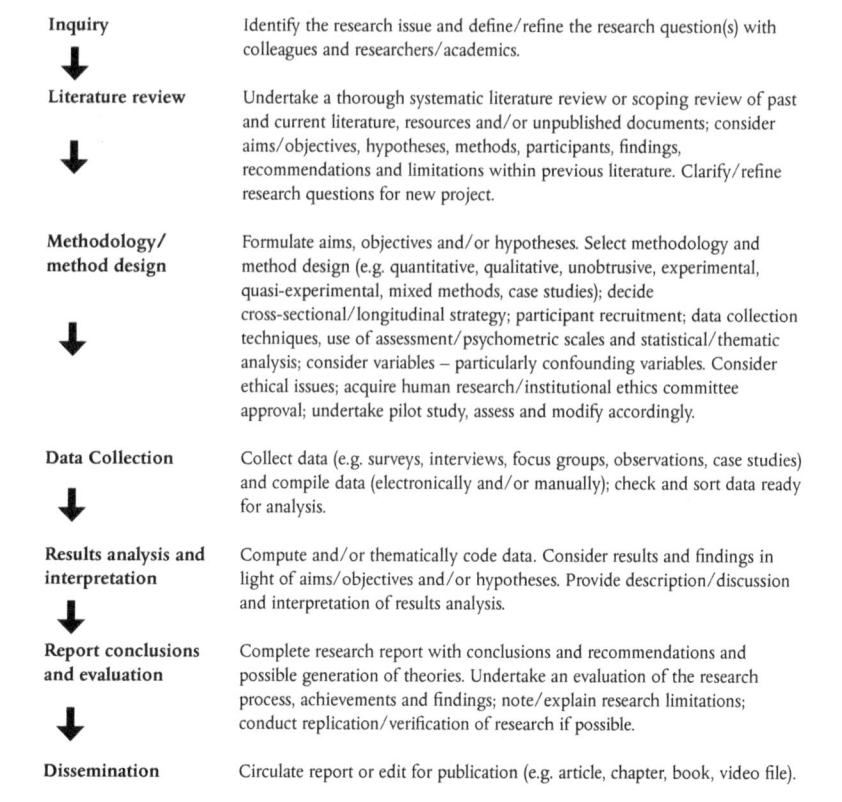

Inquiry ↓	Identify the research issue and define/refine the research question(s) with colleagues and researchers/academics.
Literature review ↓	Undertake a thorough systematic literature review or scoping review of past and current literature, resources and/or unpublished documents; consider aims/objectives, hypotheses, methods, participants, findings, recommendations and limitations within previous literature. Clarify/refine research questions for new project.
Methodology/ method design ↓	Formulate aims, objectives and/or hypotheses. Select methodology and method design (e.g. quantitative, qualitative, unobtrusive, experimental, quasi-experimental, mixed methods, case studies); decide cross-sectional/longitudinal strategy; participant recruitment; data collection techniques, use of assessment/psychometric scales and statistical/thematic analysis; consider variables – particularly confounding variables. Consider ethical issues; acquire human research/institutional ethics committee approval; undertake pilot study, assess and modify accordingly.
Data Collection ↓	Collect data (e.g. surveys, interviews, focus groups, observations, case studies) and compile data (electronically and/or manually); check and sort data ready for analysis.
Results analysis and interpretation ↓	Compute and/or thematically code data. Consider results and findings in light of aims/objectives and/or hypotheses. Provide description/discussion and interpretation of results analysis.
Report conclusions and evaluation ↓	Complete research report with conclusions and recommendations and possible generation of theories. Undertake an evaluation of the research process, achievements and findings; note/explain research limitations; conduct replication/verification of research if possible.
Dissemination	Circulate report or edit for publication (e.g. article, chapter, book, video file).

Figure 20.1: General research process

PRACTICE EXAMPLE 20.1: ROYAL CHILDREN'S HOSPITAL MELBOURNE

In one of the earliest studies exploring the role of paediatric chaplains, the team were keen to gain feedback regarding their ministry to paediatric patients and their families. From a different perspective, hospital executives were keen to know whether chaplains helped to resolve issues that facilitated paediatric discharge. One executive explained: 'If the chaplains can expedite the discharge of children, even by half an hour, we need to know how, and encourage it, because it means financial savings.' The chaplains collaborated with the Australian Health and Welfare Chaplains Association (now called Spiritual Care Australia) and researchers from La Trobe University with approval from the hospital human research ethics committee plus their hospital management to undertake an ambitious project involving both quantitative and qualitative research over a two-year period. Given that medical, nursing and allied health staff tended to engage with chaplains over a longer period than children and/or their families, the involvement of clinical staff was seen as critical to get a 'long-term' perspective about the work of chaplains in paediatric care. A total of 390 clinical staff (n=390/798:48.8%) completed a survey, and 50 staff (representing each hospital departmental area) participated in semi-structured interviews. The results for chaplains were affirming. Approximately 88% of staff interviewed believed that chaplains should be part of the hospital system and 60% of survey respondents believed that it was of 'great importance' to have a chaplain of any faith available to children and/or their families at all times. The major reasons given by interviewed participants for having chaplains were:

- teamwork
- providing religious and psychosocial support to patients/families and staff
- specialist skill support to patients/families and staff – particularly at times of death/bereavement/grieving
- specialist input with regard to (1) ethical issues/decisions, (2) being a community link, (3) providing a non-diagnostic communication role, (4) alleviating emotional discomfort for children, their families and staff within a complex and sometimes frightening institution (Carey *et al.* 1997).

Uniqueness of paediatric research

Even the most basic health care research can seem overwhelmingly complicated, yet it is even more complex in paediatric settings. Further to this, special consideration and additional time needs to be allocated to any paediatric research if the research involves unique variables that are not commonly collected as part of the usual data management process. These include variables such as exploring the role of chaplains and/or the impact of pastoral and spiritual care within a paediatric population. As summarised below (Table 20.1), when adult research is compared with paediatric research, the issues for paediatric research are unique and numerous. The particular areas in relation to paediatric research, spirituality and chaplaincy will then be discussed:

TABLE 20.1: COMPARISON OF PAEDIATRIC AND ADULT RESEARCH CONSIDERATIONS WITH REGARD TO SPIRITUALITY AND PASTORAL CARE

Paediatric research	Adult research
Patient assent/consent usually required (a)	Patient assent/consent always required
Parental/guardian consent usually required (b)	Guardian consent only required if patient vulnerable (c)
Limited number of language-appropriate research protocols suitable for paediatric population	Considerable number of language-appropriate research protocols suitable for adult population
Limited number of age-appropriate pastoral/spiritual screening tools	Considerable number of age-appropriate pastoral/spiritual assessment screening tools
Limited number of age-appropriate formal pastoral/spiritual assessment instruments	Considerable number of age-appropriate formal pastoral/spiritual assessment instruments
Limited number of pastoral/spiritual assessments instruments that have been validated	Considerable number of pastoral/spiritual assessments instruments that have been validated
Often involves research that is inclusive of parent/guardian to gain family support/perspective	Seldom involves research that is inclusive of parents/guardians unless patient requires assistance

Note: (a) Patient assent/consent: This varies depending on the age of the child and State legalities. (b) Parental/guardian consent: This varies depending upon the age and vulnerability of the child and State legalities. (c) Adult patients usually have complete autonomy of consent; however, some patients who are vulnerable due to age, illness or mental health issues often require the support or advocacy of a legal guardian.

Assent and consent

Chaplaincy associations endorse high standards of 'confidentiality' to which professional chaplains should routinely adhere (Carey *et al.* 2015). Some chaplains may think that any research data they gather will quite naturally be held in the strictest confidence. However, the conduct of ethical research requires a formal process of assent and consent. Informed consent applies only to a person who is able to agree to their own treatment or participation in research (Bioethics Committee 1995). In paediatrics, this adult concept is markedly different. Parents or other adults with legal guardianship over a child give informed permission for the child's treatment or research participation. The child's assent, their agreement to participate in the study or to have their health information accessed, is normally also required (Levy, Larcher and Kurz 2003). This is particularly important for studies which provide no direct benefit to the paediatric participant, and their persistent choice not to assent may be considered ethically binding (Bioethics Committee 1995).

Assent requirements differ across national boundaries and institutions, although they generally include ensuring that the paediatric participant has a developmentally appropriate understanding of what the research entails, and what they can expect to experience. The assent process also requires that the person obtaining informed permission and assent is suitably qualified and/or experienced in order to adequately assess the child's understanding of the research and to check whether there are any forms of coercion being utilised (Bioethics Committee 1995). Federal regulations in the United States do not specify an age at which assent is required and instead use language allowing individual institutional review boards to make their own determinations based on age, maturity, psychological status of the child and local custom (Federal Drug Administration 2000). Assent may be required through the age of 18 years, which is the typical age of maturity in the European Union and many other Western countries (e.g. Australia, Canada and New Zealand) and the age at which adolescents in the United States begin to give consent for their own healthcare (Levy, Larcher and Kurz 2003).

Despite the legal and ethical guidance on this topic, Kimberly and colleagues (2006) documented considerable variability among institutional review board approvals of consent/assent documents and study compensation. Assent documentation varied from a single line for the paediatric participant's signature on the (parental) informed permission/consent document, to completely separate assent forms; which again showed variability ranging from separate forms for specific age ranges with developmentally appropriate language for each, to a single form which used the same language as the (parental) permission/ consent form (Kimberly *et al.* 2006).

The wide variation in compensation for participating in research also raises issues of justice and biased study results, because socioeconomically disadvantaged families may feel coerced to participate due to high compensation or excluded because the compensation fails to reimburse for expenses incurred by participation (Kimberly *et al.* 2006). Another issue of concern is the respect for patient/family autonomy given the religious/ spiritual beliefs of children and their families. It is often for reasons such as justice and respect for individuals against the seemingly overriding benefits of research that some institutional ethics committees in Western countries desire or prioritise chaplains/spiritual carers to be part of the membership of ethics committees so as to ensure a professional voice of advocacy for patient participants and their families (Carey and Cohen 2010).

Spiritual screening and assessments

Although the terms are frequently used interchangeably, spiritual screenings and spiritual assessments are different. Spiritual screening is a short means of identifying persons whose spiritual condition increases their risk of poorer health outcomes. Spiritual assessments, usually performed by a professional chaplain, are more in-depth and are a means of developing a spiritual plan of care to decrease spiritual struggle and risk of poorer health outcomes (Fitchett 1999). There is generally a lack of either spiritual screening or assessment methods designed for use in paediatrics.

An exception to this is the work of Alistair Bull (2016), which utilises interactive play and storytelling to develop a shared language with the child, and which the chaplain can use clinically and interpret the outcomes to the wider healthcare team. Paul Nash and colleagues have explored the use of visual imagery, metaphor and story to understand children's spiritual needs (Nash, Darby and Nash 2013, 2015). Children and adolescents may not have developed the vocabulary to articulate their spiritual beliefs or experiences. Providing visual or metaphorical prompts may help a child to explore their spirituality and develop new language to express themselves. Many of the prompts described, such as postcards or a bracelet of beads, are left behind as visual reminders of the chaplaincy encounter and the community it created, and may spur further reflection.

One aspect to consider is that chaplains do not have to undertake screenings, assessments and research in isolation from other paediatric healthcare professionals. For example, speech-language pathologists/

therapists (SLPs) regularly use interactive play and storytelling as part of their paediatric assessments, therapy and research (Carey-Sargeant and Brown 2005). Chaplains could collaborate with SLPs to achieve multidisciplinary assessments, research and support (Mathisen *et al.* 2015; Carey, Aroni and Edwards 1997) or work with other allied health professionals who may be familiar with a bio-psycho-social-spiritual paradigm (e.g. physical therapists, occupational therapists, prosthetics/orthotists, social workers, music therapists). Such collaboration could prove to be not only more efficient but also more holistically effective for the child and their family.

Research instruments

The difficulty faced by clinical chaplains in understanding the spiritual needs of paediatric patients is the lack of available research-grade questionnaires by which to gather data from children and adolescents. Hill and Hood (1999) published a volume describing over 106 measures of religiosity, none of which were designed for use with children. A logical question to ask is simply: Can religious/spiritual questionnaires designed for adults also be used with children, or at least with adolescents? This is a particularly important question as research (whether using formal instruments or oral interviews) needs to be both age-appropriate and language/vocabulary-appropriate. Or perhaps, an alternative question should be: Are entirely new instruments needed? The answer is yes and yes. A widely used measure of religious coping styles is the Brief R-COPE (Pargament, Feuille and Burdzy 2011; Pargament, Koenig and Perez 2000) developed for use with adults. It has, however, also been used reliably with children and adolescents ages 8–19 years old (Benore, Pargament and Pendleton 2008; Cotton *et al.* 2009; Dew *et al.* 2010; Grossoehme *et al.* 2016; Molock *et al.* 2006; Reynolds *et al.* 2014; Terreri and Glenwick 2013; Westers *et al.* 2014). See also Chapter 5 which discusses tools used in screening and assessment.

The use, however, of two common adult spirituality measures (Spiritual Involvement and Beliefs Scale [SIBS] and the Spiritual Well-being Scale [SWB]) were found to produce results suggesting that these were not suitable for use with adolescents, and the authors recommended development of adolescent-specific measures (Rubin *et al.* 2009). Sara Pendleton and colleagues (2002) explored religious coping styles used by children 5–12 years old with cystic fibrosis and documented religious coping styles that were both similar and distinct from the styles presented by Pargament and colleagues. Collaborative spiritual coping, for example, is a coping style identified by Pargament (1997) and was also found in the sample of paediatric patients studied by Pendleton and colleagues. Belief that God is irrelevant is a style identified by Pendleton and colleagues; however, this was not described in the adult studies by Pargament and colleagues.

One measure, the CASST-r, is paediatric-specific although there are no established psychometric properties (Grossoehme 2008). CASST-r was developed to understand the relative balance of the spiritual needs and resources an adolescent brings to their hospital experience. It is not intended to be scored, per se, but is used as a means to judge the relative balance between resources and needs. An adolescent with moderate spiritual resources and relatively few needs may be a relatively low chaplaincy priority. Conversely, a teenager with few spiritual resources and high needs may be a high priority for chaplaincy care.

Participants

A unique aspect of clinical paediatric chaplaincy is its attention to the needs of the family, rather than focusing solely on the child patient in the bed. This is also the case in paediatric research; researchers need to be very clear who the participant will be. Children and adolescents do not live in isolation but are embedded in a family system in which parents' spiritual and religious beliefs affect their child's beliefs (Boyatzis, Dollahite and Marks 2006). Thus research in paediatrics is often and inevitably inclusive of parent/guardian perspectives – thus making paediatric research simultaneously adult research, carrying with it the points made in the table above. Parents affect their child's health, whether because they shoulder the responsibility for the child's medical care (Drotar and Levers 1994) or because their own health also affects their child's health: adolescents with cystic fibrosis whose parents were depressed were more likely to also report elevated levels of depression (Quittner *et al.* 2014).

Similarities in paediatric and parent spiritual beliefs or practices may be due to parental modelling, or similar lifestyles. D'Angelo (2017) found that parental spiritual coping predicted an adolescent's positive spiritual coping with the adolescent's chronic disease. Clarity on who is being studied, and a conceptual model which proposes who is being influenced and how they are being influenced, is important. There are times when, because of research feasibility issues or because parents strongly influence their children and adolescents, research regarding paediatric spirituality often focuses solely on parents or other family members as participants (Grossoehme *et al.* 2015). For the same reasons, research into paediatric care and spirituality or chaplaincy may only involve clinical staff and thus avoid many of the issues arising if children and/or their families are involved. Clinical staff can be a reliable source for providing the necessary feedback for chaplains/spiritual carers and hospital management (see Practice example 20.2).

> ### PRACTICE EXAMPLE 20.2: PAEDIATRIC PALLIATIVE CARE CHAPLAINCY
>
> Chaplain George Fitchett (Rush University) and his research associates wanted to explore the provision of spiritual care and chaplaincy within paediatric palliative care (PPC) programs across the United States. They asked, 'What are the roles of chaplains in paediatric palliative care?' and 'How well are chaplains integrated into PPC teams?' They launched a two-phase cross-sectional mixed-methods study involving surveys and interviews. Twenty-four of 28 (86%) surveyed PPC programs across the US reported having a staff chaplain on their clinical team. Nineteen PPC programs met inclusion criteria and eight (n=8) PPC programs were then randomly selected to study in closer detail. Following interviews of physicians and chaplains the researchers discovered that 'Among the 8 PPC programs, there was considerable variation in how chaplains functioned as members of the PPC interdisciplinary team'. Despite these variations, the interviews indicated that chaplains appeared to be well-integrated members of the various PPC teams and that chaplains were addressing children's and families' spiritual suffering, improved family–team communication and provided rituals valued by patients, families and staff. While the research concluded that further study was needed to evaluate how well the spiritual needs of patients, families and staff were actually being met, and there was a clear need to consider organisational factors that support (or do not) the delivery of spiritual care in children's hospitals, nevertheless comments by physicians about the role of chaplains in supporting paediatric care were affirming. As one physician summarised: 'A trained chaplain brings a whole other level of knowledge, skill, and comfort in dealing with these issues. That helps the team be a better team, to be more resilient in this care' (Fitchett *et al.* 2011).

Future development and research needs

There are a number of research issues relating to paediatric spirituality and chaplaincy research that need further development. Perhaps most obvious is the need to develop valid, reliable and developmentally appropriate measures of paediatric spirituality for use in research studies. This, of course, would require considerable resources and collaboration between researchers, chaplains, healthcare institutions and chaplaincy organisations – not to forget the need to recruit willing children, families and clinical staff. Also, thus far, the majority of research literature has focused on Christian children, adolescents and their parents. While there has been some research exploring the role of chaplains in interfaith spiritual care (Carey, Cohen and Davoren 2009), there is a need to understand the relationship between health and religious beliefs among child adherents of other faith traditions.

In addition, a long-standing issue that has been echoed repeatedly is the need for chaplains to become more research-literate. The majority of chaplains work in secular institutions that do not necessarily support a pastoral/spiritual paradigm, and thus chaplains need to take advantage of the available research literature and research training in order to be better informed and to develop evidenced-based professional practices relevant to the context in which they minister. There is a range of ways to begin to collect evidence and build towards a research project (Health Research Authority 2016). These include audits, service evaluations, systematic literature reviews, patient satisfaction and PROM (patient reported outcome measure) data, case studies, measuring key performance indicators, taxonomy and different approaches to recording spiritual care.

Finally, in order to utilise culturally age-appropriate spiritual measurements and implement additional training for chaplains to develop their research skills, there needs to be adequate funding and resources provided so as to ensure the future conduct of paediatric spirituality and chaplaincy research.

Summary

- Paediatric spirituality and chaplaincy research, like all research, needs to be seen as integral for the sustainability and development of both healthcare institutions and chaplaincy.

- The research process is challenging – but particularly unique and challenging when considering religiosity and spirituality in paediatric contexts.

- Assent of the child may be required based on age, maturity and psychological functioning.

- Research instruments/questionnaires that are valid, reliable and developmentally appropriate for use with children are very limited; some may be used with adolescents.

- Clarity about research participants is essential: child/adolescent, parent/guardian or whole family.

- Future development is required with regard to the development of screening, assessment and research instruments. Chaplaincy training is required to develop chaplaincy research skills for the paediatric context. Funding and resourcing is required to assist with training and research.

Questions for reflection

- What are the immediate, urgent, obvious areas where it would be helpful for you to have evidence of practice?

- How could you and your department start and develop your research strategy?

- Which clinical departments in your institution might be interested in doing a join research project with chaplaincy?

Acknowledgements

With great appreciation, we thank Dr Bruce Rumbold, PhD, OAM (Palliative Care Unit, La Trobe University), Lillian Krikheli, BHSc, MSpPath (Cabrini Health, Melbourne), Associate Professor Rabbi Jeffrey Cohen, MPH, DD, DMin (Australian Catholic University), and Clinical Research Coordinators Katrina Lewis and Alexis Teeters, Division of Pulmonary Medicine, Cincinnati Children's Hospital Medical Center, for their support (in one way or another) during the writing of this chapter.

References

Benore, E., Pargament, K.I. and Pendleton, S. (2008) 'An initial examination of religious coping in children with asthma.' *The International Journal for the Psychology of Religion 18*, 4, 267–290.

Bioethics Committee (1995) 'Informed consent, parental permission, and assent in pediatric practice.' *Pediatrics 95*, 2, 314–317.

Boyatzis, C.J., Dollahite, D.C. and Marks, L.D. (2006) 'The Family as a Context for Religious and Spiritual Development in Children and Youth.' In E.C. Roehlkepartain, P.E. King, L. Wagener and P. Benson (eds) *The Handbook of Spiritual Development in Childhood and Adolescence.* Thousand Oaks: CA: Sage Publications.

Bryman, A. (2015) *Social Research Methods.* Oxford: Oxford University Press.

Bull, A.W. (2016) *Assessing and Communicating the Spiritual Needs of Children in Hospital: A New Guide for Healthcare Professionals and Chaplains.* London: Jessica Kingsley Publishers.

Carey, L.B., Aroni, R.A. and Edwards, A. (1997) 'Health and Well-Being: Hospital Chaplaincy – A Case Study of the Melbourne Royal Children's Hospital.' In H. Gardner (ed.) *Health Policy in Australia.* Melbourne: Oxford University Press.

Carey, L B., Aroni, R.A., Edwards, A., Carey-Sargeant, C.L. and Boer, J. (1997) 'Speech pathology practice: Speech pathologists and the role of chaplains.' *Australian Communication Quarterly*, Autumn, 38–41.

Carey, L.B. and Cohen, J. (2010) 'Health care chaplains and their role on institutional ethics committees: An Australia study.' *Journal of Religion and Health 49*, 2, 221–232.

Carey, L.B., Cohen, J. and Davoren, R. (2009) 'The sacralisation of identity: An interfaith spiritual care paradigm for chaplaincy in a multifaith context.' In D. Schappani and L. Beuchardt (eds.) *Interfaith Spiritual Care: Understandings and Practices.* Ontario: Pandora Press.

Carey, L.B., Willis, M.A., Krikheli, L. and O'Brien, A. (2015) 'Religion, health and confidentiality: An exploratory review of the role of chaplains.' *Journal of Religion and Health 54*, 2, 676–692.

Carey-Sargeant, C.L. and Brown, P.M. (2005) 'Reciprocal utterances during interactions between deaf toddlers and their hearing mothers.' *Deafness & Education International 7*, 2, 77–97.

Cotton, S., Grossoehme, D., Rosenthal, S.L., McGrady, M.E. *et al.* (2009) 'Religious/spiritual coping in adolescents with sickle cell disease: A pilot study.' *Journal of Pediatric Hematology/Oncology 31*, 5, 313–318.

D'Angelo, C.M. (2017) 'Religious/spiritual coping and attributional styles among adolescents with chronic health conditions and their parents: reciprocal relationships over time.' Unpublished Masters dissertation, Department of Psychology. University of Alabama.

Dew, R.E., Daniel, S.S., Goldston, D., McCall, W.V. *et al.* (2010) 'A prospective study of religion/ spirituality and depressive symptoms among adolescent psychiatric patients.' *Journal of Affective Disorders 120*, 1, 149–157.

Drotar, D. and Levers, C. (1994) 'Age differences in parent and child responsibilities for management of cystic fibrosis and insulin-dependent diabetes mellitus.' *Journal of Developmental & Behavioral Pediatrics 15*, 4, 265–272.

Federal Drug Administration (2000) '21CFR50.55 Protection of Human Subjects.' Accessed on 13 April 2017 at www.accessdata.fda.gov/scripts/cdrh/cfdocs/cfcfr/CFRSearch.cfm?fr=50.55.

Fitchett, G. (1999) 'Selected resources for screening for spiritual risk.' *Chaplaincy Today 15*, 1, 13–26.

Fitchett, G., Lyndes, K.A., Cadge, W., Berlinger, N., Flanagan, E. and Misasi, J. (2011) 'The role of professional chaplains on pediatric palliative care teams: Perspectives from physicians and chaplains.' *Journal of Palliative Medicine 14*, 6, 704–707.

Grossoehme, D.H. (2008) 'Development of a spiritual screening tool for children and adolescents.' *The Journal of Pastoral Care & Counseling 62*, 1–2, 71–85.

Grossoehme, D.H., Szczesniak, R.D., Britton, L L., Siracusa, C.M. *et al.* (2015) 'Adherence determinants in cystic fibrosis: Cluster analysis of parental psychosocial, religious, and/or spiritual factors.' *Annals of the American Thoracic Society 12*, 6, 838–846.

Grossoehme, D.H., Szczesniak, R.D., Mrug, S., Dimitriou, S.M., Marshall, A. and McPhail, G.L. (2016) 'Adolescents' spirituality and cystic fibrosis airway clearance treatment adherence: examining mediators.' *Journal of Pediatric Psychology 41*, 9, 1022–1032.

Health Research Authority (2016) Defining Research. London: HRA. Accessed on 24/11/2017 at www.hra.nhs.uk/documents/2016/06/defining-research.pdf.

Hill, P.C. and Hood, R.W. (1999) *Measures of Religiosity.* Birmingham, AL: Religious Education Press.

Kimberly, M.B., Hoehn, K.S., Feudtner, C., Nelson, R.M. and Schreiner, M. (2006) 'Variation in standards of research compensation and child assent practices: a comparison of 69 institutional review board–approved informed permission and assent forms for 3 multicenter pediatric clinical trials.' *Pediatrics 117*, 5, 1706–1711.

Koenig, H.G. (2012) *Spirituality and Health Research: Methods, Measurements, Statistics, and Resources.* Philadelphia, PA: Templeton Foundation Press.

Levy, M.D.L., Larcher, V. and Kurz, R. (2003) 'Informed consent/assent in children. Statement of the Ethics Working Group of the Confederation of European Specialists in Paediatrics (CESP).' *European Journal of Pediatrics 162*, 9, 629–633.

Mathisen, B., Carey, L.B., Carey-Sargeant, C.L., Webb, G., Millar, C. and Krikheli, L. (2015) 'Religion, spirituality and speech-language pathology: A viewpoint for ensuring patient-centred holistic care.' *Journal of Religion and Health 54*, 6, 2309–2323.

Molock, S.D., Puri, R., Matlin, S. and Barksdale, C. (2006) 'Relationship between religious coping and suicidal behaviors among African American adolescents.' *Journal of Black Psychology 32*, 3, 366–389.

Nash, P., Darby, K. and Nash, S. (2013) 'The spiritual care of sick children: Reflections from a pilot participation project.' *International Journal of Children's Spirituality 18*, 2, 148–161.

Nash, P., Darby, K. and Nash, S. (2015) *Spiritual Care with Sick Children and Young People.* London: Jessica Kingsley Publishers.

Pargament, K. (1997) *Psychology of Religious Coping.* New York, NY: Guilford Press.

Pargament, K., Feuille, M. and Burdzy, D. (2011) 'The Brief RCOPE: Current psychometric status of a short measure of religious coping.' *Religions 2*, 1, 51–76.

Pargament, K.I., Koenig, H.G. and Perez, L.M. (2000) 'The many methods of religious coping: Development and initial validation of the RCOPE.' *Journal of Clinical Psychology 56*, 4, 519–543.

Pendleton, S.M., Cavalli, K.S., Pargament, K.I. and Nasr, S.Z. (2002) 'Religious/spiritual coping in childhood cystic fibrosis: A qualitative study.' *Pediatrics 109*, 1, e8–e8.

Quittner, A.L., Goldbeck, L., Abbott, J., Duff, A. *et al.* (2014) 'Prevalence of depression and anxiety in patients with cystic fibrosis and parent caregivers: results of the International Depression Epidemiological Study across nine countries.' *Thorax 69*, 12, 1090–1097.

Reynolds, N., Mrug, S., Hensler, M., Guion, K. and Madan-Swain, A. (2014) 'Spiritual coping and adjustment in adolescents with chronic illness: A 2-year prospective study.' *Journal of Pediatric Psychology 39*, 5, 542–551.

Rubin, D., Dodd, M., Desai, N., Pollock, B. and Graham-Pole, J. (2009) 'Spirituality in well and ill adolescents and their parents: The use of two assessment scales.' *Pediatric Nursing 35*, 1, 37–42.

Terreri, C.J. and Glenwick, D.S. (2013) 'The relationship of religious and general coping to psychological adjustment and distress in urban adolescents.' *Journal of Religion and Health 52*, 4, 1188–1202.

Westers, N.J., Rehfuss, M., Olson, L. and Wiemann, C.M. (2014) 'An exploration of adolescent nonsuicidal self-injury and religious coping.' *International Journal of Adolescent Medicine and Health 26*, 3, 345–349.

Chapter 21

Through These Dark Valleys
A Pediatric Chaplain's Response to the Problem of God and Evil

Kathleen Ennis-Durstine

> PRACTICE EXAMPLE 21.1 ACCOMPANYING THROUGH THE DARK VALLEYS
>
> I first met Ellie as a newborn on the neonatal unit. Her parents had the exhausted and stunned look of those receiving a continuous stream of test results and diagnoses – none of it good. 'Sometimes it seems as if everyone who comes brings bad news,' her mum told me. 'I don't want to hear any more bad news. How much more bad news can there be?' After that I met with them frequently during my regular visiting on the unit and supported them by listening for as long as it took to express their shock, frustrations and anxiety. It became apparent that Ellie had a serious incurable condition which meant that she would have complex special needs. Both her parents were constantly by her side. The family are Roman Catholic, so they asked for prayer, and Ellie was baptised in hospital by our Catholic chaplain.
>
> On one visit, out of the blue, her dad exclaimed to me with tears in his eyes, 'She'll never be perfect, will she?' And we explored together his hopes and dreams for his daughter and his anguish at the diagnosis and what it would mean. I was reminded of another mum facing similar issues who declared fiercely, 'My baby is not a mistake on God's production line. My baby is perfect just as he is.' We wondered together what perfection might be, for us and for God, and we accepted that there would be challenges ahead. We prayed together for big things and practical needs – for strength, for trust, for patience, for joy and for sleep – being honest with God about how they felt. Eventually, Ellie was able to be discharged home.

> Since then Ellie has been admitted regularly to the Evelina, sometimes in planned admissions, sometimes not, to intensive care or to a ward. Despite her condition, she has a cheeky smile and a mischievous sense of humour. She is not mobile but can communicate. She loves Peppa Pig and watching cartoons. I continue to support the family when they are here, catching up on their news and her progress. During one of these visits the Brexit vote was announced. Her family is not British and like many others on the ward were nervous and concerned about the future and whether they are welcome in this country. They had already experienced abuse in their neighbourhood after the vote.
>
> They don't know what the future will hold for Ellie. Her mum and dad are amazing parents, and we know each other well enough now for them to share that they are almost permanently exhausted, that Ellie has brought great joy and love into their lives and that, trusting in God, they take each day as it comes.
>
> *The Revd Sue Taylor, Chaplain, Evelina Children's Hospital, London, UK*

Theodicy is the branch of theology and philosophy which attempts to justify the reality of a good, benevolent, omniscient and fair God with the reality of suffering. Theodicy is not a defence of God. It is an attempt to show that it is rational to continue to believe in God despite the presence of evil and offers various frameworks to explain why that evil does exist. Most of us are looking for ways to understand why God 'allows' evil and suffering, or seems inconsistent in providing succour, deliverance or even acknowledgement. I will consider theories briefly, but the majority of this chapter will be looking at real-life examples of how ordinary people have explained the tragedies in their own lives, keeping the juxtaposition of God and evil in a comfortable relationship. This is ultimately what matters to us as pediatric chaplains: being with people who stand in the midst of the flood and find solid ground.

Augustine of Hippo (354–430 ce) reasoned from Scripture toward a resolution which centered on our free will. Evil, said Augustine, entered the world through the disobedience of Adam and Eve. God created a perfect realm and placed humans with free will into it. In choosing to exercise that free will in the direction of disobedience rather than obedience, sin and death entered the world and all humanity inherits the consequences – suffering (Schaff 2011).

Maimonides (1135–1204 ce), one of the great early Jewish philosophers, did not believe in an omniscient and omnipotent God who is nevertheless interested in the fate of humankind. Maimonides says that events in the natural world are purely natural and, yes, people fall ill and lose their loved ones and their fortunes. He states:

> you should not fall into error and seek to affirm in your imagination that His knowledge is like our knowledge or that His purpose and His providence and His governance are like our purpose and our providence and our governance. If man knows this, every misfortune will be borne lightly by him. (Guide for the Perplexed, Bk. III, ch. 24; Pines, p.497) (Friedlander 2010)

After the Holocaust, the Jewish approach to the question of evil and suffering became an important discussion. Elie Wiesel, a Holocaust survivor, wrote in his book *Night* (2008) of a time when a young man was being hanged in front of all the inmates and another observer asked where God was. Wiesel reports that he experienced an inner voice saying God was right up there on the gallows. Others, such as Arthur Cohen 1981), return to the free will argument: that God has established Law and it is the responsibility of humanity to choose to follow it or not.

In his classic book *When Bad Things Happen to Good People* (1981), Rabbi Harold Kushner returned to suffering as a consequence of natural laws, never God's will, and therefore God is available to help.

In Islam, evil is seen as distinct from suffering and is forbidden. But discerning what is evil often depends on the perspective of the individual and the command of God. An act itself is neutral, but if that act is counter to God's will, it is wicked. Suffering comes about through the choices of humans. Suffering is seen as a way of building character and spirituality, and God is so powerful that all suffering may be conquered with God's help (Aslan 2001).

In brief, the Hindu perspective is about enduring in order to transcend: 'Contacts with matter make us feel heat and cold, pleasure and pain. Arjuna, you must learn to endure fleeting things – they come and go!' (Miller 1986, p.31).

Buddhism also emphasizes the endurance necessary to escape from the endless rounds of death and rebirth. Suffering and evil are produced by selfish desires, cause and effect. It is the Buddhist's task to conquer these desires and the idea of the self as unique and permanent and understand that Truth and Reality are Nirvana (Rahula 1974).

The Abrahamic religions' story of Job has consistently been a source for many on the meaning of suffering and the place of God in that suffering.

When I first read Job straight through, I felt that any God who would enter into a betting match with Satan using human lives for coin was not a God I wanted to trust. It was not until I was feeling more than a little bit like Job that my perspective began to change. I grew to appreciate the faithful, heart-wrenching, questioning, the friend who sits silently; I grew to hate the advisors and the facile answers. When I finally went back to the text, I discovered 'Where were you when I laid the foundation of the earth?' (Job 38:4). What I heard was: 'I am God – I can't explain it; or, if I could, it would be in a language you don't speak. You may never understand. But, see – I showed up.' What I experienced was a sense that I ultimately had to pull the meaning out of my situation, but that I would not be totally alone in my striving. I connected with something much greater than myself, which gave me the 'foundation' on which I could build.

Chaplains call out the stories

There are several questions which arise when people experience suffering. One is 'Why?' Another is 'Why me?' Also, 'What did I do to deserve this?' and 'Where is my miracle?' These are certainly not all the questions, but they are among the most profound and difficult to answer. What happens to us today can only be explored through the lenses of past experience, of culture, of religion; of the systems from which we emerge and the authorities to which we adhere.

The essential role of the chaplain is to call out the stories. If we think we can provide any sorts of answers, we are sorely mistaken. Even if we have worked out our own explanations and justifications, what works for us is not necessarily what will ease the suffering of another. We call out the story of the relationship between the sufferer and God, between the sufferer and him or herself, between the sufferer and their worldview.

PRACTICE EXAMPLE 21.2: WATCHING
THE DA VINCI CODE

Several years ago I met the family of a four-year-old newly diagnosed with AML (acute myeloid leukemia). The mother was inconsolable; although described by family members as devoutly Catholic, she did not want to pray or ask for any relief from God. She seemed to tolerate my presence, but did not open up to talk about her distress. Several days after the diagnosis I found her alone in the child's room. She began to weep softly. I held out my hand, and she placed

> hers within it, grasping with the power of despair. Then she began to intone: 'It's my fault…'
>
> 'Why do you feel that your son's illness is your fault?' I asked.
>
> 'It is, it is. I've been disobedient. My priest told us at Mass that we should not go to see the movie *The Da Vinci Code*. That it is a lie, and sinful, and our Lord would punish us through hurting someone we loved. But I thought, it's only a story – so I saw it. But my priest was right – and look what I've done to my son!'
>
> The idea of suffering as punishment had been forced upon her in some ways, but she had also accepted it – if uncomfortably. There is no reset button, no 'escape' key. Regardless of my opinions, this morass was hers – and she needed to work her way through it. For days I simply showed up; I asked her to tell me about her childhood church and the way she learned about her faith from her family. She talked about her love of liturgy and how saying the Our Father always calmed her when she was younger. One afternoon I asked her if she would like to pray the Our Father; she did not want to pray, but she asked me to pray my version. I did so, as she continued to look out the window toward the spire of the nearest Catholic church. After some silence, I asked her what she thought would help her right now. 'Confession.' She did eventually rise above her despair, but only through the meaning-making that fit into her worldview.

One of the chaplain's biggest responsibilities is to stand in the place that is between the family and the staff. We can, and must, help staff to comprehend that the distress of a patient or a family is not necessarily the same as the distress felt by the staff. Staff may worry about the severity of an illness or injury, they may fall back on percentages and prognoses, they often are most concerned about the preservation of life, but less open to the preservation of meaningful life as understood by the patient or family. Staff can be caught up in very important things such as personal integrity, ethics, skill – and even curiosity (research) – and they may also benefit from a helping look at their backwards and sideways stories. Although professional chaplains are employed by hospitals, we are not mandated to defend our colleagues' viewpoints. We are mandated to try to understand them and to help those colleagues articulate the difficulties they are experiencing.

I began my relationship with evil/suffering early in life following my father's suicide. I started down a long road of wondering, reading, listening. Who is God and what is God up to? What is good? What is not? How might I take all the confusing possibilities and make sense of it all? But over the years it was the people who stood and faced it who taught me the most about evil.

> ### PRACTICE EXAMPLE 21.3: MURDER AND FOUR-YEAR-OLD WISDOM
>
> There are times when evil simply appears pure and undiluted. One day a friend had returned home to discover his wife and children murdered. Our sons had been born just days apart and grown up together in Sunday School. Our small town was shattered. And frightened. And angry. The general opinion was that whoever was responsible for this should be drawn, quartered, and burn in hell forever.
>
> One afternoon my four-year-old son joined me in the study. He climbed into my lap and told me he was sad that he would not see his friend again. Then he asked, 'When bad people die, do they get to go to heaven and live with God?'
>
> I was awed – and asked him if he was thinking about the person who had hurt his friend.
>
> 'Yes,' he answered.
>
> 'I don't know, sweetheart, but I guess I don't like to think about our friends having to share heaven with the person who hurt them.'
>
> 'I know, Mom, but if you want to go live in heaven with God when you die, then maybe you're not a bad person anymore.'

> ### PRACTICE EXAMPLE 21.4: DAVID AND DAD
>
> Frequently, the discussion of evil and suffering comes about because one wonders what God is doing – or not doing. Some people have a concept of God as manageable, or even manipulatable. David was born with a hypoplastic left heart. After his first surgery, the surgeons were unable to close the chest cavity. His parents were mid-20s with one older child. They each had a faith history and culture, but were not actively participating in a faith community.
>
> Early in David's hospitalization the family sought out the chaplain. They had some sense that the presence of the chaplain, and prayer, brought comfort and healing both to them and to their

son. They articulated a hopeful outlook, trusted the words and the authority of the physicians, and were attempting to live out the work of being good parents as well as possible.

One morning Dad stopped by my office to ask if I believed in miracles. He had returned to the evangelical church of his childhood and was fervently praying for his son's recovery. He was frustrated and disappointed that his prayers were, so far, unanswered. Dad talked a lot about what he was doing to better his relationship with God, because, surely, if God saw how hard he was working at this, God would respond. I asked him quietly if he had thought about David's relationship with God? He sat there stunned. In a few moments he replied that it never once occurred to him that his infant son might have a relationship with God – he thought this was all his (Dad's) responsibility. He began to spend much more quiet time with his son and wife, just touching his son and speaking softly to him. Two days later these parents came to me with a request for baptism before withdrawing the ventilator. Mom commented that she was so glad that her husband was finally able to see that David and God had worked out a different plan.

PRACTICE EXAMPLE 21.5: RELAPSING LEUKEMIA

I recall a poignant conversation with a mother of a seven-year-old girl who was nearing the end of her life following a long trajectory of treatment for her leukemia and its relapses. Eventually, the team agreed that palliative care was appropriate. As the child fitfully slept near us, the mother articulated the tension she was experiencing in her spiritual life. She admitted being angry at God, and not wanting to believe that a good and loving God could possibly exist if her child was allowed to undergo this kind of suffering. At the same time, she said, she didn't want to reject God altogether, because she wanted to hold on to the hope that her daughter would be with God, in God's embrace, when she died. The mother felt that she somehow needed to stay connected to God in order to preserve her own belief that God would be there to welcome her child upon death. The struggle of this mother was agonizing; in some mysterious way her daughter's impending death was allowing this mother to wrestle with her anger, fear, and hope all at once, with the deep conviction that although she was so angry with God, she also wanted to trust God's presence in the midst of it all. Through everything this mother was expressing, I saw how the depth of love for her child was somehow grounding her in her spiritual life, even as she journeyed through a kind of trial she had never experienced before, and I hoped that the bond of that love for her daughter would eventually keep carrying her toward a spiritual experience of deep comfort and healing.

Jessica Bratt Carle, St. Jude Children's Research
Hospital, Memphis, Tennessee, USA

PRACTICE EXAMPLE 21.6: ARJUN AND THE ELEPHANT

Children are often given simplified concepts of God, which, when some crisis occurs, become incompatible with understanding. But children are also masters at what they do best: wondering. I was paged to see a seven-year-old boy who had just been admitted after a car accident. While stopped at the side of the road, a drunken driver slammed into the rear of their car. Arjun had been thrown forward and most of the bones of his face were broken. His injuries were not life-threatening, but they were certainly painful and would require several surgeries to correct. His mother asked for chaplain help in responding to his questions about why God would let this happen to him if God loved him. Rather than answering his question, I asked him to tell me about God. He was very animated and excited to tell me much that he had learned from his Hindu faith community and from his parents. At the end of our conversation I said that I really didn't know why this accident and injury had happened to him, and that it might take us a few days to think about it together. Would he like to do that? 'Definitely,' was his response. We continued this discussion over the next several days. When I walked into his room days later, I heard, 'Chaplain Kathleen, I figured it out!' Arjun had reasoned thus: God was busy that night. He was holding an elephant in his left hand. God saw that the drunk driver was about to hit Arjun's car and knew it would take two hands to stop it. But that would mean dropping the elephant, who would surely die because it was such a long fall. But God knew that Arjun would be all right. So God loved both Arjun and the elephant.

> ### PRACTICE EXAMPLE 21.7: BETHANY AND ELIZABETH
>
> Sometimes the best plans and hardest endeavors do not appear to find favor with God's plan in our lives. When things go awry, people struggle to reconcile their hopes with the reality of their disappointment and losses. Elizabeth was a 26-week preemie. Her mother, Bethany, was a professional with a mainline Protestant background. She attended church, but she did not identify as a particularly religious person. Elizabeth had many complicating factors and after four months had developed severe necrotizing enterocolitis (NEC). I often sat with Bethany when she visited. As the NEC progressed, Bethany made the decision to withdraw support and hold Elizabeth while she died. She asked me to stay with them until Elizabeth died and say a blessing. I asked Bethany where God was for her now, in this moment. She told me she didn't think I'd like her answer, but, nevertheless, would tell me. Bethany chose to hold God responsible – for everything that was going wrong. She was very articulate about refusing to be a victim of fate, or chaos, and refusing to be a victim of Satan/evil. For her, holding God responsible meant that she was also affirming the reality of God. If God were real, then she could somehow find her way through her grief and disappointment. A world with a responsible God was better than a world without God.

Meaning-making

Each of the stories above describes how ordinary people come to understand the place of suffering – perhaps evil – in their experience. They didn't rely on books or professors. They leaned somewhat on culture and family teaching, but they relied primarily on their own experience of God in their own lives. Some of their reasoning comes close to the free will argument, some reflects that suffering is a natural aspect of creation. Some struggled with whether or not they were being tested – or punished. But none of these upheld them; no theory gave them the strength to look beyond their suffering and find hope, love, grace and meaning.

Theirs were the stories that have led me to a deeper acceptance, appreciation and understanding of suffering/evil in human life. I cannot answer the question about why evil exists, why suffering is so pervasive. Like Job, I would like to demand fairness, if not pure justice, of God. I would like to understand why goodness doesn't reach a critical mass and overtake us all. Yet I feel certain that whatever language God might use to discourse with me, it would be a language I could never comprehend, and explanations so far beyond my ability to even think about them that they would be without sense.

My son gave me an open-hearted, and open-minded, experience of a God of grace beyond what I could possibly have imagined on my own. For him, God could make anything good. But I came to appreciate that my son's thoughtfulness had an accountability side – in order for God to make a bad person good, the person had to want God. Over the years I've continued to wonder about this when faced with people who are not easy to understand and/or forgive; and wonder if God can make bad people good. Can God make bad situations good? And what is the desire toward God that needs to be present?

Between the Holy Spirit and David's dad, I began to comprehend that there may be more Godly stuff going on than I, or anyone else, can readily see. How do we stand in this seeming emptiness and trust? And Evelyn found her way to the traditional comforts of her faith. Even though she continued to think that her son's illness was, in part, her punishment, she could stand with God and face her own feelings of guilt and accept herself as still beloved.

Arjun and Bethany turned my ideas of God and suffering inside out and upside down. Are they so far from the traditional theodicies? No. But they personalize them. God becomes both much bigger than a personal God, and also a very personal God. Their lives, in the midst of their pain and grief, felt redeemed, of value.

We have to know where we stand, what gives us the strength to continue to walk into others' suffering, day after day. It is only in part about theologies and philosophies; like it or not, we are better fit to be with others in their tragedies if we know something about tragedy first-hand. Don't go looking for it – that is not what I am suggesting. Some people live a long time with no experience of significant tragedy or suffering. But if you have had some tragic experiences, learn from them. Let them lead you through your dark valley so that you may more fully understand others. If you have not had your own experiences – listen. Hear the stories of those for whom you care; read – a lot. Question. Don't accept too-easy answers. Theodicy is too deep for those.

Future development and research needs

- Working groups of children, parents and staff to explore how they understand suffering and how they would advise chaplaincy and other families in the lessons and insights they have learned.

- Produce appropriate bespoke gift and training resources out of this perceived corporate wisdom.
- Pediatric chaplains understanding and engaging in philosophical arguments of suffering.

Summary

- Tradition gives us philosophical and theological arguments for the reality of evil and the reality of a good God.
- Traditional answers do not always fit exactly into individual experience.
- Our particular experiences of tragedy, of evil, along with our particular experiences of the holy, shape the ways we have available to integrate a good God with evil as a reality.
- Don't assume people will stay in the same place in their meaning-making.
- Most people have an extraordinary ability to make sense and make meaning of the tragedies in their lives.
- Spend primary time, study and energy developing at least a starting point in your personal, religious and philosophical understanding and response to suffering. It is crucial that we have this at least in an embryonic working position to prepare, build upon and sustain our wellbeing.

Questions for reflection

- What has your particular religious/spiritual tradition taught you about God and evil? Can you identify how this has influenced the way you interact with others in the midst of tragedy? Who have you encountered in your work who has made meaning out of a terrible situation in ways that felt unusual to you? What did you learn?
- Is it all right not to have an answer to 'why'? And what do we do when our answers to 'why' are no longer are enough for us?
- How do we help others through feelings of guilt and punishment? Consider that while people may not be culpable in ways that have led to this present moment of illness/tragedy,

they may feel culpable about something important in their lives. What is the chaplain's place in helping others 'confess' as a way of moving toward atonement/redemption and closer relationship with the holy?

References

Aslan, A. (2001) 'The Fall and the Overcoming of Evil and Suffering in Islam.' In P. Koslowski (ed.) *A Discourse of the World Religions: The Origin and the Overcoming of Evil and Suffering in the World Religions.* Dordrecht: Kluwer.

Cohen, A. (1981) *The Tremendum: A Theological Interpretation of the Holocaust.* New York, NY: Crossroad.

Friedlander, M. (trans.) (2010) A *Guide for the Perplexed, by Moses Maimonides.* Kansas: Digireads.

Kushner, H. (1981) *When Bad Things Happen to Good People.* New York, NY: Anchor.

Miller, B.S. (trans.) (1986) *The Bhagavad-Gita.* Toronto: Bantam.

Rahula, W. (1974) *What the Buddha Taught,* 2nd edition. New York, NY: Grove Press.

Schaff, P. (ed.) (2011) *The Complete Works of St Augustine.* Kindle edition.

Wiesel, E. (2008) *Night.* London: Penguin.

Chapter 22

Perspectives on Suffering from Major Faith and Worldview Traditions

Emma Roberts

Introduction

Seriously ill children and their families want to make sense of why a child has to go through illness, pain and suffering, sometimes with little or no hope of recovery. They may look for an explanation of why this has happened to them, why God would allow this to happen and whether they are being punished. Many who find themselves and their loved ones in this situation turn to their faith and beliefs for comfort, while others find their faith tested in the face of suffering. A chaplain or pastoral carer is uniquely placed to provide a response to these difficulties.

In this chapter, chaplains and other faith or community representatives explain their traditions' main beliefs about suffering and why it occurs. It is important to remember that there can be a wide variation of beliefs within faith communities, so, while we have tried to capture the main viewpoints, individual families may not share all the beliefs described here. Each family's reaction to their child's illness will be a unique combination of their beliefs, personalities and experiences.

Buddhism – Keith Munnings, Chair of Buddhist Healthcare Chaplaincy Group and Medini Richardson, Chaplain at Birmingham Women's and Children's Hospital

> *Evil action springs from attachment, it springs from ill-will, it springs from folly, it springs from fear.*
>
> Sigalaka Sutta, *The Pali Cannon* (Walshe 2012)

Buddhists believe that suffering is part of the natural world. The word 'suffering' is used differently in Buddhism compared with how it is used more generally. Everything is impermanent and therefore everything brings us suffering. The Buddha taught Four Noble Truths, which are common to all variations of Buddhism:

- First Noble Truth: that we all suffer.
- Second Noble Truth: that there is a cause for our suffering.
- Third Noble Truth: that it is possible to be free from suffering.
- Fourth Noble Truth: the path to tread to be free from suffering.

This view that everything causes suffering because everything is fleeting can make Buddhism seem pessimistic, whereas Buddhists believe that it is actually an understanding of the nature of things as they are. This is seen as a tremendous insight and a release. This concept is the basis for its application in various therapies such as mindfulness-based cognitive therapy and stress reduction.

Suffering is understood as something created by humans, and so we are responsible for it. Although Buddhists may use the concept of evil in everyday language, Buddhism does not accept the idea of innate evil, as good and bad are also subject to change. Instead, the words 'unwholesome' and 'wholesome' are used.

Buddhists are taught to accept suffering, and to allow pain to pass. They believe that we cannot control it, but we can let it flow through us with wisdom and compassion. This may have an influence on how families with a hospitalised child behave when confronted with difficult experiences; however, the degree to which this teaching is understood and accepted can vary between individuals.

Anybody can support Buddhist families by offering comfort, understanding and being with them, if possible providing things that they need and offering a presence of compassion and peace. In addition to this, Buddhist chaplains can offer religious inspiration or a reminder of their faith, as well as providing reading materials and objects. If requested, Buddhist chaplains can also offer guided visualisations and meditations.

Christianity – The Revd Nick Ball, former Christian Chaplain, Birmingham Children's Hospital

> *I have told you these things, so that in me you may have peace. In this world you will have trouble. But take heart! I have overcome the world.*
>
> John 16:33, The Holy Bible (New International Version)

Christians believe that suffering is an inevitable part of the temporal world in which we live, which will give way to the kingdom of God. There are differing beliefs about why suffering occurs; some believe that suffering can be a direct punishment from God while others disagree. Some Christians believe that it is a way of testing humans.

Christianity teaches that God is powerful and loving, which for some may seem to be at odds with the existence of pain and suffering in the world. Some may even avoid using the word 'Almighty' to describe God for this reason, and in some cases believers' faith could be so severely challenged as to lead to faith being either abandoned permanently or abandoned temporarily and resumed, perhaps in a modified form, later.

There are various ways in which Christians may explain the existence of suffering; some people believe that humans were created perfect and then deliberately fell away from their state of grace and became sinners; others believe that moral evil came about because humanity was weak and immature, and we can cause suffering through different defects in our actions, intentional or otherwise.

There are differing opinions on the nature of suffering within Christianity. Some Christians believe that the Devil is the source of evil, while others may think that only God exists, and what appears to be evil has to be seen as ultimately part of the harmonious universe. In this case, evil is a privation of good and does not have a real existence in itself. A minority of Christians still believe that witchcraft can bring evil on people, or that people can be possessed by demons. This belief may be particularly prominent in cases of mental illness. The majority of Christians, however, would accept that illnesses can be mental as well as physical.

When faced with suffering, such as that of having a very ill child in hospital, Christians will often turn to prayer, asking for an end to the pain or strength to endure it. If this appears to have no effect, believers can struggle with their faith. They could question why this has happened to them, what has caused this and what is going to happen.

If you are a chaplain or volunteer of another faith caring for a Christian child and family, attentive listening is often appreciated by families. You could offer to contact someone from their faith tradition or provide a religious resource. If it feels appropriate, you could offer a prayer. If you do this, it is important to pray in a way that respects (without imitating) the family's own faith tradition. A little discussion before actually praying would be wise.

Hinduism – Rakesh Bhatt, Hindu Chaplain at Birmingham Women's and Children's Hospital

Agamapayino'nityastvam titiksva bharata.

Pain and pleasure are impermanent. Bear them patiently understanding that this is karma and nothing more.

Bhagwat Geeta

Hinduism teaches that suffering is an integral part of our lives. Our actions, both in this life and in previous lives, will determine the degrees of pain and suffering, joy and sadness, success and despair that we will attain. As long as one is attached to the chaos of *samsara*, the cycle of rebirth, then suffering will exist.

The law of karma is often used as a tool to understand the existence of suffering. This is the idea that actions taken in this life or a previous life will denote the life that one shall live now, or the idea that each cause shall have an effect. The law of karma and reincarnation is often used to explain why we are born with different advantages or disadvantages. Ignorance leads us to desire and attachment, which then lead to further karma. What one desires, one wills. What you will, you do. And what you do, you become. So being ignorant, our desires pull us in directions that lead to darkness and suffering. Suffering is therefore purely a consequence of actions, and not a punishment. Although there are variations in practice, the faith does not believe in the existence of evil as a supernatural force such as the Devil or an independent being.

Some children and families in hospital may feel guilty that it was something that they did which led to their child's suffering. Chaplains can try to remind parents that their presence and strength will give strength to their children, and that a peaceful and strong bond between families will increase their child's resilience.

Hindu chaplains support the faith of children and their parents to keep the family strong in times of turmoil and distress through whatever means possible. This may include devotional songs, reading passages from the sacred texts, discussing the many adventures of Lord Krishna, or joining hands in prayer to ask for strength to get the child and family through this time of suffering. Mindfulness may also be used to alleviate anxiety as well as yoga, not just for the patient but also for the family.

If you are a non-Hindu caring for a Hindu family, then, as with any person in distress, the best that someone can do is listen to the worries or concerns that the family has. Further to this, you can comfort the family and try to create a positive and calming environment, thus making the suffering of the family a bit more bearable.

Humanism – Simon O'Donoghue, Head of Pastoral Support at Humanist UK

> *Humanists believe that the solutions to the world's problems lie in human thought and action rather than divine intervention.*
>
> 2002 Amsterdam Declaration (http://iheu.org/ humanism/the-amsterdam-declaration)

Humanists view the answer to the question 'Why do people suffer?' as grounded in a naturalistic explanation of the world. There are at least three broad categories into which this question can be divided, but this is in no way exclusive:

1. Human psychology, and the social conditions to which people are exposed, means that some human beings become motivated to do things, knowingly or unknowingly, that cause suffering to others.

2. Our biological nature, which can sometimes malfunction or become overwhelmed, means we have the potential to develop illnesses that cause us agonising pain.

3. The physical forces that dictate the environmental conditions of the world occasionally lead to terrible and destructive natural disasters.

Put simply, suffering happens because it does: that is just the way the world is. Humanists would cite the causes for both natural and human suffering as being rooted in the natural processes in the world around us and within us. They would also suggest that although these two categories are distinct, often they can relate or have causality for one another. Humanists do attempt to understand suffering with the objective of either preventing it or dealing with it when it occurs. By accepting suffering as unavoidable, we can learn to cope with it and focus on developing ways to reduce it.

If a humanist family had a seriously ill child in hospital, their main questions would be about how suffering can be reduced in that moment and in the future. As humanists believe that this is the one life we have, the focus would be on how suffering can be relieved in the here and now. For example, they would want to find out the most effective medical interventions to overcome the illness, as well as the pain management techniques to keep them comfortable.

The intervention of a humanist pastoral carer in hospital is person-centred and focuses entirely on the narrative of the individual for whom they are supporting. There is no agenda or dogma, and they will look to build trust and intimacy by being present, empathising, actively listening, and by demonstrating unconditional positive regard, using a whole range of finely tuned and highly developed interpersonal skills. Unlike religious chaplains, the humanist pastoral carer does not attempt to offer hope of salvation in the next life. The focus, instead, is on empowering people to be happier, confident and more fulfilled in this life by opening up meaningful discussions about universal aspects of the human experience: hopes, dreams, relationships, love, fear, morality, meaning, purpose, values, forgiveness, etc.

Islam – Dr Aftab Parwaz, Imam at Birmingham Women's and Children's Hospital

> *And whoso has done an atom's weight of good shall see it. And whoso has done an atom's weight of evil shall see it.*
>
> 99:7–8, The Qur'an (Arberry 1996)

The prevalent Islamic belief is that suffering is from God to serve a wiser purpose which fallible humans are unable to acknowledge. Jackson (2010) identifies some of the significant Islamic beliefs from the variant schools of Islamic theology regarding the nature of suffering. He states: 'Yet, while God can, according to the Maturidites (orthodox theology school in Sunni Islam founded in tenth century), create evil and human suffering, God cannot and does not create evil that does not ultimately serve a wise purpose.'

The remaining two dominant theodicies in Islam are that of the Mu'tazilites (theological school that flourished from the eighth century to the tenth century in Basra and Baghdad) and the Ash'arites (orthodox Sunni theology founded in the tenth century). The famous Mu'tazilite belief that it is essential upon God to be just to creation (*adl'*) meant that they disassociated evil from God entirely. The Ash'arites, however, maintained that God is the originator of suffering as he is with goodness, whilst emphasising the subjective nature of suffering; it could serve an ulterior purpose which the transcendent God knows.

Regarding the source of evil and suffering, Muslims believe it to stem both from a supernatural force, from God in this case, and from human actions. Humans are to react to suffering by humbling themselves. The Qur'an states: 'We have sent no Prophet [who was denied] to any city but that We seized its people with misery and hardship, that haply they might be humble' (7:94; Arberry 1996).

The majority of Muslims believe that God has granted free will to humans, through which they are able to determine good and evil actions. Muslims also believe that everyone is born upon a state of *fitrah* or natural disposition which inclines towards belief in a creator and basic moral principles. Humans, therefore, are given the ability to actively commit evil as well as goodness, with the condition that they are to be judged accordingly in the hereafter.

Muslims believe that every soul shall be judged according to their own actions. This comes with the conditions, however, that an individual is *Mukallaf*, a term used to describe an individual who has passed puberty, is sane and is physically able. Children, therefore, are not to be punished for any acts which may oppose Islamic beliefs. Further, children are not put into suffering as a result of the actions of another individual, as clearly indicated in the Qur'an: 'Every soul shall be pledged for what it has earned' (74:38; Arberry 1996).

Islam draws a distinction between suffering in general and that in relation to children. Looking at some of the explanations for the suffering of children, Watt states: 'A common view in later times was that God allowed children to suffer in order to warn adults and that then in order to compensate for their sufferings he gave them an indemnity such as entry into Paradise' (1979, pp.6–7). The faith's beliefs regarding the nature of suffering would have an impact on how believers react to suffering in that it would advise them to adopt patience and return to God, humbling themselves in so doing. The doctrines of the faith that could be used to respond to a child and their family include but are not limited to the Hadith (meaning peace be upon him, a salutation used by Muslims upon hearing, reading or uttering the name of the prophet) related by al-Bukhari in which the Prophet (a prophetic teaching collated in books of Hadith) said: 'If Allah wants to do good to somebody, He afflicts him with trials' (vol.7, no. 548).

A common question that is posed by believers who are suffering, or have a child who is suffering, is what they did to deserve the suffering. In accordance with the doctrines of Islam, one would respond by answering that not all suffering is an immediate result of evil or one's actions. Humans are taught to adopt patience in the wake of suffering and return to God in prayer. Believers are further taught to pray to God to alleviate the suffering and are to be rewarded for their patience.

Judaism – Rabbi Yossi Jacobs, Chief Minister at Birmingham Hebrew Congregation

> *The Lord has given and the Lord has taken away; blessed be the name of the Lord*
>
> Job 1:2

Followers of Judaism believe that the reason for suffering may not always be apparent to humans; we cannot understand everything that God does. They do, however, believe in an after-life, and that we do not know how things will be after death. Jews believe that children become responsible for their actions when they reach a certain age (12 years old for a girl and 13 years old for a boy), but do not tend to see suffering as a form of punishment, instead focusing on rewards for good behaviour.

It does not follow from this that humans have no control over suffering. God created the world with both good and bad in it, and each person has both good and evil parts within themselves. Each person, therefore, has a choice about which part of themselves to follow. Judaism places a responsibility on people to do everything they can to save a life, even if it means breaking a commandment. For example, Jews would be able to work on the Sabbath if it meant saving a life, even though this is usually forbidden in Judaism.

One of the ways in which human agency can lessen suffering is through medicine and the care given to children in hospital. Jewish children and families who are in hospital may therefore believe that humans do have the power, and therefore the responsibility, to alleviate suffering, and it is a religious requirement for each person to do what they can to help others.

As with many religious believers, Jews will often fall back on their faith as a support in difficult times, although they naturally can have questions of why this has happened to them. Judaism's answer is that we cannot know the ways of God, and it is not always possible to know why something has happened to a particular family, but that it is important to have faith. Any chaplain can support a Jewish family by spending time with them and showing love and kindness. In their support of a family, Jewish chaplains will often include prayer and encourage a person's faith.

Sikhism – Parkash Sohal, Sikh Chaplain at Birmingham Women's and Children's Hospital

As someone sows, so he reaps.

Bhai Gurdaas Vaaran (p.1)

A core belief of Sikhs is that of Karma. Sikhs believe that each person's actions determine what will happen to them, and that good is rewarded with good fortune, and bad deeds are rewarded with suffering. People carry their deeds from past lives with them, so young children who are suffering could be being punished for something that they have done in a previous life. It is not the fault of the parents, and children are not punished for what their parents have done.

Suffering is given by God, and so Sikhs believe that it is a part of life which should be accepted. However, this does not mean that there is nothing that people can do to alleviate their suffering. Illness and suffering can be relieved through good deeds, faith and, in particular, meditation on God and prayer. There are set prayers to recite in times of illness and other suffering. These can take up to an hour and a half to recite, but can be much shorter (for examples of prayers to use with families with an ill child, see Bakhshi and Sohal 2013).

Hospitalised Sikh children and their parents naturally often question why they are suffering, especially when a child is so young that she is unable to have done anything in her life deserving of punishment. In these cases, Sikh chaplains would stress that sometimes there is no clear explanation for why a child is suffering, but that God knows best and has a reason for sending suffering to this family. It is important to note that the parents are not to blame for what is happening. A chaplain could offer and encourage prayers, as well as pastoral support.

If you are not of the Sikh faith and meet a Sikh child or family, pastoral support will be appreciated, such as a listening ear or any prayer resources that your chaplaincy department might have. If you do not have a Sikh chaplain who is able to provide religious support to the family, you could try to contact a local Sikh temple (*Gurdwara*), who will provide support to a member of their community who is in need.

References

Arberry, A.J. (1996) *The Koran Interpreted: A Translation.* London: Simon & Schuster.

Bakhshi, S.S. and Sohal, P.K. (2013) *Sikh Prayers for an Ill Child.* Birmingham: Red Balloon Resources.

Jackson, S.A. (2010) 'The problem of suffering: Muslim theological reflections.' *Huffington Post.* Accessed on 24/11/2017 at www.huffingtonpost.com/sherman-a-jackson/on-god-and-suffering-musl_b_713994.html.

Walshe, M. (2012) *The Long Discourses of the Buddha: A Translation of the Dīgha Nikāya.* Boston, MA: Wisdom Publications.

Watt, W.M. (1979) 'Suffering in Sunnite Islam.' *Studia Islamica 50*, 1, 5–19.

Conclusion

If you are a paediatric chaplain, we hope that as you have read this book you have felt a sense of being with kindred spirits, listening to people who you don't have to explain yourself to or who might put you on a pedestal or think you are weird! We hope we have celebrated the distinctiveness of what makes paediatric chaplaincy paediatric chaplaincy, even if we cannot agree how to spell it! We are grateful for the inspiring stories from around the world, illustrating the unique contributions of our discipline, and appreciate our contributors' willingness to share. We have so much to be encouraged by and we seek to share that but also to give some direction of global travel as individual chaplains, teams and as a universal vocation. Even this week, I have just heard about another paediatric chaplaincy network in Germany having their 30th year celebration!

We hope it has inspired, challenged and motivated us to raise the bar even higher, which is a challenge, given much of the wonderful work that already happens in contributing to the wellbeing of our patients, families, institutions and communities. It is our responsibility to integrate, triangulate and critique our practice, with relevant theory, patient stories and our faith and values, to set our own standards, competencies, capabilities, guidelines and good practice. We do this for the safety of those we seek to serve as well ourselves.

To summarise, we have tried to highlight the particular Skills, Attitudes, Knowledge and Ethics (SAKE) around different elements of paediatric chaplaincy which include:

- distinctiveness
- spirituality and development
- spiritual, religious and pastoral care of sick children and their families
- loss and attachment
- supporting staff and the life of the institution

- engagement with the natural life of our patients: play, development, transition, family, community
- understanding some of the wider dynamics which impact our work
- empowerment, participation and safe engagement with children
- pros and cons of working in multifaith and religious and spiritual constructs
- dealing with and supporting families through times of injustice and unnaturalness
- perspectives on suffering, religion and evil
- differences between caring for multifaith and spiritual needs of neonates, babies, children and young people as opposed to adults
- challenges of different patient groups
- exploring sacred space and places
- screening and assessment models
- affirming assets and offering love and compassion to those struggling
- being able and comfortable in the silence, the liminal, the saddest places of life
- duty of care in positions of power, powerlessness and voicelessness
- creative development of our service
- responding to emergencies and trauma
- ethical framework and principles
- personal and professional conduct of boundaries, wellbeing and resilience
- integration to add value into all relevant aspects of the life of our institution
- research and evidence-based practice.

We celebrate our progress so far and commit ourselves towards more contextual paediatric chaplaincy and spiritual care, to hear more stakeholder patient, family and staff voices. There are significant areas where further development would be helpful:

- Research – more evidence-based practice:
  - efficacy of paediatric chaplaincy
  - patient, family and staff satisfaction audits of precise aspects of our work
  - patient reporting outcome measures (PROMs), with PROMs also for families
  - clearer understanding of the spiritual and religious needs of sick children and their families
  - a taxonomy of what paediatric chaplains actually do
  - how a child's illness and their spiritual life interact
  - effective screening, assessment and intervention tools
  - child- and family-centred models of working in multicultural settings
  - elements that add value to our institution
  - spiritual abuse and how to mitigate against it or address it
  - universal standards, competencies and capabilities
  - generalist and specialist spiritual care roles
  - cost and savings implications of our work
  - what is a significant spiritual encounter with those who cannot speak.
- Contextual resources and rituals:
  - developing, sharing and disseminating more multifaith, spiritual and pastoral care resources: comforting gift booklets, spiritual play activities, prayer and reflection booklets for chaplains, staff support and training activities
  - more research centres to develop specialist aspects of our distinctiveness

- e-learning modules and specific training courses
- meaning-making resources and rituals that take illness, lament, grief and loss equally seriously.

- Initiating, building and maintaining relationships:
  - that are empowering, flourishing, life-giving and safe
  - chaplaincy e-contact and support spaces
  - robust referral processes
  - contextually appropriate patient and family recording platforms
  - cultivating people of peace
  - joined-up community support
  - international community of paediatric chaplaincy practice.

These are the things that will bring us life in more fullness. We might be emotionally and physically exhausted at the end of the day, but we are simultaneously renewed and replenished by being in the privileged position of caring for sick, dying, bereaved children, their families and staff, looking to meet religious, spiritual and pastoral needs in hospital, hospices and community institutions.

Chaplaincy has naturally grown out of and been perceived as being about support around bereavement, dying and death. We hope this book has shown how we have matured into so much more without leaving behind our rightful heritage. We are now offering the same elevated level of care to those who are sick or who have long-term conditions or life-threatening illness. In the same way as paediatric chaplaincy is not chaplaincy to little adults, paediatric chaplaincy is more than an imitation of chaplaincy to grown-ups. We are growing into an established, recognised discipline in our own right and for the benefits of the child in our midst.

Appendix 1
Being a Paediatric Specialist in a General Hospital
Deborah Louise Wilde

For the past ten years I have been privileged to serve as lead chaplain at Oxford Children's Hospital, and alongside this leading in other specialisms such as transplant, renal, heart centre and critical care areas across the main Oxfordshire University Hospital sites.

The Children's Hospital forms a 100-bed block in the centre of the largest site, with outpatients, day treatment and specialist units. Yet, because of their access to emergency departments, our intensive care and high-dependency units are deep within the core of the main adult general hospital site. Similarly, our women's hospital, which cradles the maternity and neonatal units, lies alongside both the adult and children's hospitals. As a team, we cover the four hospitals and hospice in the Trust and, naturally, we see patients and families over the span of many years and multiple admissions or visits. For this reason the transition between services and stages is something that is a constantly growing area of the hospitals' oversight, and two groups I sit on regularly look at developing this potentially difficult bridge.

Working in the same area for any length of time, caring for each generation, means our lives journey together. One night recently I was called to a toddler who had died suddenly in his cot at home. As soon as I entered the emergency unit I saw the family who I had sat with, visited and supported during the teenage daughter's admission for meningitis. The teenager, now a young mother, faced the cruel loss of her only child. That night, and in the bleak days ahead, the family began to find their new way surrounded by those who they had trusted and received care from eight years before. Similarly, coming on to the neuroscience ward a few months ago, an elderly man, newly diagnosed with a brain tumour, immediately reached out for my hand, for we had met on the night his small grandson was admitted dead after a car collision.

Our work as part of the child death team is perhaps one of the very distinctive pieces of work that we have given a lot of time and energy to in recent years. From a very palpable need evolved the provision of rapid-response support in the event of sudden and unexpected child death. The regional boundaries for care provision extend over three counties, and we see on average 52 sudden child deaths every year. Chaplaincy services have been part of the team that delivers this care as it developed essentially because of the nature of the supportive care required to families and also to staff. From the emergence of the earliest model of rapid-response care for sudden and unexpected child death, chaplaincy has had a fully integrated role in the care provision. Initially, this involved ensuring all supporting staff and professional groups were contacted, that there was effective liaison between each group, and that there was one identified person (central point of contact) to which the family could relate to guide them through the processes ahead. This more functional role opened the way for relationships to be built that recognised the need for pastoral, spiritual and religious care not just for the family but supporting all involved. The chaplain involved in each incident is now part of a rapid-response meeting which advises and responds to planning care within the next 48 working hours, incorporating schools, Child and Adolescent Mental Health Services (CAMHS), general practitioners, social services and other agencies where appropriate. As team lead in this service, I also sit on the Child Death Overview Panel which examines all child deaths in the area, looks at areas of learning and how we can care for families after child death and develop better practice both locally and nationally.

Learning together is very much at the core of our chaplaincy team. Each member has specialist areas of work and responsibility, and thus I have developed a confidence in what chaplaincy can offer children's wards in the everyday pastoral, spiritual and religious care as well as in bereavement. Our learning and our development in these areas complements and informs the whole team ministry, our teaching and our vision. We share in regular times of reflection, case review and, very essentially, peer support. In a multifaith team we naturally bring our own faith perspectives and cultural understandings, but in a very honest way of offering insights that hold a breadth of narratives through which we and our patients journey. Together we draw parallels, we evaluate practice, and alongside one another we recognise the distinctiveness of each stage in life, from first breath to the last.

For some we care for, ours will be brief intervention, sometimes acute and deeply meaningful. Occasionally, we will see patients and families over many years. In a highly medicalised and academic institution, we rediscover our sense of self, our need for soulfulness almost daily. In recent years, teaching on spirituality, spiritual care and spiritual assessment across the Trust has grown. We have been amazed by the waiting list for places on our first course in Practical Philosophy for staff and have celebrated the demand for two further terms to continue. For similar reasons I regularly teach mindfulness taster sessions in Healthy Hospital days and in-reach sessions on mindfulness at ward handovers.

Here, as a clustered community, we come together to recognise difference and alikeness. As many cultures, many faiths, and embracing each age in this life's journey, we recognise the significance in holy days, in community celebrations and occasions of shared importance from Eid to Easter and Passover. What we find in each is the discovery and recognition of shared truths, the presence of soul, spirit and meaning together.

Understanding our stories and recognising the journey is very much part of the chaplain's role within a healing community. In a large acute Trust, we see clearly motifs, marks of our shared spiritual reality, embedded in the fabric of life, illness, wellbeing and death.

Perhaps what is most profound and deeply powerful – in the rawness of disease and death but also in the steady path back to physical wellness – is the drawing from who we are and the caregiving of the community around us to identify our humanness, our faith and our hope.

Appendix 2

Useful Websites for Paediatric Chaplains

Chaplain specific organizations

Association of Hospice and Palliative Care Chaplains (UK) – www.ahpcc.org.uk
Association of Muslim Chaplains (USA) – www.associationofmuslimchaplains.com
Association of Professional Chaplains (USA) – www.professionalchaplains.org
Chaplaincy Australia – www.chaplaincyaustralia.com
College of Health Care Chaplains (UK) – www.healthcarechaplains.org
European Network of Health Care Chaplaincy – www.enhcc.eu
HealthCare Chaplaincy Network (USA) – www.healthcarechaplaincy.org
Healthcare Chaplains Ministry Association (USA) – www.hcmachaplains.org
National Association of Catholic Chaplains (USA) – www.nacc.org
Neshama: Association of Jewish Chaplains (USA) – www.najc.org
New Zealand Healthcare Chaplains Association – www.nzhealthcarechaplains.org.nz
Paediatric Chaplaincy Network (UK) – www.paediatric-chaplaincy-network.org
Pediatric Chaplains Network (USA) – www.pediatricchaplains.org
UK Board of Healthcare Chaplaincy – www.ukbhc.org.uk

Resources

Baker Ross craft supplies – www.bakerross.co.uk or www.bakerross.com
Bible Gateway (with many translations available) – www.biblegateway.com
Godly Play – www.godlyplayfoundation.org or www.godlyplay.uk
Happy – religious and cultural festivals – www.happy.co.uk/about-happy/free-publications/festivals
Holidays on the net – www.holidays.net
Held in Hope Videos – www.paediatric-chaplaincy-network.org/media/online-videos
Hello Holy Days (Muslim) – www.helloholydays.com
Illustrated Children's Ministry – www.illustratedchildrensministry.com
Pathways Bereavement Video, Winnie Palmer Hospital – www.youtube.com/watch?v=Ru-CIi0Rx20
Religious festivals and events – www.reonline.org.uk/supporting/festivals-calendar
Therapist Aid – www.therapistaid.com
World Prayers Project – www.worldprayers.org

Pinterest has boards for all different sorts of festivals, crafts, etc.

Research and learning

Association for Clinical Pastoral Education – www.acpe.edu
Beliefnet – www.beliefnet.com
Center for Spirituality, Theology and Health – www.spiritualityandhealth.duke.edu
Center for the Spirituality of Children – www.childrens.com/patient-resources/visitor-patient-guide/family-support-services/pastoral-spiritual-care/center-for-the-spirituality-of-children
Centre for Paediatric Spiritual Care – www.bwc.nhs.uk/centre-for-paediatric-spiritual-care
European Network of Research on Religion, Spirituality and Health – www.rish.ch/en
GW Institute for Spirituality and Health – www.smhs.gwu.edu
Health and Social Care Chaplaincy [Journal] – https://journals.equinoxpub.com/index.php/HSCC
Health and Social Care in the Community [Journal] – www.onlinelibrary.wiley.com/journal/10.1111/(ISSN)1365-2524
International Journal for Children's Spirituality – www.tandfonline.com/loi/cijc20
Journal of Health Care Chaplaincy – www.tandfonline.com/loi/whcc20
Journal of Pastoral Care and Counseling – www.uk.sagepub.com/en-gb/eur/journal/journal-pastoral-care-counseling
Search Institute – www.searchinstitute.org

Author Biographies

The Revd Carl Aiken was the Manager of Spiritual Care at the Women's and Children's Hospital in Adelaide, South Australia. He has served as an Australian Army Reserve chaplain for 24 years and is a founding board member of Spiritual Care Australia. His Doctor of Ministry thesis was on how chaplains support staff.

Chaplain M. Karen Ballard is Director of Chaplaincy Services at Akron Children's Hospital in Akron, Ohio, where she also serves at the palliative care chaplain. Karen is board-certified by the Association of Professional Chaplains (APC), previously served on the Board of Directors for APC and chaired the task team to develop Standards of Practice for Palliative Care and Hospice Chaplains. She is Chair-Elect for the Leadership Team of the Network on Ministry in Specialized Settings. She is a contributor to *Palliative Care for Infants, Children, and Adolescents: A Practical Handbook* (Johns Hopkins University Press, 2011).

Chaplain Mark Bartel is the manager of Spiritual Care at Arnold Palmer Medical Center in Orlando, Florida. Mark is board-certified by the Association of Professional Chaplains. He is a charter member of the Pediatric Chaplains Network (USA), for which he has served as President. He has received medical ethics training at Stanford Medical School and the Kennedy Institute of Ethics at Georgetown University, and served a term on the US Department of Health and Human Services Secretary's Advisory Committee on Infant Mortality in Washington, DC.

The Revd Wyatt Butcher is Chaplain to the Mental Health Service of the Canterbury District Health Board and Association President of the New Zealand Healthcare Chaplains Association (NZHCA).

Chaplain Ryan Campbell received a B.A. in Philosophy from Austin College in Sherman, Texas and a Master of Theological Studies from the University of Dallas in Irving, Texas. He completed his Clinical Pastoral Education training at Children's Medical Center and Texas Scottish Rite Hospital for Children, both in Dallas, Texas. He has been board certified by the National Association of Catholic Chaplains. He has completed a graduate certificate in the Spiritual Guidance of Children at General Theological Seminary in New York, New York, studying under the Revd Dr Jerome Berryman. He is currently on staff at Children's Medical Center Dallas as Program Manager for the Center for the Spirituality of Children. Ryan also ministers to patients, families and staff in the Gill Center for Cancer and Blood Disorders (CCBD) and the inpatient psychiatry unit. Ryan is a member of the Pediatric Chaplain's Network national advisory council and is currently studying for his Doctor of Ministry at the Pacific School of Religion in Berkeley, CA.

Dr Lindsay B. Carey is Head of the Bachelor of Health Science Public Health Discipline and Research Fellow with the Palliative Care Unit within the School of Psychology and Public Health, La Trobe University, Melbourne, Victoria, Australia. Dr Carey has served as an industrial chaplain, health care chaplain, welfare chaplain and military chaplain.

The Revd Claire Carson is an Anglican priest with a special interest in paediatric spiritual care. She is Head of the Chaplaincy–Spiritual Care Department at St George's University Hospitals NHS Foundation Trust in London, UK.

Chaplain Kobena Charm is a board-certified paediatric chaplain with ten years' experience at LeBonheur Children's Hospital in Memphis, Tennessee. He has a BA in communications from Evangel University, Springfield, MO, and Master of Divinity and Doctor of Ministry degrees from Memphis Theological Seminary.

The Revd Kathryn Darby is a chaplain at the Birmingham Women's and Children's Hospital, UK. A Canadian, she has co-authored a book and articles on the spiritual care of sick children with Paul and Sally Nash. She is an Integrative Counsellor, leads a hospital staff choir and is involved in offering Ignatian retreats and spiritual direction.

The Revd Kathleen Ennis-Durstine is the Manager of InterFaith Pastoral and Spiritual Care at Children's National Health System in Washington, DC. Kathleen is a board-certified chaplain in the Association of Professional Chaplains and holds a certification in paediatric bioethics from the University of Kansas (Children's Mercy Hospital) and certification with the Critical Incident Stress Management Foundation. She has published articles on both children's spirituality and ethics. She is the Dean of the Pediatric Chaplains Institute, the educational branch of the Pediatric Chaplains Network.

The Revd Dr Edina Farkas is a paediatric chaplain at Velkey László Center for Child Health in Miskolc, Hungary. Edina's PhD is in Pastoral Psychology and Spirituality from Boston University School of Theology and she completed four units of Clinical Pastoral Education (CPE) at Massachusetts General Hospital and Baystate Medical Center, USA. She completed her theological studies at the Reformed Theological Academy of Sárospatak, Hungary, and earned a Master of Theology degree at Louisville Presbyterian Theological Seminary, USA. She is an ordained minister of the Hungarian Reformed Church.

Chaplain Bob Flory has been the Director of Spiritual Care and Bereavement Services at Children's Hospital Colorado since 1997. He previously served as Director of Spiritual Care at Children's Hospitals and Clinics of Minnesota from 1987. Bob is a founding member and past President of the Pediatric Chaplains Network (USA) and one of the founding faculty of the Pediatric Chaplains Institute.

The Revd Krista Gregory is a board-certified chaplain with the Association of Professional Chaplains, is an active member of the Pediatric Chaplains Network and has served on the faculty of the Pediatric Chaplains Institute in Washington, DC. She is the Director of the Dell Children's Resiliency Center at Dell Children's Medical Center in Austin, Texas.

The Revd Dr Daniel H. Grossoehme is an Associate Professor of Pediatrics (Division of Pulmonary Medicine) at the University of Cincinnati Academic Health Center, and board-certified Staff Chaplain III at the Cincinnati Children's Hospital Medical Center, currently serving the cystic fibrosis team.

The Revd Stephen Harrison is a Baptist Minister who was Chaplain of Helen and Douglas House (www.helenanddouglas.org.uk), the world's first children's hospice, in Oxford, UK, from 2012 to 2017.

Rabbi Naomi Kalish ACPE BCC has served since 2009 as the Coordinator of Pastoral Care and Education at the New York Presbyterian Hospital/Morgan Stanley Children's Hospital and ACPE supervisor. Kalish is a Past President of Neshama: Association of Jewish Chaplains. She teaches the course Spirituality in Health at the Columbia University Medical Center. Kalish has taught chaplaincy programmes and courses at the Jewish Theological Seminary, Yeshivat Chovevei Torah, Yeshivat Maharat and the Academy for Jewish Religion. She is a doctoral candidate in Education and Jewish Studies at New York University and is writing a history of the Jewish entry into the fields of CPE and Chaplaincy.

The Revd Jim Linthicum is Senior Chaplain to Great Ormond Street Hospital NHS Foundation Trust. Originally from Baltimore, Maryland, USA. Jim is Chair of the Bloomsbury Research Ethics Committee and Vice Chair of the Great Ormond Street Hospital Clinical Ethics Committee. He has a strong interest in bioethics, multifaith working and the role of spiritual care to the health care institution.

The Revd Paul Nash is Senior Chaplain at Birmingham Women's and Children's Hospital; co-founder and convener of the Paediatric Chaplaincy Network; founder of the Centre for Paediatric Spiritual Care including Red Balloon Resources; member of the UK Board of Healthcare Chaplaincy; member of NICE Centre for Guidelines Expert Advisors Panel; Chaplaincy Services Advisory Committee member, Health Care Chaplaincy Network (USA); tutor in chaplaincy, ethics, ministry and practical theology for the Midlands Institute for Children Youth and Mission. Paul has published books and articles on paediatric chaplaincy, bereavement, spiritual care, multifaith care, ethics, ministry and work with young people.

The Revd Dr Sally Nash is the research lead for the Centre for Paediatric Spiritual Care and the Birmingham Women's and Children's Hospital Chaplaincy Team, is Director of the Midlands Institute for Children Youth and Mission at St John's College, Nottingham, coordinates the Centre for Chaplaincy with Children and Young People and is Associate Minister at Hodge Hill Church in Birmingham. She has completed two doctorates in practical theology, a Masters in Education and has published a range of books and journal articles in the fields of work with children and young people, spirituality, ministry, reflective practice and spiritual care.

The Revd Dr Daniel Nuzum is a board-certified Healthcare Chaplain and Clinical Pastoral Education Supervisor at Cork University Hospital and Marymount University Hospital and Hospice, Ireland. In addition, Daniel is an adjunct lecturer at the College of Medicine and Health and University College Cork. Daniel's PhD thesis was on the spiritual and professional impact of stillbirth. Daniel and his wife are also parents to five children, including twin boys who were born prematurely and spent their first two months in a neonatal unit.

Dr Rebecca Nye is a children's spirituality researcher and consultant. Her work addresses schools, churches and hospital contexts. Originally a psychologist, she conducted a landmark study of spirituality with David Hay (The Spirit of the Child, 1998/2006). She introduced 'Godly Play' to the UK, and is National Coordinator of its training programmes. Rebecca is also an Associate Lecturer in psychology and childhood studies at the Open University.

The Revd Dan Roberts, M.Div., BCC, is the chaplain supervisor at McLane Children's Medical Center–Baylor Scott & White Health in Temple, Texas. He is board-certified by the Association of Professional Chaplains (APC). He currently serves as the business manager for the Pediatric Chaplains Network (USA).

Emma Roberts is a Research Assistant in the Birmingham Women's and Children's Hospital Chaplaincy team. Her work focuses on research into paediatric spirituality and chaplaincy, and she leads on the multifaith Celebrate project. She has a Masters in Global Ethics from the University of Birmingham.

The Revd Mary Robinson is Director of the Chaplaincy at Boston Children's Hospital. She completed her AB at Vassar College, MA in Psychology at the New School for Social Research, M.Div. at Drew Theological School, and a fellowship in Medical Ethics at Harvard Medical School. An ordained minister in the United Church of Christ, Mary Robinson is a board-certified chaplain through the Association of Professional Chaplains.

Deacon Deborah Louise Wilde was ordained in 2000, belongs to the Methodist Diaconal Order and has served in sector and circuit appointments including healthcare chaplaincy, chaplaincy in education, young people's ministry and multifaith community leadership. For the past ten years she has been chaplain at Oxford University Hospitals specialising in paediatrics, transplant, renal, critical care areas and the heart centre.

Subject Index

absolution 241
abstract religious thinking 26
acceptance 198
accessibility
  to chaplaincy 126
  staff and self-care 115
adolescence 44–6
age, and assent 156
agency 41
agreements/rules, family systems 101–3
Aiken, Carl 116, 120, 215
aloneness 92
altrupreneurialism 141–3
Amsterdam Declaration 287
Andrzejewski, Joshua 29, 157–8
angels 252
anxiety 92
Aquinas, St Thomas 155
art and craft 172–3
assent 156
  and consent 262–3
assessment, sacred space 253
Association of Professional Chaplains (USA) 125, 145
attachment 39
Augustine of Hippo, St 272
Australian Health and Welfare Chaplains Association 260
authority 14
  and autonomy 158
autonomy 155
  and authority 158
  of children 41
  transition to adult care 236
awareness-sensing 31

Babchuck, Elan S. 209
Bartel, Mark 14, 131–2, 174
beads, spiritual assessment 76–7
behaviour contracts 236
beneficence 154
bereavement care
  context and overview 225
  funerals 228
  future development and research 232
  memories and memorials 228–30
  presence 226–30
  relationship building 225–6
  role of faith 230
  summary 232–3
  team membership 231–2
bereavement care rooms 248
bereavement support, staff and self-care 117–18
best interests of patient 156
Bhagwat Geeta 286
bibliotherapy 79
bite-size strategies, staff and self-care 115
blessings, discharge blessing 57
book
  aims 11–12
  hopes for 293
  overview and structure 18–19
  readership 12
  themes 15
  use of 18
Boston Marathon bombing 202
boundaries
  appropriate 87
  crossing 69–70
  staff and self-care 112
  transition to adult care 236–7
boxes, spiritual assessment 77
Bratt Carle, Jessica 118–19, 248
Brief R-COPE 264
Bryson, Liz 173
bubbles, spiritual assessment 77
Buddhism, view of suffering 284–5
Bumstead, Heather 210

care
  future development and research 58
  personal experiences 51–5
  summary 58
  see also pastoral care; religious care; spiritual care; staff and self-care
care plan meetings 243
caring at the limits 92–3

CASST-r 265
Celebrate project 182
celebrations
    festivals and culture 182–3
    and memorials 146–7
Centre for Paediatric Spiritual Care (UK) 145
ceremony, patients unable to speak 174–5
chapel chaplaincy 126
chaplaincy census 82
charting 81–2
child-centred care 66–8, 168
child death 194–5
Child Death Overview Panel 298
child development insights
    adolescence 44–6
    context and overview 37
    future development and research 46
    infancy 39–40
    pre-school 41–2
    school age 42–4
    summary 47
    toddlerhood 40–1
child protection 86–7
child spirituality
    context and overview 23
    in everyday life 31–2
    future development and research 34
    non-verbal 32–3
    perspectives 30–1
    principles 31–4
    privacy 33
    relational awareness 33
    research, principles and applications 31–4
    summary 34
    unpredictability 33–4
    and wellbeing 32
child spirituality checklist 35
children
    in religion 167–8
    spiritual strengths 30–1
Children's Hospital Melbourne (RCHM) 247
children's wards, in general hospitals 149
Christianity, view of suffering 285–6
Churches' Child Protection Advisory Service (CCPAS) 86
Code Lavender 115–16
codes of ethics 161–2
Common Burials 229
communication
    palliative care 221
    spiritual assessment 81–2
communitarianism 155
community relations, major incidents 209–10
competence 156
complementary therapies 117
confidentiality 262
connecting 50–1, 56
consent and assent, for research 262–3
continuing professional development (CPD) 148–9
coping styles 264–5
core concepts
    child protection 86–7
    empowerment 96
    equal opportunities 95–6
    loss 87–8
    spiritual abuse 86
    voluntary participation 95
corridor and coffee conversations 119–20
Cotterrell, Jodie 95
counselling, sacred space 254
creativity 11
crossing boundaries 69–70
culture, celebration 182–3
CURE International 71

Davis, Mary D. 23, 37, 128, 159, 229
death of a child 194–5
    staff and self-care 118
death of a colleague, staff and self-care 118–19
decision making
    medical ethics 160
    triangular relationships 104
defuse/debrief groups, staff and self-care 115
dependency 236–7
    patients unable to speak 169
development stages 132–3
development theory 25–6
differentiation 105
dignity, innate 167–8
disaster planning 202
discharge blessing 57
discharge, mental illness 186
distress, major incidents 211–12
dolls, spiritual assessment 77
D.R. 15
drawing, spiritual assessment 80
dying 230–1

eating disorders 178
education
    informal 96–7
    sacred space 254
Einstein, A. 124
Elkerson, Synchana 67–8
Elliot, Murray 251
embedded chaplaincy 61, 127–9
emergency supply kits, major incidents 211
emotional responses, to illness 43
empathy 88
empowering 41, 66, 96
engagement, with institution 127–9

SUBJECT INDEX

equal opportunities 95
ethical codes 161–2
ethical practice 75
  patients unable to speak 167–8
  see also medical ethics
ethics committees 160–1
EVER model 128–32
evil
  Buddhist perspective 284
  Christian perspective 285
  Hindu perspective 288
  Islamic perspective 288–9
  Jewish perspective 290
  perspectives on 272–4
  see also good and evil
evil eye 183
existential limits 92–3
experience, and wisdom 88–9
experiments and trials 138–40
expertise, external 145
expressive play, spiritual assessment 76–81
external expertise 145
eye level talking 40

fairness 42
faith development
  context and overview 23
  development stages 25–30
  implications for practice 27–30
  perspectives 23–5
  principles, values and research 25–7
  stages of faith model 26–7
family relationships, challenges to 50–1
family systems
  agreements/rules 101–3
  autonomy and control 239–40
  context and overview 99
  defining 99–100
  future development and research 108
  metaphors in 106–7
  multifaith perspective 108
  palliative care 219–21
  relationships with staff 275
  researched approaches 99–101
  summary 108
  transition to adult care 238–9
  triangular relationships 103–4
family systems theory 99–100, 103–6
Farkas, Edina 140–1, 225, 229
fears, transition to adult care 236–7
festivals 182–3
FICA screening tool 74–5
Fitchett, George 266
Fleenor, David 203
forgiveness 198
Four Noble Truths 284

4 Rs 144
friendship 87
funerals 228
futility 156–7
future development and research, summary of areas for 295–6

gender transition 238
general hospitals
  children's wards in 149
  working in 297–9
generalist/specialist model 73
generic spiritual care model 64–6
genetics 154
Godly Play 23, 35, 67, 77–8, 93–4
  see also story telling
good and evil
  context and overview 272–4
  future development and research 280–1
  meaning-making 279–80
  perspectives on evil 272–4
  questioning suffering 274–9
  questions 274
  role of chaplain 274–9
  suffering 274–9
  summary 281
good practice, relationship building 50
grants 142
Gray, Marino 251
Great Ormond Street Hospital 126
Green, Kathy 68–9, 110, 124
Guide for the Perplexed (Maimonides) 273

Hadith 289–90
Harrison, Stephen 226
Hasan, Yusuf 67–8
Hatton, Jane 65
healing processes, major incidents 209
Health Care Chaplaincy Network (USA) 145
Hildebrand, Alice A. 111
Hinduism, view of suffering 286–7
Hippocrates 153–4
holding environments 86–7
honorary chaplains 146
hope 221
hospital choirs 121
hospitality 69
hospitals, development 12
Huber, Peggy 38, 56, 171
humanism, view of suffering 287–8
humility 75
Hurricane Sandy 201, 202, 203
Hussan, Yusuf 220

identity development 45
illness
  emotional responses to 43
  talking about 43–4
independence, transition to adult care 236
individual responsibilities 149
infancy 39–40
infection-control protocols 40
informal education 96–7
innate dignity 167–8
Insley, Susy 85
institutional policies 50
institutions, chaplaincy to
  accessibility 126
  context and overview 124–5
  contribution to institution 133
  development stages 132–3
  embeddedness 127–9
  engagement 127–9
  EVER model 128–32
  future development and research 134
  love 126–7
  meaning of 125
  paediatric specifics 132–3
  space creation 132
  summary 134
  understanding 127
  uniqueness 127
  VALUE 125–8
  visibility 125–6
  wider relational context 132
integration 146–7
interconnection 100
interfaith model 63–4
Interpretive Spiritual Encounters (ISE) 66–8, 76, 81
intuitive-projective faith 26
intuitive religious thinking 25
Isaiah 60.20 209
Islam, view of suffering 288–90

Job 1:2 290
Jones, Maggie 63
journals, spiritual assessment 81
Judaism, view of suffering 290–1
justice 155

karma 286, 291
keepsakes 181
Kelly, Lavender 60
Kifner, Hadley 57
Kosberg, Robin 70

lament 185
language
  major incidents 208
  religious/secular 74

life-limiting chronic disease 234–5
  see also transition to adult care
Lillehei, Walton 162
limbic resonance 88–9
listening, attentive 49
literal religious thinking 25
literature review 15
loss 87–8
  finding meaning 230–1
loss theory 87

magic visiting bags 40
major incidents
  advance planning 203–4
  after the incident 206–10
  chaplain's role 203–4
  community relations 209–10
  context and overview 201
  disaster planning 202
  emergency supply kits 211
  emotional and spiritual distress 211
  emotional and spiritual processing 206–7
  future development and research 212
  healing processes 209
  language, spiritual and theological 208
  multidisciplinary working 204–5
  multifaith services 207–8
  Pastoral Care Emergency Preparedness Plan 203–4
  personal disaster plans 211
  personal experiences 210–12
  psychological needs 211–12
  resources 213
  responding to 202
  self-care 210–12
  spiritual care 205–6
  summary 212
  what to expect 202
making sense, of suffering 283
management *see* team management and development
Manchester Arena attack 208
Mark 10:13–16 167–8
Maslow's hierarchy 111
meaning-making 279–80
medical ethics
  acceptable/tolerable/intolerable behaviour 159–60
  codes for chaplains 161–2
  common issues 157–8
  context and overview 152–3
  decision making 158–9
  decision-making grid 160
  ethics committees 160–1
  future development and research 162–3
  history 153–4
  resources 163

summary 163
terminology 154–7
see also ethical practice
medically inappropriate treatment 156–7
medication, mental illness 178
meditation 38
memorials 229–30
  and celebrations 146–7
  staff and self-care 118
memory making 194, 229–30
Mental Health Act 2007 182
Mental Health First Aid 191
mental health, resources 178
mental illness
  activity ideas 179
  celebrating festivals and culture 182–3
  chaplains' contribution to care 183
  context and overview 177–8
  discharge 186
  expressing lament 185
  future development and research 187
  keepsakes and messages of hope 181
  medication 178
  positive and negative aspects of religion 183–4
  religious perspectives 182–4
  safe practice 181
  safe spaces 180–1
  self-care 187
  self-esteem 179
  staff support 186–7
  stigma 179
  struggles and tensions for chaplain 186
  summary 187
  support for parents 184–5
  support for siblings 185
  supportive spaces 185
  training and skills 187
  use of term 178
  vertical habits 180
messages of hope 181
metaphors, in family systems 106–7
mindfulness 116–17
mission not evangelism 68–9
models of chaplaincy
  child-centred care 66–8
  context and overview 61–2
  crossing boundaries 69–70
  future development and research 71
  generalist/specialist model 73
  generic spiritual care 64–6
  hospitality 69
  interfaith model 63–4
  Interpretive Spiritual Encounters (ISE) 66–8
  mission not evangelism 68–9
  multifaith model 62–3
  non-judgemental 69

partnership 70–1
summary 71–2
values 66–71
moral development 42
mortality 240–1
multiculturalism 61
  see also models of chaplaincy
multidisciplinary working 147–8
  major incidents 204–5
multifaith model 62–3
multifaith perspective, family systems 108
multifaith services, major incidents 208
multisensory life story approaches 170
Murrup Biik 247
music, self-expression 171–2
mutual blessing 89
mutual pretence 103
mystery-sensing 31
mythic-literal faith 26

Nakah, Victor 71
Nash, Adam 154
Nash, Paul 11, 13, 114
Nash, Sally 114
National Consensus Project of Quality Palliative Care Guidelines 216
National Institute for Health and Care Excellence (NICE) 216
National Quality Forum 216
navigation 14
need-to-know criterion 82
Newborn Individualized Developmental Care and Assessment Program (NIDCAP) 171
Newtown, Connecticut, shooting 209
NHS UK Chaplaincy Guidelines (DOH) 13, 125, 126
Night (Wiesel) 273
non-accidental trauma (NAT) 195–7
non-judgemental attitude 69
non-maleficence 154–5
non-managerial supervision, staff and self-care 119–21
non-verbal care *see* patients unable to speak
non-verbal spirituality 32–3
not knowing 92
Numbers 6:24 252

Oak Creek, Wisconsin shooting 210
Oxfordshire University Hospital 297–9

paediatric chaplaincy
  background 12–13
  compared with other ministry 13–15
  definition 11
  embedded chaplaincy 61
  future development and research 19
  scope of care 16–17

paediatric chaplaincy *cont.*
  spectrum of work 15–18
  standards and competencies 17–18
  summary 19
  variety 61
  working across generations 297–8
Paediatric Chaplaincy Network (UK) 149
Pali Cannon, The 284
palliative care
  communication 221
  context and overview 214–15
  defining 214
  family care 219–21
  future development and research 223
  patient care 218–19
  relationship building 218–19
  role of chaplain 214, 217
  spiritual care 216
  summary 223
  team care 221–3
parental modelling 265
parents, interaction with 39–40
participation 66
  voluntary 95
partnership 70–1
pastoral care 15–16, 49
Pastoral Care Emergency Preparedness Plan 203–4
Pastoral Intervention Codings 253
patient and family led development 143
patient's best interest 156
patients unable to speak
  art and craft 172–3
  context and overview 167
  creating and telling stories 170–1
  dependency 169
  ethical rational 167–8
  future development and research 175
  hearing and learning stories 170
  multisensory life story approaches 170
  music 171–2
  recording stories 175
  relationship building 169–70
  ritual and ceremony 174–5
  story telling 168–75
  summary 175
  theological rationale 167–8
  touch 171
  toys 173–4
peace trees 210
Pedersen, Lynn 55–6
Pediatric Chaplains' Network (USA) 145, 149
peer groups 42–3
people of peace 143–4
permission, and child autonomy 41
person-centred care 168
personal disaster plans 211

Personal Preparedness Plans 201
Platter, Janette 193–4
play
  properties of 89–90
  relationship building 40
political awareness 144
practice examples
  absolution 241
  anger with God 277–8
  Arjun and the elephant 278
  assumptions 105–6
  autonomy and control 239–40
  behaviour contracts 236
  bereavement care 225, 226
  bereavement care rooms 248
  booklets 13
  butterfly bush 118–19
  callings 14
  care pathway 142
  celebrating festivals and culture 182–3
  challenging decisions 159
  child development insights 37
  child's insights 29
  church/hospital partnership 71
  Common Burials 229
  concepts of perfection 271–2
  contribution of chaplaincy 140–1
  creativity 136–7
  crossing boundaries 70
  discharge blessing 57
  emotional space 65–6
  engaging 85
  equal opportunities 95
  evil and suffering 276–7
  faith and doubt 45
  family systems 100–1, 102
  gender transition 238
  generic spiritual care model 65
  God and Buddha 60
  Godly Play parable box 23
  God's ears 80
  God's responsibility 279
  Gregory's heart 152, 162
  improvising a response 11
  informal supervision 120
  interfaith prayer 64
  Janna's doll 90–1
  maintaining connections 56
  major incidents 201, 203, 207, 208, 209, 210
  medical ethics 157–8
  meditation 38
  memorials 229
  mental health 177
  mental illness 180, 187
  mission not evangelism 68–9
  murder 276

music 172
non-accidental trauma (NAT) 196–7
organ donations 138
palliative care 214, 215, 218–19, 220
patient-focused care 67–8
patients unable to speak 171, 174
prayer blankets 231
prayer scarf ministry 63
preparing a room 78
presence 227–8
reflecting back 128
relationship building 51–5
religious sensitivity 131–2
research 260, 266
rural South Africa 55–6
sacred space 247, 251, 252
self-care 114
sexual relationships and orientation 241
social cues 43–4
staff and self-care 116
staff care and support 110
suffering as punishment 274–5
Taco Bill 78–9
teaching spiritual screening 74–5
transition to adult care 236, 237, 243
trauma 190
trauma and abuse 193–4, 197–8
triangular relationships 104
Why does God hate me? 27–8
prayer blankets 231
prayer scarves 63
pre-school children, child development insights 41–2
presence 61, 89, 226–30
primal faith 26
Primum non nocere 154–5
principle of Respect 182–3
privacy 82
Private Worlds of Dying Children, The (Bluebond-Langner) 103
progress, celebration of 294
provision, developing 141–4
psychological needs, major incidents 211–12
punishment, suffering as 274–5

questions for reflection
  approaches and skills 97
  bereavement care 233
  care 58–9
  child development insights 47
  child spirituality 35
  family systems 108
  good and evil 281–2
  institutions, chaplaincy to 134
  introductory 20
  major incidents 213
  medical ethics 163
  mental health 187
  models of chaplaincy 72
  palliative care 223
  patients unable to speak 175
  research 268
  sacred space 256
  spiritual assessment 83
  staff and self-care 123
  team management and development 151
  transition to adult care 244
  trauma and abuse 199
Quinlan, Karen Ann 153–4
Qur'an, The 288

rapid response, staff and self-care 115–16
re-traumatisation 112
referrals, indicators for 74
relational awareness 33
relationship building 37, 50–1
  adolescence 46
  bereavement care 225–6
  between families and staff 275
  palliative care 218–19
  patients unable to speak 169–70
  role of play 40
  rural South Africa 55–6
  transition to adult care 242
relationships
  as key 144
  staff and self-care 113
  triangles 103–4
  wider relational context 132
religiosity, measures of 246, 264
religious care 15, 49
religious perspectives, mental illness 182–4
religious thinking, development stages 26
remembering and rituals, staff and self-care 119
remembrance 228–9
research
  assent and consent 262–3
  confidentiality 262
  context and overview 258
  difference of paediatric research 261
  family systems 265
  future development and research 267
  instruments 264–5
  paediatric palliative care (PPC) study 266
  participants 265–6
  process 259–60
  recognition of 145
  resources 267
  spiritual screening and assessment 263–4
  summary 267–8
resilience 112, 120–1
resources
  context-specific 145
  major incidents 213

resources *cont.*
    research 267
    sacred space 251–4
    for support 149
    trauma and abuse 200
    trialling 140
    websites 300–1
responsibilities, individual 149
retreats 117
right and wrong, sense of 42
rites of passage 46
rituals 145
    patients unable to speak 174–5
    sacred space 251–4
    staff and self-care 119
    transition to adult care 243
rotation 149
rule of double effect 155
rules/agreements, family systems 101–3

sacred space
    activities 251
    assessment 253
    bereavement care rooms 248
    best practice standards 249
    chaplaincy roles 252–3
    child's spiritual space 250–1
    conclusions 254
    context and overview 246–8
    counselling 254
    creating 253–4
    education 254
    future development and research 255–6
    neutrality 246–7
    physical space 248–9
    protecting 249–50
    rituals 254
    rituals and resources 251–4
    silence 250
    simplicity 250
    slowness 250
    solitude 250
    stillness 250
    support 254
    use of 247
    ward and bedside 249–50
    worship 254
safe practice, mental illness 181
safe spaces 180–1
safeguarding 86–7
safety 75
safety and security, trauma and abuse 191–2
samsara 286
Sandy Hook Elementary School 208
Saunders, Cicely 216
school age, child development insights 42–4
Schwartz Rounds 206–7

screening *see* spiritual screening
self-actualisation 111
self-audit 137–8
self-belief 140
self-care 121–2
    major incidents 210–12
    mental illness 187
    palliative care 221–3
    principles 113–14
    spiritual practice 122
    trauma and abuse 198–9
    see also staff and self-care
self-expression
    art and craft 172–3
    music 171–2
    touch 171
    toys 173–4
self-identification 74
senior chaplains 149
sexual relationships and orientation 237–8, 241
Sikhism, view of suffering 291–2
Silberman, Jeffrey 209
silence 250
simplicity 250
skills
    being ready 90–1
    caring at the limits 92–3
    experience and wisdom 88–9
    future development and research 97
    Godly Play 93–4
    informal education 96–7
    play 89–90
    summary 97
    working in mental health 187
    youth work principles 94
Skills, Attitudes, Knowledge and Ethics (SAKE) 293–4
Skype 56
slowness 250
smart phones, spiritual assessment 81
Snellgrove, Samantha 136–7
social cues 43–4
social networks 42–3
solitude 250
space creation 132
spiritual abuse, core concepts 86
spiritual assessment 75–81, 263–4
    assessment models 75
    beads 76–7
    bibliotherapy 79
    boxes 77
    bubbles 77
    charting 81–2
    communication and sharing 81–2
    dolls 77
    drawing 80

expressive play 76–81
future development and research 82–3
Godly Play 77–8
journals 81
smart phones 81
stuffed toys 78
summary 83
video games 80
videos 81
virtual trip home 78–9
see also spiritual screening
spiritual care 15, 16
  defining 48
  generic model 64–6
  major incidents 205–6
  palliative care 216
Spiritual Care Australia 260
Spiritual Care Interventions 253
spiritual communities 168–75
spiritual crisis, trauma and abuse 192–4
Spiritual Involvement and Beliefs Scale (SIBS) 264
spiritual practice 122
spiritual screening 73–5, 263–4
  see also spiritual assessment
spiritual themes 76
Spiritual Well-being Scale (SWB) 264
spirituality
  expression of 249
  innate 39
  as protective 44
  staff and self-care 113
  transition to adult care 240–1
  see also child spirituality
staff and self-care
  accessibility 115
  approaches to 114–19
  bereavement support 117–18
  bite-size strategies 115
  boundaries 112
  complementary therapies 117
  context and overview 110–11
  core skills 122
  death of a child 118
  death of a colleague 118–19
  defuse/debrief groups 115
  enhancing self-care 121
  expressing care 112
  future development and research 122–3
  hospital choirs 121
  informal supervision 119–21
  issues in 112–13
  memorials 118
  mindfulness 116–17
  non-managerial supervision 119–21
  principles 113–14
  rapid response 115–16

referrals to other resources 121
relationships 113
remembering and rituals 119
resilience 112, 120–1
resources 122
retreats 117
spirituality 113
staff care and support 110
summary 123
wellbeing 112, 120–1
staff, relationships with families 275
stages of faith model 26–7
standards and competencies 17–18
'Standards of Practice for Professional Chaplains' (APC) 125
stigma, mental illness 179
stillness 250
story telling 40–1, 168–75
  see also Godly Play
stuffed toys, spiritual assessment 78
Substance Abuse and Mental Health Services Administration (SAMHSA) 191
suffering 274–9
  Buddhist perspective 284–5
  Christian perspective 285–6
  context and overview 283
  Hindu perspective 286–7
  humanist perspective 287–8
  Islamic perspective 288–90
  Jewish perspective 290–1
  making sense of 283
  Sikh perspective 291–2
supervision, non-managerial 119–21
support
  in mental illness 184–5, 186–7
  resources for 149
  sacred space 254
  team and individual 148
synthetic-conventional faith 27

talking, about illness 43–4
team care, palliative care 221–3
team management and development
  altrupreneurialism 141–3
  building on strengths 140–1
  celebrations and memorials 146–7
  children's wards in general hospitals 149
  context and overview 136–7
  continuing professional development (CPD) 148–9
  developing provision 141–4
  experiments and trials 138–40
  external expertise 145
  4 Rs 144
  future development and research 149
  grants 142
  individual responsibilities 149

team management and development *cont.*
  integration 146–7
  multidisciplinary working 147–8
  patient and family led 143
  people of peace 143–4
  political awareness 144
  pro- and reactive 143
  rotation 149
  self-audit 137–8
  senior chaplains 149
  summary 149–50
  support resources 149
  team and individual support 148
  track record 143
  volunteers 146
teddy bears 252
terminology, medical ethics 154–7
Texas Advance Directives Act (1999) 160
theodicy 272
theology of children 28–9
time, effective use 242
toddlerhood 40–1
Together for Short Lives 216
total pain 216
touch 39, 171
toys, self-expression 173–4
track records 143
training 73, 187
transition 14
  adolescence 44
transition to adult care
  autonomy 236
  challenges 235
  context and overview 234–5
  dynamics 235
  future development and research 244
  graduation celebration 243
  independence 236
  mortality 240–1
  parental/familial issues 238–9
  parental/familial loss of control 239–40
  patients' fears 236–7
  relationship building 242
  service changes 239
  sexual relationships and orientation 237–8, 241
  spirituality 240–1
  summary 244
  team work 242–3
  time use 242
  trust 241–2
trauma and abuse
  acceptance and forgiveness 198
  chaplains' responses 195
  death of child 194–5
  future development and research 199

information gathering 192
listening 192
long-term effects 197
non-accidental trauma (NAT) 195–7
resources 191, 200
safety and security 191–2
self-care 198–9
spiritual crisis 192–4
summary 199
support for colleagues 198
support planning 190–2
trials and experiments 138–40
triangles, relationships 103–4
trust 75, 230–1, 241–2
Tweddle, Matthew 219

UK Board of Healthcare Chaplaincy 145
understanding 127
undifferentiated faith 26
uniqueness 127
Uno 136–7
utilitarianism 155

VALUE 125–8
value-sensing 31
vertical habits 180
video games, spiritual assessment 80
videos, spiritual assessment 81
virtual trip home, spiritual assessment 78–9
virtue 154
visibility 125–6
'Voicing My Choices' 219
voluntary participation 95
volunteers 146

wandering with intent 61
Weiss, Robert 208
wellbeing
  and child spirituality 32
  staff and self-care 112, 120–1
When Bad Things Happen to Good People (Kushner) 273
wisdom, and experience 88–9
Wollschlaeger-Fischer, Linda 27–8, 65–6
World Health Organization codings 253
worship, sacred space 254

youth work principles 94
youth workers, as friends 87

Zhang, John 154
Zones of Proximal Development (ZPD) 37–8

Author Index

Adams, K. 75
Aging with Dignity 219
Alexander, S. 155
Als, H. 171
American Academy of Pediatrics 217
Amini, F. 88–89
Arberry, A.J. 288, 289
Aroni, R. 252–253, 264
Aslan, A. 273
Association for Children with Life-Threatening or Terminal Conditions and Their Families 214
Association of Professional Chaplains 125, 222

Babchuck, E.S. 209
Bakshi, S.S. 291
Balboni, M.J. 73, 230
Baldacchino, D. 73
Ballard, M. 221–222
Bandini, J. 75
Barata, I. 226
Bartels, J.R. 198, 206
Beardsley, C. 249
Beauchamp, T.L. 156
Bello Belasco, J. 156
Benore, E. 264
Bentley Stewart, J. 159–160
Berger, J. 111
Berryman, J. 35, 76–77, 89, 92, 93
Berryman, T. 93
Betz, C.L. 234, 237
Bioethics Committee, 262
Bluebond-Langner, M. 103, 156
Bodó, S. 230
Borneman, T. 74
Bowen, M. 99, 103–106
Bowlby, J. 39
Boyatzis, C.J. 265
Boyce, G. 69
Bresson, L. 161
Briller, H. 229
British Broadcasting Corporation (BBC) 246

Brown, A. 178
Brown, P.M. 264
Brown, S. 89–90
Bryant-Davis, T. 183–184
Bryman, A. 259
Bull, A. 15, 263
Bumstead, H. 210
Burd, R.S. 197
Burleigh, B. 15

Cadge, W. 75, 128, 246, 247
Caldeira, S. 169
Campbell, R. 94, 226, 249
Carey, L.B. 252–253, 260, 262, 263, 264, 267
Carey-Sargeant, C.L. 264
Carson, M.L.S. 178, 179, 180, 186
Catholic Standard 208
Catlin, E.A. 169
Cavaletti, S. 27
Centre for Paediatric Spiritual Care (CPSC) 34
Childress, J.F. 156
Clark, P.A. 235
Clift, S. 121
Cobb, M. 49
Cohen, A. 273
Cohen, J. 253, 263, 267
Connell, S. 249
Cotton, S. 264

D'Angelo, C.M. 265
Darby, K. 34, 76, 127, 132–133, 172, 250, 253, 263
Davoren, 267
de Souza, M. 31
DeMesquita Wander, M. 156
Department of Health, UK 125, 126
Dew, R.E. 264
Doehring, C. 87
Dollahite, D.C. 265
Drain, M. 235
Drotar, D. 265

Edwards, A. 252–253, 264
Ellison, C.G. 178
Erikson, E. 26, 40, 41, 45

Fabricant Linn, S. 122
Farkas, E. 226, 227
Federal Drug Administration 262
Feldstein, B.D. 227
Ferrell, B. 74, 216, 217
Figley, C.R. 212
Fitchett, G. 73, 74, 217, 263, 266
Ford, D.F. 62
Fosarelli, P. 15
Fowler, J. 26–27, 28, 75
Friedlander, M. 273
Friesen, M.F. 15

Gable, J. 235
Garros, D. 230
General Synod of the Anglican Church of Australia 86
Gersch, I. 32
Gilbert, P. 33
Glenwick, D.S. 264
Goldman, R. 25, 27
Gopee, N. 119
Gordon, T. 113
Granqvist, P. 39
Grossoehme, D.H. 15, 40, 41–42, 264, 265
Günay, S. 179

Hall, J. 169
Hamzelou, J. 154
Hancox, G. 121
Handzo, G. 73
Harris, B. 86–87
Haslam, S.A. 246
Hay, D. 30–31, 33, 34, 249
Health Research Authority 267
Hein, I. 156
Henderson, A.K. 178
Hesch, J. 15
Heschel, A.J. 117
Hess, D. 221
Hill-Brown, R. 70
Hill, P.C. 264
Hood, R.W. 264
Hopkins, T. 61
Hull, J. 28–29
Hussain, Z. 44, 49, 183, 184
Hyde, B. 32, 75

Institute for Mental Health in England 182

Jackson, S.A. 288
Jan, S. 235
Jecker, N.S. 157
Jeffs, T. 96
Jonsen, A. 155, 157, 161

Kabat-Zinn, J. 116–117
Keating, T. 122
Kelly, E. 48, 54, 113
Kendrick, K. 178
Kerr, M. 103
Kevern, P. 125
Kimberley, M.B. 262–263
Kinsella, A.K. 178
Kinsella, C.G. 178
Kirkpatrick, L.A. 39
Knight, J.S. 96
Knox, J. 161
Koenig, H. 73, 259, 264
Kohlberg, L. 26
Kurz, R. 262
Kushner, H. 273

Lannon, R. 88–89
Larcher, V. 262
LaRocca-Pitts, M. 75
Lartey, E.Y. 49
Leach, J. 187
Levers, C. 265
Levy, M.D.L. 262
Lewis, T. 88–89
Liebrich, J. 249
Lindner, E. 29
Linn, D. 122
Linn, M. 122
Lipscomb, A. 32
Lucas, A.M. 15

McAnulty, G.B. 171
McFadden, R.D. 154
McSherry, W. 15, 125
Madson, P. 92
Magee, J. 208
Maimonides, M. 273
Malone, M.P. 235
Marks, L.D. 265
Maslow, A. 111
Massey, K. 15–16, 73
Mathisen, B. 264
Meaney, S. 226
Meert, K.L. 229, 231
Merton, T. 122
Miller, B.S. 273
Miller, G.W. 152–153
Miller, L. 39, 44

AUTHOR INDEX

Minor, C. 94
Mitchell, D. 113
Molock, S.D. 264
Mooney, C.G. 39
Morton, T.A. 246

Nash, P. 14, 15, 15–16, 34, 44, 49, 62, 76, 125, 127, 132–133, 172, 183, 184, 250, 253, 263
Nash, S. 34, 76, 96, 127, 132–133, 172, 250, 253, 263
Nee, R. 76, 81
New Zealand Statistics Department 246
NHS Education for Scotland 48
NHS England 13
NICE 216
Nuzum, D. 226
Nye, R. 25, 27, 30–31, 33, 34, 35, 249
Nyirő, J. 226

O'Connell, D. 94
O'Donoghue, K. 226
Oelofsen, N. 119
Oliver, R.C. 197
O'Malley, P. 226

Palmer, R. 96
Pargament, K.I. 183–184, 264, 264–265
Parkes, M. 44, 49, 183, 184
Paterson, M. 187
Pediatric Chaplains Network 137–138
Pendleton, S. 264, 264–265
Penman, D. 117
Perez, 264
Peteet, J.R. 230
Pew Research Center 74
Piaget, J. 25, 26
Pilling, J. 229
Pines, 273
Poon Zahl, B. 39
Proffitt, M. 99
Puchalski, C.M. 74, 216, 217, 227

Quittner, A.L. 265

Rahula, W. 273
Ramshaw, E. 243
Reynolds, N. 264
Richards, S. 87
Rippon, S. 61
Risk, J. 74
Risse, G.B. 246
Roberts, N. 14
Roberts, P. 73
Robinson, M. 73, 74, 231, 232, 248

Robinson, S. 178, 180
Rosenbaum, J.L. 168
Rosenblatt, P.C. 106–107
Rothman, D.J. 154
Royal College of Paediatrics and Child Health 214
Rubin, D. 264
Rushton, C. 221–222

Schaff, P. 272
Schneiderman, L.J. 157
Schwartz Center for Compassionate Healthcare 206–207, 211
Sercombe, H. 94
Shelly, J.A. 15
Sherwood, H. 246
Siegler, M. 161
Simpson, J. 99
Singleton, A. 246
Smith, J.R. 168
Smith, M.K. 96
Smith, T. 74
Snow, S. 226
Sohal, P.K. 291
Steinway, C. 235
Stewart, S. 77
Sulmasy, D.P. 253
Surr, J. 30
Swift, C. 12
Swinton, J. 186

Tacey, D.J. 247
Terreri, C.J. 264
Thayer, P. 76, 81
Thiel, M.M. 73
Thienprayoon, R. 226, 249
Threlfall-Holmes, M. 61
Thurston, C.S. 229
Torry, M. 227
Trousdale, A. 31
Turiel, E. 42

Vandecreek, L. 15
Vygotsky, L.S. 37

Walshe, M. 284
Watson, J. 31
Watt, W.M. 289
Weiner, E.S.C. 99
Westers, N.J. 264
Wicks, R. 111
Wiesel, E. 273
Williams, M. 117
Winick, N. 226, 249
Winslade, W. 161

Woolley. R. 75
World Health Organization (WHO) 214
www.calvin.edu 180

Young, K. 87, 96
Ysseldyk, R. 246
Yust, K. 75

Zimmerman, M. 29
Zollfrank, R. 168